WITHOUT RESERVATIONS

Peter — Santa Fe's
loss will be Hendersonville's
gain. May your new
chapter in your life's
journey include excitement,
love and worthy health.
Sam 6/03

WITHOUT

RESERVATIONS

From Harlem to the End of the Santa Fe Trail

by

Samuel B. Ballen

A Legacy Edition • OCEAN TREE BOOKS

First Public Edition, 2001

Inquiries about this book should be addressed to:
Ballen & Co., P.O. Box 2263, Santa Fe, New Mexico 87504

OCEAN TREE BOOKS
Post Office Box 1295
Santa Fe, New Mexico 87504

ISBN 0-943734-36-3

Library of Congress Cataloging in Publication data:

Ballen, Samuel B., 1922-
        Without reservations: From Harlem to the end of the Santa Fe Trail /
by Samuel B. Ballen.
        p.   cm. – (A Legacy Edition)
        ISBN 0-943734-36-3
        1. Ballen, Samuel B., 1922- . 2. Jews – New Mexico – Santa Fe
–Biography. 3. Hotelkeepers – New Mexico – Santa Fe –
Biography. 4. Jewish businesspeople – United States – Biography. 5.
Santa Fe (N.M.) – Biography. I. Title. II. Series.
F804.S29J533 1977
978.9'5605'092
[B]–DC21   97-1151
                                                                CIP

Contents

ETHEL

My greatest challenge – my deepest reward

1/ A PERIPATETIC WAY

It is 8:15 a.m. on September 22, 1994, and I am sitting on a ridge 150 feet above Cottonwood Wash, one mile north of Arizona into Utah. Below me the Navajo Mountain Trading Post founded by the Four Corners pioneers Ben Wetherill and Ray Dunn lies abandoned. There is not a cloud in the sky. In the western heavens in daylight a full moon tries to dip behind Navajo Mountain. The air is crisp, and a light wind blows from the east suggesting that fall is taking over. I am here to record my journey toward maturity. The last time I was on this ridge was 1962 when my wife, Ethel, and I prevailed on the trading post proprietors Madeline and Ralph Cameron to let us take horses to the top of the mountain by ourselves. It was there and then that our youngest daughter was conceived. We should have named her Naatsisaan (Navajo Mountain) instead of Marta Shya. Her entry into life there is manifest in her love of the outdoors and its untamed inhabitants and her disdain for the conventional. She's a true westerner and doesn't possess a single dress.

In 1953 and a week later into September my California buddies and I were exploring the Navajo Canyon complex when a chap from St. Louis introduced himself. He had spent the day at this spot on the ridge secretly photographing the Navajos sitting on the bench and gossiping and going in and out the trading post. The intervening forty-one years have brought stark changes. Back then horses and wooden wagons were the only mode of transportation on the western reservation and only a handful of the Navajos were comfortable in English. There were no Chapter Houses, no medical clinic, and no road graders, and no electricity other than that provided by a gasoline-powered generator for the store and the small boarding school. And, of course, there were no propane heaters and no communication devices other than two hand-cranked emergency radios. But the principal change was that each Navajo hogan was then supported by some form of subsistence agriculture plus a herd of sheep, whereas today most of the locals have a good pickup truck and Cape Cod type single-family houses and survive on some form of government support. They may work for Tribal or State or the numerous U. S. government educational bureaucracies or the Environmental Protection Agency or depend on welfare. Even Navajo Mountain itself has been "improved." A difficult jeep road carries communication service personnel to the top to repair and maintain the three transmission towers belonging to the Utah, Arizona, and Navajo police agencies plus a commercial cellular tower that connects Chapter members through 100 gratis phones! But the California company which negotiated this deal had not properly informed the residents of ongoing toll charges!

My last two days at Navajo Mountain made reminiscences more poignant because of the house visit of long-time friends Bob and Dottie Walker. They were returning to Santa Fe from the Grand Canyon with the harpsichord Bob had made and loaned for use during the annual fall Grand Canyon Concert Series. During World War II Dottie was a technician at Los Alamos. She once pricked her finger with a plutonium source, but here she is today—fit as a fiddle. Bob did neutron measurements at Los Alamos and carried the first plutonium micrograms in his pant's pockets to the Laboratory. After the war he was professor of mathematical physics at Cal Tech but admits he doesn't understand General Relativity. The *enfant terrible* phenomenon Richard Feynman was best man at their wedding. Until a few years ago Bob was the halest outdoor camper I knew; at the age of 72 he and his son used cross country skis to climb Mount Wheeler (the highest peak in New Mexico) on the first day of January. Two days ago the Ballens and the Walkers succeeded in finding near Paiute Mesa a cliff dwelling that the teacher Lisbeth Eubank, at Navajo Mountain Boarding School, had mentioned to me thirty years ago. Lisbeth had heard about this Anasazi dwelling but had never seen it. It was not a particularly hard climb to this once-inhabited cave. Bob, Dottie, and I reached the site first, and Ethel made it just a few minutes later. We also found large potsherds and even an ancient fabric sandal. We left everything as we found it. To protect such sites the USGS no longer identifies ruin locations on its maps, and I will follow that practice in these pages.

Yesterday we tried to find Hawk Eye Bridge on our own. After several trips down side canyons proved fruitless, we asked the handsome Henry Stevens, who was facing his hogan with Navajo sandstone and wearing a mask because of the hantavirus threat from some mice trash piles, to lead us there. He readily agreed. We were pleasantly surprised at the beauty and isolation of the arch. Back at Mr. Stevens' hogan we offered our courteous guide a few greenbacks to compensate for diversion from home improvements and to offset his loss of three sheep who died after consuming loco weed. But now Henry Stevens is promoting a guide service to the surrounding spectacular sights, but hindered by health concerns.

Today, soothed by the tranquility of the Rainbow Plateau, I am drawn to reflect on why I'm even attempting to write this book. The mathematician Stanislaw Ulam used to tell of three monks who were talking about their achievements. The first said, "I'm good at piety." The second said, "For me it is charity." The third said, "I'm tops in humility." George Cowan, a retired Los Alamos chemist and the first president of the Santa Fe Institute, was overheard to say of me that I was "laid forward." Despite George's assessment I don't think I can be accused of braggadocio. My dad used to carry around a *New York Times* clipping when my chemist cousin Jacob received the Ernest O. Lawrence Award, and my sister was the one my parents always proudly displayed. So why this book? To start, the genius, Stan Ulam, encouraged me to write down these descriptions of the people and events central to my life experience. None of Stan's ideas could be ignored Nor did I want to ignore the suggestion.* The man I am today grew from strong family relationships and the good fortune to develop close friendships with exceptional people from all walks of life.

I remember in the early days of my leadership at the oldest hotel in North America, La Fonda, in Santa Fe, New Mexico, the physical plant was in such a deteriorated state that I dreaded coming down to work. I wouldn't know whether the ceiling plaster had fallen or whether there was hot water, or whether the steam radiators would be clanging. Sometimes the locks on the guest room doors wouldn't work, and occasionally I might find that some vagrant had defecated in the hallway. One morning my wonderful secretary, Dayle Pond, now assistant manager at Rancho Encantado, said that an irate guest wanted to see me. In marched this well-coiffed and well-jeweled lady from Texas. "I was here for my honeymoon forty years ago," she began, "and this place is not the same." Without thinking I spurted, "And neither are you." All she could do was turn on her heels and storm out, while I wanted to vanish into my office walls.

---

* But this book would not have come to completion without the encouragement of Cormac McCarthy, Priscilla McMillan and Francoise Ulam. And my debt to talented editor Mary Mann and my administrative aide Eliza Vigil Williams, assisted by the Bertelli twins, must also be mentioned. And I have benefited from the critical reviews of Ron Klein and Marvin Wise and Patricia Dietrich plus my focused agent Joyce Blalock.

Those complaints are now rarely heard. Now guests come in to compliment the staff, to praise the ambiance of the hotel, to tell us how wonderful the rooms and the maids and the waitresses and the food are, and to express thanks that they were able to have their holiday at La Fonda. And then a fair number of them cannot control their curiosity and ask, "How did someone raised in Harlem end up as the owner of La Fonda?"

In this condensed recitation of my life story, I will try, without reservations, to answer that question. In writing about my life I have posed my personal quest for absolute honesty against my human desire not to be cruel. A compromise between truthfulness and kindness is not easy. Just ask Mary Branham, to whom I am indebted for my title. That lovely redhead from Fort Sumner, New Mexico, who ran, unsuccessfully, for Secretary of State and now is an executive with the Wheelwright Museum, once authored a handbook on how to turn your marriage into an affair. But before that she had worked at La Fonda's front desk and was sufficiently intrigued by the goings-on to produce her own manuscript titled "With Reservations." Her potential agent in New York sent it to the Fred Harvey headquarters in Chicago for review. Mary was promptly fired, and her manuscript remained unpublished until now.* Fortunately I cannot be fired. However to balance truthfulness and to avoid causing unnecessary pain to them, I have preserved the anonymity of some individuals by resorting to the use of initials only.

Of course, the real story of the goings-on in Santa Fe in the 1940s is in an out-of-print book called *The Spider in the Cup.* Most of the copies were bought up by a physician in Española, and the State Library copy was stolen.

I have few regrets for following my Peripatetic Way. Some people may learn from others, but I have learned only from my own mistakes and my own twists and turns. They have been sufficiently numerous that possibly I am now approaching wisdom. But I cannot join with Edith Piaf's *Je ne regrette rien.*

Kierkegaard was right on with "It is not true that the scientist goes after truth. It goes after him. It is something he suffers from." Since inhibition will be denied, this journey is intended for my family and friends.

---

* Mary wrote "With Reservations" in 1954 when La Fonda was operated by Fred Harvey as part of a large chain of hotels and restaurants throughout the Southwest. Now, hopefully, we will assist getting Mary's wonderful spoof published.

2/ HARLEM

MY MOTHER AND FATHER were part of that great Jewish emigration from Poland-Russia before World War I. My mother came from Radaschitz, northwest of Crakow and Kielce. As a teenager, she entered Ellis Island as Monya Chelmnitski and exited it into America as Mary Friedman. Her original surname is somewhat strange since King Chelmnitski was a notorious anti-Semite responsible for some of the most vicious pogroms against Jews in Poland. My mother did not have a happy childhood. Her widowed father had married a woman with children from a previous marriage. The new wife apparently favored her own children, even providing larger portions of food to her own brood than to her spouse's. Radaschitz was predominantly a Jewish village with stone and log homes that were taken over by Poles after the obliteration of the Jewish community during the Holocaust, which included burning the Jewish synagogue. The Jewish cemetery was similarly destroyed by the Germans although some beautiful sculptured headstones did survive.*

My mother had only unpleasant recollections of her father and spiteful recollections of her stepmother. Her older sister and younger brother were already in New York and that undoubtedly encouraged my mother's emigration.

My father, Max Biegelaisen, from Uzakuf west of Warsaw and north of Lodz, and his brother Harry Bigeleisen (*sic*) had been teenage partners as tailors. They managed to save enough money to come to New York, where one of my father's cousins carrying the adopted name Sol Sherman had married one of my mother's sisters. When we visited Uzakuf in 1994, we discovered that, like Radaschitz, it had been a place of violence for the Jewish community during World War II. The Jewish cemetery was about 99.9 percent destroyed by the Germans, and the Poles were a trifle hesitant to point out its location

---

* When Ethel and I with our daughter Lenore visited Poland in 1994, I wore my beat-up black cowboy hat. One of the Poles we met at Radaschitz wrote me three months later, "I was too embarrassed to ask while you were here but could I have a hat like yours?" So we sent one for him and one for his wife.

to us. After the Holocaust the Poles wanted to set up a memorial but didn't have the money so instead they planted a grove of fast-growing trees which is all that remains other than a very few broken pieces of stone.

My father managed to avoid military service in the Russian Army by voluntarily submitting to an operation which created a hernia causing him to fail the medical examination. He told me that in the war with Turkey a Russian general had received a medal for winning a battle in which he had crossed a stream using drowned soldiers from his own division as the bridge. For Jews, life in the Russian Army must have been hell, commencing with consumption of treif (nonkosher) food, which would have been a harsh violation of the biblical commandments. On the other hand my father always remembered warmly the civilized cordiality of Amsterdam, Holland, where he embarked for the United States.

The name Biegelaisen is a play on two German words meaning "to iron with an iron," so the ancestors must have some transient German roots and they undoubtedly must have been tailors. The name must date to 1812 when the Jews were emancipated in Prussia and names were then assigned. The only contemporary who survived from my father's generation is a cantor in Haifa, Israel, who has taken the name Shlomo Barzilon, which means "iron" in Hebrew. Another cousin, Yeidel (John) Bigeleisen, became a Lutheran and ended up as professor of religion at Washington University in St. Louis. Since the Germanized names must have replaced former Sephardic and former Hebrew names, they continued to adjust as the country of residence changed. One was anglicised to Smith and Tarunchik became Turner in the United States.

I was born Schmuel ben Mordecai on March 3, 1922, three years after my sister Marian. My father had started out as a garment worker in New York City, but motivated by his added family responsibilities, he joined his other cousins and a nephew and opened a grocery store in Harlem. It was located at the corner of 142nd Street and Lenox Avenue, diagonally across from the Cotton Club. We lived four blocks away. My earliest recollections are of my third birthday when my mother had seated me on a dining room table and was dressing me. My mother was short and heavy, with hair that reached down to her knees. She was very proud of her hair, and we always enjoyed watching her luxuriously comb the strands. She said that if she had remained in her orthodox environment in Poland, she would have had to shave her hair at marriage, and that this contributed to her decision to leave for the United States. My mother had great inner and outer strength, and my sister and I and our father all loved her deeply, even if many others found her strongmindedness too much to take. She was notoriously late for every appointment. But she and my father had only one goal in life—to sacrifice for me and my sister. Although she kept a kosher household (but not to the point of having separate dishes), she really had no empathy with religious notions, and I do not recall her ever attending a synagogue other than the day of my own bar mitzvah. She could neither read nor write and didn't harbor the slightest feeling of inadequacy as a result. To the contrary, she often stated, "Paper has patience, you can write whatever you want on it." She actually felt superior to those who could only traverse life's paths by being literate. She had very strong feelings of opposition to Christian churches and in our household never referred to Jesus but frequently to *mamza*, which in English is bastard. My most kind mother had no inkling of the place of neighborly love in Christian theology and certainly could not relate to Gertrude Stein's statement, "The Jews have produced only three geniuses: Jesus, Spinoza and myself."

My father was kindhearted and soft-spoken and lived a terribly demanding life, opening his grocery at 6 a.m. and closing at midnight, six days a week. On Sunday he closed about 2 p.m. In those days there were blue laws, which forbid commerce on Sunday morning. So it was a standing practice for a police car to drive up about 10 a.m. and for a tall Irish police captain to solemnly walk across the very wide Lenox Avenue and approach the cash register where my father would hand over the necessary bounty. My father was in all respects, of lower middle-class orientation without any real intellectual expressions. At that time most immigrant Jews read either the Communist Yiddish paper, *The Freiheit*, or the Socialist Yiddish newspaper, *The Forward*. But my father read *Der Tag*, which was bourgeois in its concerns. I don't recall that he ever read a book. He took a passive role in the Lodzer Lodge, a social club of Jews from the Lodz area. At one club event he was encouraged to drink beyond his capacity by a rascal of a cousin, and my sister and I were ashamed at his antics. This cousin also had a store in Harlem where it was rumored he entertained black females in the back of the shop. Father always lovingly remembered his mother and worried over the difficult poverty that faced her back in Poland. Even during the Depression he periodically would save a few dollars and write a letter back home and hand the envelope to a courier who would be making a trip back to Poland and distributing these small gifts. Sometimes my mother would grudgingly comment on my father's charity to his family, but she never seriously objected.

Back in those days before World War II, all the shops in Harlem were owned by Greeks or Jews or Japanese. The customers, of course, were exclusively Black. Many had migrated north from the southern states; others were West Indians from the Caribbean and were more emotional and a little tougher to deal with than the transplanted southern Blacks. They all trusted my father implicitly, since simple honesty was his hallmark. The conflicts in Harlem at that time were between the more educated West Indians and the American Blacks, with the animosity toward the Whites taking second place. For me Harlem was excitingly exotic.

From a very early age I worked in my father's store on Saturday and Sunday and continued to do so through college. Starting at the age of eight or nine, I would deliver orders to the Cotton Club, where I met Cab Calloway, Dizzy Gillespie, and Charlie Parker and, of course, caught glimpses of those beautiful and sensuous light-tanned chorus girls. At night, outside the Cotton Club would be Packards and Dusenbergs and Cadillacs with chauffeurs waiting for their white employers who were tourists from Kansas City or Ft. Worth and whose mischievous highlight of their visit to New York would be coming to the Cotton Club. It wasn't until much later that I learned black customers were not admitted to the Cotton Club. I don't believe the movie "Cotton Club" caught the glamour and excitement of that cabaret since it overemphasized the presence of the gangster Dutch Schultz. The kitchen at the Cotton Club was always leased out, usually to a Chinese or a Japanese operator, who would come into my dad's store to make supplemental purchases. I learned an early lesson in merchandising when my father used a ticket of purchases amounting to about $8.00 (a lot of money in those days) to prepare a supplemental invoice adding up to perhaps $9.50 for the messenger to take back to the chef.

The main highlight of working at dad's store was the routine each Sunday morning when I would deliver an order to a bordello midway up the street between Lenox and 7th Avenues. This request was generally for two dozen eggs, a pound of bacon, six bottles of Guinness Stout (quite a luxury in the Depression) and a dozen bottles of Coca-Cola. Now no one told me the nature of this place, but I almost immediately recognized something unusual since the elevator operator would press a particular button that probably rang a bell in the apartment and then accompany me from the elevator to the apartment which housed about a half-dozen very appealing "high-yellows." The madam was not too careful about the security of her silk robe, and I could not help notice that the point of her breast was concave. For some time I had the feeling that was normal for women. Periodically a white detective would move into that apartment and remain there for about a week. As I got older, my mother would ask, "What took you so long coming back with that order?" My mother must have had a very peculiar notion about the possible risks of delivering to the apartment because one day she told me, "Now when you go up to that apartment and bring back the empty bottles, grasp them from the bottom of the bottle and not from the lip."

There was never any antiblack prejudice from my parents. Rather they expressed concern at the effects of the hard times of the Depression on Blacks and appreciation of the mothers who held the family together after working like dogs as domestics and then meeting the responsibilities of homemaker. The black women really were the heroines, applying the cement that now seems eroded from so many Afro-American families. We always packed boxes and bags half full with their purchases and then put in their purses with more groceries on top to discourage purse snatchers. My dad experienced about one armed hold-up a year. I was in the store during one such robbery and, without thinking, stopped the leader of the two burglars from pushing my mother. She then pleaded with the armed thief not to hurt me since he would protect his mother the same way.

An apartment inhabited by Blacks typically contained two locks on the door plus another lock that controlled a four-foot steel bar that ran on a metal track inside the door plus an enormous German shepherd or two. And then there were the "hot beds" in apartments where tenants rented a bed for one of three eight-hour shifts and this on a consistent basis. I was never assaulted when delivering orders to these apartments but was always suspiciously alert. One day when I was walking to the "El" at 145th Street and 8th Avenue, a young future "Mohammed Ali" provoked a fight. His right to my jaw lifted me off my feet, and I still carry a scar from that altercation.

The black mothers assembled daily outside the subways in the Bronx, waiting to be selected for housecleaning work. Locally this was called "the slave market." Some of the swankier, dolled-up ladies did more than clean house after inspection by single men. Crimes of passion were not infrequent, and about every fortnight some man would rush into the street with a razor slash across his neck or some young chippie would come screaming with her pretty face cut with a knife. Despite the rough lifestyles the church was really important to the sanity of Harlem life. At 145th Street and 7th Avenue the second floor of the Baptist Church over the movie marquee burst with the strong gospel melodies while the rhythms made the wood floors and brick walls almost explode in cadence.

I was a workaholic at my dad's store, rapidly scooping out one-pound bags of sugar or flour from 100-pound sacks or slicing layers from huge slabs of butter. Periodically, I would clean up the storeroom in the back. One day I recoiled in horror at the corpse of a rat almost entirely composed of moving maggots. Everyone was afraid to go down to the basement storeroom that accessed from Lenox Avenue because of the darkness and rodents, but they did not stop me. One day a near riot developed that only my mother could quiet. I was about fifteen years old and had climbed up the ladder from the basement when a five-year-old black girl screamed I had "sexed" her. I had never seen this youngster before and cannot imagine how she zeroed in on me, but a huge, angry crowd assembled and I was really in danger. My father would never have been capable of soothing that mob, but my mother did.

Early in 1939 we started repacking the storeroom as tightly as possible. My father was overstocking the groceries because "a war is coming and we will need to be prepared." And of course my dad did profit from inventory inflation during World War II. This prosperity was offset by the 1943 Harlem riot, which utterly destroyed all the stores. No compensation from the City of New York was ever offered. The previous source of good business during Prohibition days was routinely selling one customer 300 pounds of brown sugar, twenty pounds of yeast, and several cans of malt syrup; there was little arguing about prices in these transactions. Nor was there any arguing concerning a nervy incident with another customer. In the store a large barrel of mackerels stood near the bags of rice. One day a buxom mama was checking out with my father, who was noting the charges with a stub pencil on the brown bag. When the lady asked, "What's that five cents?" My father replied, "That's a mackerel." She followed with "What mackerel, Mr. Max?" My dad then reached down her bodice and extracted a sizable fish and ended all discussion with "that one."

I happened to be down in the store the night of the Joe Louis-Max Schmeling return bout. Schmeling, of course, had won the first fight, and the Nazis had openly spouted snide slogans of the White Hope's victory. When Louis knocked out Schmeling in the first round, all of Harlem exploded in a communal fiesta and the streets were packed solid with ecstatic humanity. My dad reacted quickly and said, "Let's close and go home." Ordinarily, in those Depression days a taxicab would wait for my dad's departure. Dad paid only 70 percent of the meter reading for the ride home. This arrangement guaranteed the driver would be able to show some gross to his boss in those bleak nights when few could afford taxi fare.

In those days many people in Harlem received welfare in the form of what was called a relief check. Such a check was actually a three-inch by eight-inch piece of ruled paper that the grocer filled out, ostensibly to report purchases limited to essentials and not extended to luxuries like cookies or Pepsi or cigarettes. Every Sunday evening at home, as we listened to Amos and Andy and Walter Winchell on the radio, my dad would dictate fictitious purchases out of the blue to me and my sister. We would subtotal the costs and the results were presented to the authorities for reimbursement. Blind obedience to regulations that violated common sense was not part of our upbringing. The other big affair of some regularity was going down to Steinbergs, a Manhattan dairy restaurant, on Sunday afternoon for early dinner with members of our extended family. The three or four fathers would fight to pay the bill while all of us first-generation Americans squirmed in embarrassment at the loud uncouthness of our parents. My uncles all had cars but my father did not. Although he was tolerated as somewhat of a failure, he outlived them all, respected and loved.

My sister was the apple of our parents' eyes. She was sensible from infancy and took care of me since my mother returned to the store and stayed till closing after she fed us supper. Looking back I now recognize that jealousy was in me. I was a very late bed-wetter and a persistent nail-biter. But my sister was a worry bird and we had to change apartments after a break-in through the fire-escape window. Just prior to adolescence we experimented with some groping petting, which probably is not that unusual when siblings are left alone. When I entered third grade, in order to provide better education for my sister and me, our parents moved to a solid white middle-class neighborhood, Highbridge, just between the Yankee Stadium and the Giants' Polo Ground. This entailed a difficult commute for my father. My short sister had skipped three grades. This so impressed the principal that when I went to register in PS73 she said, "This must be a smart family, so we will start the young boy in the Rapid Advance class." This meant that I would also advance three grades before graduating. Practically every day our teacher would say to us, "You are the best elementary school in New York City and you are all the smartest in this RA class." In my senior year our class advisor was the science teacher, Miss Feick (you can imagine how the class delinquents played with that name on the chalkboard). Miss Feick wanted me to go to Stuyvesant High, which emphasized science, but I wanted to be with three buddies. We took the exam for Townsend Harris Preparatory School, and to my surprise, I was admitted. This was a unique adjunct to the City College of New York. The prep school occupied three floors in the School of Business. It was an elitist boys school that granted a high school diploma in three rather than four years and provided an automatic entry to CCNY. I did receive the science medal at PS73, with my father clapping loud and long in the back of the auditorium.*

There were many street corner orators in Harlem, ranging from the back-to-Africa nationalist Marcus Garvey to the charlatan evangelist Father Devine, who surrounded himself with wealth and white lady followers. The Communists made little inroads into the Harlem scene although they did promote some token black politicians. I don't recall visceral hatred from our black customers; several of them corresponded with me when I was an overseas GI.

In preparation for my bar mitzvah, I went every afternoon to an orthodox synagogue with Rabbi Rabinowitz as teacher. We ended up reading the Five Books of Moses and the Book of Joshua in Hebrew. (No, I do not know Hebrew now!) In no time at all I became a true believer of orthodoxy. Here was the answer to all life's perplexity, and a sweet glow of superiority accompanied this faith. I was Rabbi Rabinowitz's star pupil and would accompany him to his apartment for lunch after the Sabbath Service. But I failed the critical test in my bar mitzvah speech when I forgot my lines and had to be prompted by the rabbi. For more than a month after my bar mitzvah I laid t'fillin each morning, lacing the leather thongs or phylacteries on my arms and saying prayers. By the thirty-fifth day I could not escape the realization that this was a simplified god and the grandeur of the strange universe was much more wondrous than bending my knees and repeating by rote the ancient prayers. My abandonment of orthodoxy hurt Rabbi Rabinowitz deeply, but I could not sacrifice

---

* At the 1995 Indian Market, Ruth Schultz of Albuquerque and Paul Furgatch of North Carolina and Harvey Furgatch from California all put on the PS73 hats Harvey had made and were his guests for a grand dinner at the Inn of the Anasazi.

what seemed painfully clear to my intellect. It was the start of my ultimately appreciating how the quantum mechanics innovator Max Born concluded his Nobel acceptance speech: "For the belief in a single truth and in being the possessor thereof is the root cause of all evil in the world."

3/ THE BEST AND
THE BRIGHTEST

THERE'S MUCH TALK of the Minta High School in Budapest that produced Szilard and Teller and Wigner and Von Neumann and of Boston Latin in Massachusetts and of the Lowell School in San Francisco. But in New York, Townsend Harris Preparatory School was unsurpassed. Its alumni include Cornell Wilde, Kenneth Arrow, Robert Jastrow, Bennet Cerf, Joseph Flom, Hobart Rowen, Elliot Janeway, Sidney Kingsley, Bernie West, Eugene Lang, Frank Loesser, Ira Gershwin, Edward G. Robinson, Jonas Salk, Richard Rogers, David Schoenbrun, Julian Schwinger, George Weissman, Seymour Lipset, Adam Clayton Powell, and Herman Wouk. This tiny school of fewer than 10,000 alumni has already produced four Nobel Laureates. Hans Bethe once asked if I were one of them. I said, "Not yet." In those days there was no Bronx High School of Science, and all of the young male elementary graduates at the top of their class took the entry exam trying to get into Townsend Harris. The Nobelist Leon Lederman failed and was rejected. For me it was an educational experience absolutely unsurpassed.

At our very first orientation lecture the corpulent Latin teacher, Dr. Roy Begg, said that we were the cream of the crop and nothing less than excellence would be tolerated. He concluded his little talk by saying, "There will only be two reasons for absence. The first will be sickness and the second will be death." And we all roared with laughter. Later my classmate Richard Rothstein mentioned this to his father, who said that was how Dr. Begg had greeted his own class twenty-five years previously.

The school was named for the man who opened up Japan to the Western World, and it was intended to be a haven for the intellectually elite. It was under the jurisdiction of the New York Board of Higher Education. Physically, it was located in the middle three floors of the downtown CCNY School of Business at 23rd Street and Lexington Avenue, but students came from all of the five boroughs. The school was restricted to boys, and they were scheduled to graduate in three years. The required curriculum included Latin and one other language and several years of mathematics, plus a year of science. The teachers were untenured, but with their dedication and brilliance they represented the school's essential talent. Periodically, students who could not keep up would be flunked out and sent to Evander Childs or Stuyvesant.

It seems to me that everyone in my class was Jewish, with the exception of a Black, Robert Mangum, and a Catholic, Carrol. Mangum was a respected combination of scholarship, athletics, and leadership. He ended up with a successful career in the New York police force and would have gone to greater heights, but he was caught up in one of the New York City bureaucratic imbroglios and became a judge. Carrol was a complicated specimen. He was a good student who directed his anger at being surrounded by so many Jews by coming to school every day dressed entirely in black to mimic the nazi black shirts who were then marching in Yorkville. By alphabet, I normally sat next to him and we got along fine. I appreciated his good mind. Of course I had no inkling of his ultimate plight. He broke his leg on a skiing trip (the rest of us had no idea whatsoever of this uppercrust sport of skiing). While he was in the hospital, his girl-friend ended one of her visits to him by becoming pregnant. They entered into a suicide pact, but after he shot her, he underwent a change of priorities. This notoriety was the highlight of our class for quite some time. I do not know what happened to Carrol after he got out of juvenile detention. We had no idea what having a girlfriend meant, so that added to the intrigue.

We followed a demanding scholastic program and normally went to bed at 10 p.m. after trying to keep abreast of the homework load. The school combined a magnificent student body and a no-nonsense faculty. I looked up in awe to one of my classmates, Jerome Entis, who I really thought would at least become president of the United States. He was inspired excellence from top to bottom and was the quickest in our class. His father was a salesman for National Biscuit Company and would always regale my father during his visits to the grocery store. So my stature within the family was diminished some-what with the knowledge that I was nowhere up to Jerome Entis. At the end of World War II while Jerome was an officer in the navy, his ship picked up some White Russian refugees off the coast of Shang-hai. They included a beautiful young lady who became his wife. Surprisingly, Entis' career capped off with his being an advertising executive with R.H. Macy. Later, he had his own advertising agency before suffering a premature fatal heart attack.

My first introduction to leftist thinking was under the instruction of the English teacher, Dr. McQuen, who included in the class sessions political arguments about the Japanese invasion of China and the Fascist support to Franco in Spain. This was a strange tone to me since concern for society was very secondary to my family and Eretz Yisroel, the land of Israel.

Across 23rd Street from THHS was a highrise commercial hotel, and all of us learned together (by watching specific guest rooms) the unaesthetic technology of procreation, which appeared rather sordid. Our camaraderie, I should also say, extended to using the window lift pole to write equations on the dusty top windows prior to examinations in physics. Some of our classmates were so young they graduated wearing short pants. Unfortunately, in 1941 Mayor LaGuardia proclaimed that an elitist school did not conform to the struggle for equality in a democracy, and he succeeded in abolishing the school. Recent research suggested there may have been some political deal making with certain black aldermen. The professors did not have tenure and there were no real pensions so they were forced to go into other careers after twenty or thirty years of successful tutelage at Townsend Harris. For some, of course, it proved to be a fortuitous bonanza. One switched into accounting and became a famous authority.

About 1980, several of the alumni started a movement to activate an association of former classmates and to promote the reactivation of Townsend Harris. Ethel and I went up to the first reunion of all alumni. The program included the famous physicist William Nieremburg, who said that a certain professor had given him a grade of 89. When he appealed in protest and asked, "Couldn't you have found at least one additional point to give me?" the professor replied, "I am surprised at you. Surely you would prefer to be the highest of the B's than the lowest of the A's." On the program was the well-known Communist, Morris U. Shappes, who had gone to jail at the time of the Rapp Coudert loyalty hearings. I was a little dismayed to see him included on the program, but after he had concluded his remarks, I joined everyone with a loud ovation. Shappes said that he had left Europe as a refugee with his family and had gone to Argentina where they remained for several years before they were able to get up to New York City. His mother worked the angles, and he was somehow admitted to Townsend Harris, which psychologically was a disaster for him. He was confused by the Germanic Jews and became ashamed of his background and his parents and of his orthodox religion. He said that his emotional confusion was so great that he failed Spanish even after having resided in Argentina. He finally found solace in Marxism and for many years was an apologetic Stalinist before he finally saw the light, but it seemed to me he had replaced that anchor with Jewish nationalism.

The campaign to reestablish Townsend Harris was partially effective and in the mid 1980s a coeducational four-year school was established as part of Queen's College. I don't believe there is any vigorous entrance exam although the school apparently had more science finalists in the Westinghouse Science Fair than the Bronx High School of Science. Some of our alumni groan that it is coeducational, but most of the stars are turning out to be ladies.

I had become fascinated by Dr. Truesdale's classes in physics, and even though I was not too careful in the elementary experiments, I did go on to read Einstein and Infeld's book on relativity. I wanted to enroll in college as a physics major, but my sister pointed out that I had to give some thought to earning a livelihood. She thought the only job that could be secured in New York City at that time was teaching bookkeeping in the high school. "How will you ever get a job as a physicist?" "Well, Doc Truesdale is quite up in years and before too long there will be a vacancy." "No, you just can't depend on his mortality for your own career." Now that sixty years have passed, it is apparent that my true calling was science and not commerce.

One of the benefits of graduation from Townsend Harris was automatic entry into City College, and except for those few from more affluent families who could go on to colleges that required tuition, that is where most of us went. And so I decided to remain downtown at 23rd Street and Lexington Avenue and pursue a degree that would enable me to teach commercial bookkeeping. A number of my Townsend Harris friends did the same thing.

4/ STURDY SONS
OF CITY COLLEGE

MANY GRADUATES OF CITY COLLEGE have published their paean of praise to the effect that they could not have achieved their subsequent success in life without having had the benefit of that free tuition. The latest to have gone public with such a manifesto is General Colin Powell, who very frankly described his successes in ROTC and his failures in engineering at Uptown City College. So he switched his major to military science. His revelations ten years ago suggested a rare bird with inner strength. For me the school was absolutely a disaster, and I have no one to blame but myself.

In my freshman year it was apparent that one could coast on the superb education from Townsend Harris and earn B's without doing anything. That, more or less, is what most of my high school buddies succumbed to. The very worst subject was the introductory course called Methods of Education, which was pure repetitive simplicity. I knew I could not take much more of this and decided to switch majors. So I carved out a unique banking and finance program, even though it was not listed as one of the alternatives. Professor Aaron Sokolsky was much taken by my economic arguments when he wasn't concentrating on Selma Levy's crossed legs. Many years later the respected chemist Joel Hildebrand, who I believe was still teaching a considerable load in California at the age of 90, pointed out as one of the indictments of American higher education that a famous university (probably Columbia) listed more courses in education than in chemistry. I would have died remaining in the supercilious education curriculum.

The four Foner brothers were a phenomenon in Marxist circles then and possibly still are. The oldest were the twins, Jack (downtown) and Phil (uptown), who taught history. Phil was generally considered the more scholarly of the two. Maybe they were like the Panofsky twins–the smart one with a grade of 100 and the dumb one with a grade of only 99.5. Henry Foner, downtown, was recognized for his leadership qualities and became president of the student body, and later had a successful career as president of the Fur Workers Union. I understand there is now a new-generation Foner, who is a respected historian at Columbia. The twins were charismatic Marxist historians and many suspected that they were disciplined members of the Communist Party, but this was denied under oath to the Rapp Coudert Committee. However, those were confining times, and it is quite possible that false testimony may have been rationalized, but I certainly do not know the facts.

Like so many others, I was captivated by Jack Foner's brilliance and success as a history teacher. By my sophomore year, I had joined the American Student Union, which was the popular organization of liberal students across the United States. It was headed by Joseph Lash, who was a close protege of Eleanor Roosevelt. Some FBI agents claimed the closeness was more than intellectual, but that's a peculiar tossup. Ultimately, the ASU was taken over by communist sympathizers, and then as a victim of the erratic line coming out of Moscow, it disintegrated. I was present at an all-day debate where the Marxists headed by Witt defeated Lash. I was swept up by Marxist thought and devoured all of the writings of Marx and Lenin and Leo Huberman and John Strachey and David Guest. I found Marxism a comfortable faith. It was based not on revealed truth, but on "the science of society," which provided good answers to all questions ranging from philosophy and political action to the hard sciences. My time was spent at the mimeograph machine or in political demonstrations instead of at class. After failing to show up at introductory Science Survey for two weeks I wandered one day into class midway through the hour and curiously started to play with a Toricelli vacuum tube, which sputtered as I pulled it up from its mercury bath. Professor Shaw's attention came my way, and he shouted, "You dirty bastard!"

I became the leading leftist radical in downtown City College in my junior year. I actually read the three volumes of *Das Kapital* but recognized Marx as a sociologist and not a disciplined economist. Despite his brilliance he was ignorant of bureaucracies and of the evil that self-perpetuating corrupt leaders are capable of. In 1863 Marx was a correspondent for the *Herald Tribune*. It was the same year in which Jules Verne and Edgar Allen Poe were predicting wicked government bureaucracies would emerge, but that never occurred to Marx. Most of the ten demands of the *Communist Manifesto* have by now been adopted by all the Western democracies. I tell my liberal friends that society will probably similarly adopt Newt Gingrich's ten points in his Contract with America. But young people need to realize that in the 1920s when Communist William Z. Foster led the steel strike at Gary, Indiana, the standard was twelve hours per day, seven days a week, for starvation wages.

My disenchantment with Marxism was accelerated by essentially two developments. My close friend Alvin Gouldner refused to follow the party line and accept the Nazi-Soviet Pact, and the YCL higher-ups accused him of being a social fascist (yes, that was the characterization then). They ostracized him, and one was not permitted to talk to him. This violated every modicum of common sense within me, and I continued my friendship with Alvin Gouldner on a clandestine basis. He was a hot-headed rebel who went on to become a famous sociologist and first editor of the magazine *Transactions*. He always married girls named Helen. Just before he died (in the early eighties) he wrote a critical monograph on Stalin with a footnote to the effect that Stalin was one of those arch criminals known as statesmen. Alas, he sent me that pamphlet with a notation, "Why don't I hear from you?" He was then on sabbatical from Washington University and there was no return address.

The second and deeper development involved the periodic mass rallies at Madison Square Garden, where every seat was sold and the principal attraction would be either the orator Earl Browder or the black baritone Paul Robeson. Browder was a cut above the run-of-the-mill bolshevik and it was pleasant many years later to meet his two talented mathematician sons, both members, I believe, of the National Academy of Science. It was frightening to see respected Ph.D.s join at Madison Square Garden to chant for more than fifteen minutes, "Browder is our leader. We shall not be moved. Browder is our leader, we shall not be moved. Just like a tree that's standing by the water, we shall not be moved." This mass psychosis from otherwise respected and decent people was reminiscent of the newsreel scenes of the fanatics in Berlin in front of Adolf Hitler. Blind obedience was a preparation ground for the same people, ultimately like robots, trying to explain the 180-degree shift coming out of Moscow from the United Front to the Nazi/Soviet Pact. I felt the same way when we were at the Wailing Wall in Jerusalem one Friday night, and I told Ethel I couldn't watch those orthodox true believers putting written pleas to God into cracks and that I had to leave. "You are silly—you stay for the Indian dances." But I left in a cab while Ethel met an acquaintance from Santa Fe.*

Most of those I ran into in the Marxist tide were first-generation American Jews who were trying to find some viable answer to the spread of Fascism. This was certainly not provided by our own Congress, which did not come to the assistance of the legitimate government of Spain but permitted Germany and Italy to use the Civil War as a training ground for their ultimate plan of world conquest. Many of the best students from City College volunteered and went to fight for the Loyalists. They included John Gates, who became the leader of the Abraham Lincoln Brigade. Gates finally left the Communist movement in the 1960s after Kruschev's speech revealing the crimes of Stalin. Those were the days when every Sunday the radio waves carried the screeching of the Detroit Priest, Father Coughlin, whose openly anti-Semitic attacks were not very far removed from those frightening speeches by Hitler. Coughlin's oratory did not produce any condemnation from Cardinal Spellman or any of the other top leaders of the Catholic Church.

Most of my intimate leftist friends went on to very successful careers in real estate or finance or other areas of corporate America or the military. Their professional achievements underscore Eric Hoffer's later statement that the radicals of the 1930s became the landlords of the 1960s. It was unnerving in later years to occasionally come upon a die-hard still adhering to the evil god of Marxism. They'd attached so much of themselves to this faith that it would have been spiritual suicide for them to open their eyes to its folly. It is frightening to realize that, during my junior year, I was a subservient apologist of the greatest mass murderer in history.

My second class with Jack Foner included as a classmate the precocious and outspoken Daniel Bell, who became a highly respected Harvard sociologist and the author of *The End of Ideology* and *The Post Industrial Society*. Whereas most of us in those college days were more or less blindly sympathetic to Stalin's dialectic, Danny Bell was unique for criticizing it for what it was. But the Communist hierarchy labeled him a Trotskyite and someone to be avoided. Bell had as good a

---

*Of course with ingenuity the rigid mindset could be avoided. For instance, a Soviet archeologist colleague of Southern Methodist University Professor Tony Marks quoted Marks in his doctoral thesis, and that sufficed for the obligatory quotation of Marx. They are spelled the same in Cyrillic.

mind and as lucid a vocabulary as I had come across, and many teachers feared having him on their class rolls. About 1967 when he was invited to Dallas to be an honorary lecturer at Southern Methodist University, Ethel arranged a dinner party for him. She invited our most intellectually skilled friends. At that time Bell was somewhat sympathetic to our country's efforts in Vietnam and claimed that "favorable surprises could occur." But the impressive, brainy Bill Garrett (he turned down editorship of the *Harvard Law Review* saying he came from Tulsa to Cambridge to study law) responded, "Unfavorable surprises can occur." When I drove Bell back to his motel, the only guest whose address he asked for was Ann Richards, who, of course, went on to become governor of Texas.

I was, fortunately, able on several occasions to renew my friendship with Bell, but he is proof that even the most talented are not perfect. In the late 1970s he was invited to be the annual lecturer for the J. Robert Oppenheimer Memorial Committee in Los Alamos. On the afternoon of the lecture I took him and his wife Pearl to lunch at El Paragua in Española. The conversation got around to the oil fields in the middle east and the threat of some terrorist groups destroying them. After listening to Dan and his wife, I suspected that they were making a gross error. "Dan, you seem to think an oil pool is a void space like a swimming pool." "Why, yes. Isn't that the case?" I then pointed to the limestone rocks next to our luncheon table and said, "No. Oil is normally produced from the minuscule void spots in sandstone or limestone and the rate of flow is governed by the degree of connection or permeability between these porous spots." Dan mentioned that a friend of his probably wasn't aware of this and, as it turned out, the friend had just left Harvard to head the Persian Gulf desk at the CIA! Bell's lecture at Los Alamos drew a large crowd since his title was "The Return of the Sacred" and "The Hill," as Los Alamos is familiarly referred to by the locals, oddly enough is packed with churches. But you needed a good-sized English dictionary to stay with him as well as an Italian one for his favorite word, *recoursos*.

I ended up taking a number of courses in economics, a subject in which I got respectable grades. I didn't have the patient discipline for accounting but captured its essence for future use. In my last semester my classes started at 8 a.m., and after commuting by subway I remained at school to attend a 9 p.m. course taught by John T. Ryan and titled the History of Economic Thought. Professor Ryan, who had studied in Ireland, was appreciated as having one of the sharpest minds in the faculty. Unfortunately, he was a victim of alcoholism and we never knew whether he would show up. Some considered him the Irish Morris Raphael Cohen. He'd lost his tenureship in the main college but was finally given an opportunity to reestablish himself in this course in the evening session. The first two lectures were magnificent, and I knew I had made the correct decision to stay through the evening.* He did not show up for the next four lectures, and by then the administration realized that he was a hopeless case and brought in a substitute teacher of conventional abilities. There were no quizzes whatsoever until the final exam. To the puzzlement of the other students, I got up five minutes after the exam was distributed and walked out. I had written something to the effect that the exam was a disgrace to the memory of Dr. Ryan and that I thought I should receive an A. The substitute instructor was tolerant of the extreme arrogance of youth and gave me a B.

My most significant achievement at City College was establishing a close friendship with Ethel, who would become my wife. While the main CCNY Campus was restricted to men and Hunter College was restricted to women, downtown CCNY was coeducational. Ethel finished her studies as a statistics major and in the last years of the war she took advanced courses including chi square and analysis of variance at Columbia. She promoted herself into a mail-order firm that advertised dress patterns in newspapers and sold them for 10 cents to 25 cents each. Postmen staggered in each morning with orders from all over the country. The business was booming, and an excess-profits tax of 90 percent encouraged the luxury of research, so the boss was elated with Ethel's theory that she could determine which patterns would sell best in different parts of the country and which were the best days to advertise. Soon she headed up a department with three statistical clerks, and no decision could be made without her. The boss urged her to hire a professional assistant, and the finest of applicants turned out to be a math graduate girl who was Black. Ethel hired her, and the next day Ethel was called into the boss' office. "What's this I hear about your new assistant?" "She's the best of the applicants." "Well, I don't care about that. Fire her." "Then I go too." There was a long, long pause before the boss capitulated. He saved face by concluding the meeting with "don't let it happen again."

Ethel awoke one day in rather angry confusion. She insisted the

---

* When the Nobelist Willie Fowler got to Cal Tech on a scholarship, he saw Millikan and Einstein in the hallway and said to himself, "Ah, I've come to the right place."

formulae she had fitted to the business were incorrect and she would have to close down the department. Nothing I could say would dissuade her and that's exactly what she did. I still wonder why she wanted to run from her problem. Perhaps she psychologically was trying to adjust to macho me.

I had been working for Lehman Brothers when in 1949 I resigned to experiment with self-employment. We needed some regular earnings, so Ethel tried, unsuccessfully, to get a job. After fruitless searches, I suggested she amend her resume to exclude college studies, and in no time at all she was hired by the actuarial firm Quackenbush as a statistical clerk. One evening she revealed a serious problem: her superior, whom she admired, was submitting an insurance quotation, but Ethel detected errors in his mathematics. After we analyzed the predicament through the night, she approached her chief the next morning and innocently asked whether the crucial calculation was accurate. After his reexamination, he looked at her quizzically since he recognized the essential error. Well, when she subsequently resigned so we could move to Texas, she revealed to him her advanced courses in statistics. He then admitted to her that he was relieved it was not really a junior clerk who had stumbled on his mistake.

Our college anthem was "Sturdy Sons of City College..." and Ethel was and is a sturdy daughter. I met her in the leftist movement, and we were in a number of classes together. She was a cheerful and open young lady from the *Shtetl* of the East Bronx, with a humanitarian psyche throughout her family. Her father took in several homeless people and supported them in Depression days until they could recover. He was the last White to leave the neighborhood after it turned Black. It seems to me that she wore the same red sweater for four years at college. Although we were close classmates, our very first date was two weeks after graduation. She had not attended the ceremonies because she was recovering from a deep gash in her leg from a bicycling accident in New England.

She has become the central focus of my life, and now that she is over seventy she is more beautiful than when she was thirty, a better mother than earlier, a better tennis player, skier, swimmer and hiker, a more passionate lover, a talented hotel decorator, and a more confident and independent soul. That does not mean that our times together have been a bed of roses. The sculptor Janet Schroeder, who for a while was a permanent guest at La Fonda, wrote a story about her idyllic marriage to her second husband, who developed the first pressurized space suits. I told her the tale was either a gross falsehood or she was uniquely blessed. She said it was the latter. Ethel and I have shared many joys and many anguished sorrows, but our commitment and loyalty to each other have become the central facet of my life. I take in stride the challenges that face me almost daily in trying to cope with her. Rabbi Leonard Helman said it was a miracle that two such diverse personalities could survive together but that we could learn from each other. I know I have learned from her but often wonder...how much she has learned from...me.

My grades at City College were not exceptional, and I guess the motivation was lacking. After the war, when I enrolled in an MBA program at NYU Graduate School of Finance in the evening, I received only A's even though NYU seemed like a trade school compared to City College. The dialectical arguments in the student lounge on the fourth floor of City College where I and my student friends settled the grand fundamental philosophical disputes of the planet were never to be matched in my academic life.

Out of admiration for Robert Taft and Jacob Javits, I registered in the Republican Party in 1946 and have remained so enrolled even though those radical weirdos currently in the catbird seat cause one to reflect. In the 1980s one of the great shocks in my life was to realize the Republicans can be as crooked and dishonest as the Democrats. But I remain a green Republican.

5/ ENTERING MANHOOD

IT WAS LATE 1943, and I was just twenty-one with corporal stripes on my left sleeve. I was stationed in the verdant Sila Mountains in southern Italy with the 800th Engineering Forestry Company. We were laboring through unbelievable snowfalls at civilian sawmills that had been commandeered by the U.S. Army to resume production of lumber at pre-war prices for immediate transport by narrow-gauge railroad to the main line in the valley. At the same time the 800th's own portable sawmill, tested in Virginia and carted from Louisiana to North Africa to Cosenza, was working three shifts down at the railhead. The local pine timber was cut into dimensions deemed urgent by the Fifth Army 200 miles up the peninsula. The 800th's portable groaning sawmill was spewing out lumber 500% above rated capacity while the ball-bearing line for discarded slabs was surrounded by Italian laborers. Our morale was high, as was that of the Calabrian day laborers who had both wages and a hot lunch. Even the liberated Jewish and Yugoslav refugees from the nearby Fascist Feramonti concentration camp, hired as white-collar workers, were forgetting their traumatic times of yesterday.*

To the 160 GIs of the 800th the time spent in Italy was so much better than the nine months spent in Western Tunisia, where we cut one million board-feet in the oak woods at Ain Drahm. This destruction of one of the few forests in North Africa was an abject lesson in military stupidity. The wet lumber was not stacked properly, and most of it ended up in tent stoves at a fighter air base near Tunis. The protesting Vichy colonel was told by me (requisitioned as interpreter), "*Lentement* (slowly) *s'il vous plait, c'est la guerre.*"

Each week a charcoal-powered civilian truck with a hot water tank behind the cab would come into our main camp from Tunis. Sgt.

---

* I met the family Tusak with their infant daughter in this most southern of Europe's concentration camps and then met them again years later in Dallas with their daughter, who had earned a math scholarship to Rice. Strangely, Ethel, Lenore and I also visited the Nazi's most northern rail shipment point to Auschwitz, Nordkap, Norway.

Schultz and I got permission from Captain Ericksson to hitch a ride into Tunis provided, "If you're not back by Monday roll call, you are both privates." We toured the churches, mosques and synagogues and then had some titillating experiences in the Casbah. Sunday afternoon we got a ride from the Casbah to the outskirts of Tunis and waited there five hours with not a vehicle in sight. We wondered whether this excursion was worth losing our stripes. Finally at about 11 p.m. a truck slowly chugged up. We queried the driver (in French), "Where are you headed?" "To Ain Drahm near Tabarka." We made it back to camp with fifteen minutes to spare.

After landing in Naples, another soldier and I were sent south to Vibo Valencia with instructions to write a report on lumber facilities there. We were scared silly and hugged our guns and crept into Cosenza late at night. We finally cornered an Italian young man who couldn't understand that we wanted him to take us to the police station. Finally with a look of dawning recognition, he directed us to a madam. But her den of pleasure was not our frightened menu that evening. At the hotel where we spent the night we told the innkeeper we would give him a US army chit. He climbed to a shelf and pulled down a handful of unpaid German and Italian army chits. But we convinced him we were the victors and he had no choice.

The Sila climate was exhilarating, the wine was good, the public bathhouse an unexpected luxury, the Cosenza professional ladies were inviting and the matter-of-fact brutes from Washington and Oregon who composed the 800th were making playful sport of the Calabrian brave ones in the nightly "fist-fetes" outside the mountain bistros. In this single respect the natives compared us unfavorably with the members of the Luftwaffe, who had previously manned a nearby fighter strip. But we were all welcomed otherwise as distant relatives of those who had migrated to Philadelphia or Newark. I got along well with the Calabrese who insisted I was really Italian. When I protested that my family were Jews from Poland, they countered, "Oh your parents were ashamed to reveal you were Italian."

The Fifth Army's appetite did not stop at ammo, fuel, grenades, and plasma. The bridges and corduroy roads up at the Arno demanded more and more timber. So the 800th was ordered to search for additional civilian sources. Herbert Gildow, Luigi C., and I headed for Lago Arvo up in the mountains with our two-and-a-half-ton truck and spent the night at the Milano owner's guest cabin. A vicious storm raged all night and by morning everything was so white we could barely see the truck. For twenty-seven days we were nourished by resident managers Pasquali diBuono and Guido. Each night they outdid one another in providing a feast for us, replete with red wine. One night I stumbled in a stupor into a snow bank, but fortunately Herbert asked where I was before turning in. They found me, but I came down with pneumonia. Pasquali saved my life with warm goat's milk. After twenty days Pasquali and his wife were in heated discussion as to whether they should bring back some female companionship for us from San Giovani en Fiore through four feet of snow. But I convinced them it wouldn't be necessary.*

While we were snowbound I was the ranking NCO and I finally decided we had to get word to our unit. Fortified with wine, cheese, salami, and bread, Pasquali and I started off on snowshoes (a new experience to this New Yorker). After ten hours of fatiguing hiking through drifts we finally came to our caterpillars, which were trying fruitlessly to break a trail through the snow. I wanted to return ample GI food stocks to Guido and Pasquali but our Italian-American food sergeant was giving me a hard time until I reminded the captain that we had passed up 243 food rations in our absence.

Luigi C. was from New York and was a fascinating fellow utterly content with himself. He was an expert in opera, and there he concentrated his intellectual talents. Before the war he had been a printer on cruise ships, and he had assembled a photo album of luscious harlots he had known throughout all the world's seaports. If he learned there was an enticing redhead in Singapore, he'd sign up for a ship with that destination. As our translator, he always drew a crowd whenever he opened his mouth in a town square to ask directions. They would ask him many questions. How do you speak Italian? Where are your parents from? Do you have relatives here? Finally he went

---

* In 1970 Ethel and I went to Italy with the Santa Fe Opera tour and we drove down to Calabria. The Lago Arvo where I had spent nearly a month was unrecognizable; it was filled with high-rise ski chalets where formerly there were sawmills. No one had ever heard of Pasquali diBuono—not even the carabinieri after checking their conscription lists. We were dejected at first, but I remembered they used to talk of Isola Capo Rizuito. We drove down there but met with the same lack of success. As we were about to depart, I saw in the town square diBuono's Auto Parts and in we walked. When I inquired about Pasquali, his 28-year-old daughter squealed with delight and said in Italian, "You are Corporal Samuel." She had remembered the stories of when she was two years old. Pasquali had moved north 100 miles to Spezzano Albanese and after she telephoned him he promised to wait for us on the highway and we found Pasquali and his family at Spezzano Albanese where his greeting words were "Is this your first wife?"

into a Cosenza print shop and thereafter would hand out printed cards with his life story in Italian.

After our rescue Captain Ericksson said, "Sam, you are to proceed to Corrigliano on the Adriatic coast and arrange for the local sawmill to sell us all its output. The British Eighth Army controls that railroad and will be tough to deal with. But they have instructions to drop three empty flatcars a day at Corrigliano. Make an accurate count of the lumber every day, give a receipt to the Italian millowner from which he will be paid, and see that the cars are securely loaded and anchored. Come back every two weeks to pick up rations for yourself and the Italian chauffeur assigned to you. It should be an interesting experience and Lord knows how long this war will last."

And so the 25-year-old chauffeur Carlos in his Italian army uniform, with me as passenger in his Fiat pickup, pulled into Corrigliano. Hailing from North Italy, he was blond and blue-eyed, with aquiline features and a taciturn nature. Our good rapport was marred only by the unconcealed disgust in which he held the local Calabrese. Since there was not another soldier within an 80-mile radius of Corrigliano and the roads were utterly devoid of motorized transport, Carlos would tear heedlessly around the curves—inevitably running into the native men and women walking arm in arm from road shoulder to shoulder, as well as pigs, goats, mules, cows, dogs, cats, and chickens. Carlos left his mark on the countryside. He would charge at the flotsam and curse the fact that these locals were part of his own nation. My trifling of Italian picked up when snowbound permitted some discourse. Thus we enjoyed each other's company and hardly had a disagreeable moment in the months we spent together in one commandeered hotel room in Corrigliano.

Of course, we did not subsist on the issued GI rations. After each trip back to headquarters, we handed over our invaluable coffee, sugar, soap, cigarettes, spam, chocolate, and canned eggs to the hotel proprietor and in return feasted thrice daily gratis at his family's table. And, of course, I did not spend my time at the railroad siding counting the pieces of lumber loaded onto the flatcars. "Roberto, now you are sensible and so am I. There is no reason we should both count this lumber, particularly since you know that only my count is the official receipt and that's how you will be paid, regardless of my overage or underage. Therefore, let us agree to some ground rules. You will make the count daily in my absence. Periodically I will make a spot or partial or total count and I warn you, if you ever cheat by one measly one-by-four, I will deliberately screw you thereafter in the accounts I turn in to American Military Government. Come, let us have a glass of anisette and celebrate our arrangement."

On return to Lago Arvo one day I learned that the British had stopped two cars with extended lengthy poles. My mission was to go north with a crew of Italians and reload the cars with peaveys for leverage. That night at Cosenza Station I saw a clean Littorina (a diesel-type trolley car) and told the station master we would take that in the morning. He protested spiritedly and said it was reserved, but I told him our work was the most important and to have a conductor there at 7 a.m. The Italian laborers were thrilled—never before had they ridden in luxury in a Littorina. The station master was blocking the train, but I fingered my revolver and off we went. All of us worked hard under the hateful eyes of the British sergeant, who could not understand my fraternization with the laborers. The British NCOs could easily qualify as the most arrogant of the species on the planet. Everyone was singing joyously when we rode into Cosenza at night, but one of the 800th GIs said, "Now you've done it, Sam. The Captain is waiting for you." At company headquarters Ericksson exploded, "Dammit! That Littorina was reserved for an inspection of southern Italy by a general—we are all in hot water." "Reloading that car was more important than any general's visit, don't you think, Captain?" So he winked and let me go.

The countryside was beautiful, Corrigliano was quaint with its ancient cobblestone streets, and the nearby beach was a delight afforded few troops. Occasionally we witnessed a bit of excitement as when an RAF fighter made a forced landing on the beach, which was deserted but for Carlos and me. I liked the people; they liked me and tolerated Carlos. A local capo pointed out what a fortune we could both make letting him use our idle pickup to transport the oranges of the countryside rotting on the trees to the distant metropolis of Taranto, where people were crying for citrus. "One hand washes the other, and they both wash the face," he pleaded. But the black market suggestion was promptly rejected. Back at Cosenza, headquarters had their own excitement involving a Yugoslav private named Matt Sizgorich. He had been sunk three times as a merchant sailor and was given the option of returning to sea or enlisting in the US army. He joined the 800th just before we left the states. Now in Cosenza he learned through a displaced person's grapevine that his wife and children were in a refugee camp in Taranto. Captain Ericksson said this latrine rumor was nonsense. But after Matt threatened to go AWOL, he was given a three-day pass. Astoundingly, he arrived in Taranto as his family were on the gangplank boarding a ship to Egypt. He brought them back with him, and they unofficially joined the 800th's roster. The mess sergeant manipulated the daily rations to make sure they were well fed.

Yet, a cloud of guilt gradually enveloped me after each trip back to headquarters from Corrigliano when I could catch up with the war's progress in the latest issue of *Stars and Stripes*. The Anzio beach bloodbath was now in full fury, and I knew I had not joined this army to spend my days in paradise on Corrigliano's beaches. So it was that confusion finally suggested a grand tour. "Carlos, we have things well in hand and have a satisfactory and reliable arrangement with Roberto. Without notice, let's slip down to Catanzaro and then by the back country in a wide swing up to Taranto and then home. We have two 55-gallon drums of gas so let's leave at the break of dawn without a word to anyone. I know how the lumber count averages each day so if Roberto pulls any Mafia stuff I will know straight out."

Before the war Catanzaro, 150 miles to the south, had been a long-established winter spa for British tourists. Now its principal high-rise hotel had served as the bull's eye of an air strike so that it was hanging together like a tinker-toy construction. Yet the British were using it for one of their casualty retreats and mezzo-mezzo on its bulletin board a typed notice read, "Due to the exigencies of the times, service will not be up to normal." Nevertheless the chef's mess was better than we were used to and we left in much improved spirits. But the return swing through the mountains gnarled away our good cheer. In one of the isolated villages, home to perhaps several hundred civilians, our pickup's entry on the one and only street created a near riot. Women with infants at their breasts and half-draped in rags of garments swarmed into the road screaming, "Pane, pane, pane, pane." But we cleared out quickly since we had no bread to provide. Hours later with our discomfort still churning inside, we reached Taranto and sought shelter.

What a thriving, bustling, energetic city Taranto seemed as I strolled the main streets while Carlos went off seeking some hoped-for dalliance. But suddenly one black-marketeer of watches appeared at my side. He was slenderer, straighter, suaver than the others. Carefully and tentatively he whispered, "Jehudi." When with a self-conscious smile I said, "Si," he burst forth like the coming of dawn. I could see that he was dressed better than the others, had better shoes, had better color. In a mixture of French, Italian, Yiddish, and English, he excitedly told me that he and his wife were refugees from East Europe and had escaped the Nazis. One way or another, they had survived and now had an apartment in Taranto. He begged me to go there with him. I entered his one-bedroom apartment to meet his wife. A beautiful, elegant, sensuous woman in her thirties, she was finely dressed and adorned with jewelry. Yes, they had escaped across Europe, suffering starvation and humiliation. Yes, they were now deep in the black market to scrape whatever lire they could in order to bribe their way to Tunisia. They had now found a fellow Jew, a conquering American who would help them with money and would bring merchandise for them to sell.

In a stupor I heard this tale while simultaneously viewing the silken sheathed bosom before me, and recalling the emaciated breasts of the starving villagers of yesterday. My sympathy for this couple gradually turned to loathing. What right had this elite couple, so better off than anyone I had seen for months, to demand a priority of my aid and succor. Alas, just as Carlos could not conceal his disdain for his Calabrian brethren, so I could not hide my anguish and confusion. As I awkwardly backed out of their room, they showed only astonishment—never hostility, just astonishment. At an unremitting and silent pace we returned to Corrigliani, picked up the receipts, and the next morning loaded our belongings and drove until dusk when we reached headquarters at Camilliatella in the Sila.

"Captain Ericksson, I want a transfer to a combat unit." He never looked up but put his papers down, and in a slow voice replied, "Fine, Corporal, you will leave for the front tomorrow."

So it was that I found myself participating in maneuvers preparatory to the invasion of Southern France. Our daily exercises consisted of hiking down a cliff to a narrow beach where we would spend the day in conditioning exercises and then at dusk climb back up the cliff. After a few days a pimp appeared on the beach with two protegees. He had gauged the market well and a queue of certain GIs across the beach was thereafter a fixture at lunch time; it was labeled the alternate chow line. Our daily routine was interrupted one day by a visit from an inspiring hunk of an officer seeking volunteers for the First Special Service Forces, a joint Canadian-US Commando Unit in which every volunteer had to shed his rank and enter as a private. I found myself with a devil-may-care group of ruffians who found such prospects appealing, but I chickened out of the volunteer line a minute or so before swearing in. (Whatever sixth sense of survival prompted that decision was clairvoyant since every single one of these volunteers was killed on a raft assault outside of St. Tropez off the French Riviera.)

The Replacement Depot north of Naples was like a mix-master from which recruits would hourly whirl out to the fighting units. But six weeks went by and here I still sat, now No. 2 in longevity. Puzzlement turned to a chill fright when I learned that No. l, a signal corps master sergeant, had joined the Repple Depple in Casablanca two years previously and he was still waiting for his assignment. With this specter before me, Corrigliano began to look mighty enticing as I appeared before the Depot's Chief of Classification to inquire why I was becoming a permanent boarder of his transient hotel. "Let's see, your spec number is lumber statistician, and we have only one such post in our theater. That's with the 800th Engineer Forestry Company!" I quickly explained that Catch-22 twist to this Chief of Classifications.

"We have lots of shortages now for mortar squad leaders. How does that sound?" I assented to this change in classification without mentioning that I had never seen a real mortar.

By summer's end the invasion fleet was on its way to Southern France to meet with a glorious reception from the populace whereby all daydreamed tales of heroic war came true. In this manner, still in a Repple Depple, I found myself bivouacked in Grenoble. We were guarding a group of Mongolian captives, part of the Turkoman division of Siberian POWs who had been conscripted into service by the Wehrmacht. At this point, the local Maquis came down from the hills, burning for revenge since the Germans had only recently massacred some hostages in the suburbs. The apathetic Mongolians did not flinch even at the trigger-happy Maquis who, at the slightest infraction of rules, would pull the unfortunate aside and a rifle shot rang out.*

By September 1944 I and the other assigned replacements were riding north compressed in the back of a two-and-a-half-ton troop carrier. Out of excitement at the change and just because any new assignment has the charm of the unknown, all the replacements were joking as is, no doubt, the way of soldiers for time immemorial. That

---

* Recent revelations of the complicity of significant segments of the French populace in accepting German occupation have been a sad awakening. We in the invasion force were convinced every Frenchman was in the resistance. The actuality is that most of the resistance Maquis and underground FFI were communists.

truck could have been mistaken from its carefree sounds for a busload of skiers returning from the exhilaration of the day's slopes. But suddenly the background theme changed with the very first sounds of dull, deadly, unmistakable artillery. From the time of that first sound—and until we reached our destination two hours later—not a word was spoken. Each man became an impotent captive of his thoughts—as he finally came to a stark realization of what was in store and wondered how he would respond, how his subconscious would dictate his accommodation to this foreboding-unrelenting artillery.

Company headquarters of the 117th Cavalry Reconnaissance Squadron was in an abandoned two-family dwelling on a side street of some worked-over French town in the Vosges Mountains. The captain and his aides were leisurely draped across the sofas and exhibited as little concern as the occupants of a steam room in a Turkish bath. Their elegant, confident manner was in keeping with that of the Essex Troop of East Orange, New Jersey, men of the National Guard who had enjoyed the right side of the tracks and really didn't know that there was another side. "Christ, I'm glad we finally got a mortar man for Troop C." "I'm sorry, Captain, but I've never seen a mortar. I'd like to go to your Troop C and will gladly tear off these stripes until I earn them." The captain only chuckled, and I was shipped into the 2nd Platoon, Troop C, still sporting two stripes. My good reaction to combat and the game of death was undoubtedly influenced by the blessed fortune of being surrounded by a close group of men, gentlemen who demonstrated that there was some good after all to be conceived in gentility. By now nearly seventy percent of the ranks were filled by replacements from the recesses of our melting-pot nation. But the hard core of Essex Troop respectability still placed its elevating stamp on the periodic newcomer.

Reaction to combat is unpredictable. Performance in rear-echelon maneuvers is no guide to behavior under the real thing. It was my pleasant surprise to learn that I was a superior combat soldier. Perhaps I was helped by the knowledge that my 20/200 uncorrected vision was an exit visa in reserve any time combat got too rough for me. When squads were picked for a particularly dangerous probe, it was flattering to know that my comrades could feel secure having me alongside. Our close-knit and highly efficient decimation squad included Robbie, a sanitation worker from Newark who was the finest of battle leaders and who ultimately earned his lieutenant's bars in Alsace; J., a dull, imperturbable Yakima Indian from the Pacific Northwest who could stand before any barrage oblivious to everything but his mission; Mulligan, a Cajun from the bayou country utterly devoid of introspection but a good man to be with in a fire fight; Bienstock, our capable and dependable radio operator, an accommodating Jew from Brooklyn; S., a hulking erect rancher from Wyoming, straight out of the "shoot' em ups," for whom life was divided into the good guys and the bad guys and who was fortunately on our side; Sandy, a handsome clean-cut youngster from Oklahoma with ice in his veins when the going got rough; and Pancho, a Mexican transplanted to southern California who was not yet reconciled to wearing khaki in a war on distant shores, a war that didn't concern him, but whose "macho" side always enjoyed a gory, bloody fight.

There is nothing like the baptism of combat to bring out the courage, altruism, kindness, self-sacrifice, and camaraderie in a group of men. People call this *esprit de corps* and it is one of the grandest experiences in life to know your buddies will come regardless of risk to your aid and you to theirs. Five days under combat turns a man into a veteran. To those who've experienced that baptism and survived, no amount of writing can contribute one iota of understanding. No descriptive power can enlighten that sensation for those still innocent to the doughboy's moment of truth.

The only cancer that marred our small squad's unity followed the arrival of P., a veritable SS trooper in GI drag. He hailed from the Midwest, was six feet, two inches tall and built proportionately, seemed moderately intelligent, but was an opportunistic power seeker. The fact that he was a superb combat soldier did not lessen one's sense of the abasement he reserved for all humanity. He had picked up in some abandoned German supply warehouse the leather uniform of a Luftwaffe pilot. He wore it constantly. I was concerned about the "H" on my dog tags in the event of my capture, but the prospects facing P. with his leather togs never seemed to have entered his head. One disgusting incident vividly revealed P.'s inner temperament. We were told to make a surprise midnight visit KKK-style on a captured German village and line up all the males and, after a talk by an AMG representative, force the civilians to surrender their arms, including hunting pieces and knives. The group assembled before us were the aged, infirm, and crippled inasmuch as by that time the Wehrmacht were scraping the real bottom of the barrel for manpower. One slender octogenarian German did not move fast enough when directed to make an about-face. P. lunged at him with a crushing slap across the face. Although P. was proud of this chastisement and none of us uttered a word of rebuke, discomfort remained a collective undercurrent in our squad.

The battles raged from the Vosges Mountains of France to Strasburg in Alsace Lorraine and to Ludwigshaffen in Germany. Fortunately, the human psyche retains the pleasurable sensations and, having survived the gory part of war, our memory of that winter is one of grand sport. We gloss over the new faces required in our ranks—in five days they will be old reliable comrades. We forget the dismemberment of Troop A when caught in a minefield, with six casualties suffered in the attempt to rescue the first soldier. We remember bivouacking in the warm, three-story farm houses in prosperous Alsace. We chuckle at Mulligan's reply when asked why he always picked the house with the oldest woman when we all first reconnoitered to pick the house with the youngest: "Well, dey tink it's de last time at dere age and dey put everyting into it."

One of our missions was to enter a town at night with three jeeps and reconnoiter and then return to base. Naturally, there were no lights and it was a pitch-black moonless night. As we slowly traveled the road, having previously memorized a map of the village, we all could see out of the corner of our eye a tank standing perpendicular to the road with a muzzle brake on its cannon—*ergo*, a German Tiger tank. Nothing happened. Hardly breathing, on the return we again slipped by the Tiger tank. Was he asleep? Was he puzzled at what went by? Did he assume we were Wehrmacht vehicles? On another occasion two armored cars were ordered into a village for inspection. We quietly inched in and the lieutenant told our gunner to put a shell through a substantial water tower. "Wait a minute," I interjected. "If you do that, you will flood out the houses below." "Oh yes," said the Lieutenant. "But there may be some snipers up there." "Granted. But why don't we button up our command cars and sneak in?" Well, it was a draw: fire came from across a ravine but not from the town. So we quickly turned around and fled and I was not scolded for insubordination.

On another occasion we were ordered to survey a mountain road. We parked the vehicles on the near side of a bend and on foot proceeded around the corner where we all fell flat after attracting mortar fire from a near hilltop. Our inclination was to hug the earth but the mortars would have killed us all. So after one barrage, we all jumped up and ran for cover. Our Lieutenant radioed to headquarters that we couldn't proceed—because the Jerries had the road zeroed in for mortar fire. "Lieutenant, proceed ahead with your vehicles." "Like I told you Captain that would be suicide." "Lieutenant, you have your orders. Proceed ahead on your mission." We all stared apprehensively at our lieutenant with his microphone, then shouted hurrah as the lieutenant spoke loudly, "Captain there's something wrong with this radio. You are garbled and I can't hear you. We are returning to base."

All ground troops resent the air force and navy with their hot meals and clean sheets. As a matter of fact, ground combat troops are resentful of headquarters personnel one mile back. There was a world of difference between the "front" and the protection of a mile back. However, we all saluted the air force one winter day when they came to our rescue. We were camped under a highway bridge in snowbanks with a long open field ahead when here came three German Tiger tanks leaving a wooded area and heading straight for us knowing that our 37-millimeter shells would bounce off a Tiger tank. Should we surrender? Should we put up a fight? Should I throw my dogtags away? But happily two American dive-bombers responded to our distress call, and the tanks turned tail.

During the frigid Battle of the Bulge we were ordered to withdraw from our positions in a forest to shorten the Seventh Army lines. Finally, we were able to start one vehicle and then used it to start the others. But our convoy drew to a halt in a woods about 3 a.m. when a very intense fire fight raged for thirty minutes before quieting down. I'm not sure, but I don't believe any enemy was opposing our barrage of fire. However, one newly arrived twenty-year-old recruit stepped over the barrel of our armored car's exterior 50-caliber machine gun when someone inside brushed the foot-activated trigger and a shell went through the young man's lung. The pathetic lad lay on the ground. "I don't want to die. I don't..want to die. I...don't...want....to....die......!

While I was still with the 117th Cavalry Recon Squadron in the Vosges Mountains, we were in Foret Le Bitche in foxholes and subjected to an intense artillery bombardment of Neberwoufus. These eight mortars lie in a circular pattern. They fire in sequence with a frightening distinctive sound of boom—eight times. The soldier next to me had logs and dirt over his foxhole, but he did not creep out with the rest of us when the shelling ceased. Then we pulled him out by his legs—a piece of iron had pierced his helmet and brain. I was waiting to pray to God during those fearful moments but did not do so. The conventional statement that there are no agnostics in a foxhole was not completely true.

A few of us got lost and joined another unit for several days. A short twerp called me a dirty Jew. I told him if he didn't apologize right then, he wouldn't see daylight. All night I tossed and turned because I wanted to waste him when my own guard duty tour came, but I realized others had heard my challenge and I would end up in the brig or worse. I could still see his smirk when the sun rose, but he never saw my relaxed sigh when he was killed the next day in an artillery attack. I had placed wooden personnel mines around the perimeter of our position and didn't have a chance to deactivate them when we suddenly pulled out. Many is the time I've wondered if some post-war picnic turned into a tragedy from those "bouncing betties."

Europeans are experienced in warfare. Stoically, the citizenry endured the starvation, the killings, the pillaging, the fleecing, the fleeing. Stoically, they knew it must ultimately come to an end and then would be time to settle accounts and switch to old values. The fact that our bombers missed the bridge but hit the church and school, the fact that the Germans reentered Strasburg and slaughtered those who had shown enthusiasm for the Allies, the fact that valuables from both corpses and chateaux were often "liberated"—all this was understandably covered by the trenchant comment, "C'est la guerre."

Strasburg had been selected by Nazi bigwigs as a destination for their wives or mistresses. It seemed the town was filled with sex-starved frauleins but some of them were shills to entrap GIs to their apartments where they were killed by accomplices. General Juin of the French Armored Division announced that a German POW would be executed for each Allied soldier so murdered. But this order was revoked by General Eisenhower back at Nancy. He understood that leadership requires better judgment from the detached. At the Battle of the Bulge we were ordered to pull out of Strasburg, but those loyal to the Allies climbed on our vehicles and we were ordered to club them off with our rifle butts. This was one of the saddest moments of my military service.

The 117th Cavalry had the distinction of being the first unit of the Seventh Army onto German soil. The first day all we found were some stragglers who wanted to surrender. Although the previous 100 days on the front line had hardened us, it was jolting to enter Mannheim. This residential city on the Rhine was utterly flattened by mass bombing. A new infantry division of teen-agers had just arrived from the States and came in a day behind us. These young-sters sensed that the war was in its final inning. Those who feared they would not get a chance to use their Garands were trigger-happy, and it did not bode well for any aged German civilian to venture forth for water or food and come into such youngsters' gunsight.

The next day we entered Heidelberg. It was absolutely normal: not a blade of grass, not a pane of glass showed any mark of war. Then moving south to Bavaria, each team of soldiers selected a home for the night and invited itself in. Apparently our selection had been that afternoon's choice of a group of Moroccan Ghoums attached to Le Clerc's Tank Division. Here was a middle-class respectable home with a comfortable middle-class respectable family. The aging father's reaction to our making ourselves at home was a mixture of resigna-tion, petty condescension, and another quality that I could not put my finger on. We each selected our sleeping space and spread our bedrolls and enjoyed the seduction of hot water and a bath. Our behavior seemed to have more or less convinced the father that we were tolerably part of homo sapiens.

However, this man soon approached me and excitedly insisted I follow him to the upper floor. As we climbed the stairs this elderly fellow became more and more agitated. He beckoned me to follow quickly. I did not know what the source of this excitement was and could not help but release the safety on the Luger in my belt. Finally, we came to a closet on the upper landing. He swung the door open and, with a mild oath, pointed inside. With one eye peering into the closet and with the other scanning the landing for some treachery, I dumbfoundedly surveyed the scene but could not see the source of irritation. The agitated father kept up a steady stream of incoherent German, and finally in exasperation at my stupidity he pulled aside several of his suits. Then I saw that each jacket had been vertically slit by some sharp knife. From the continuing froth of German sentences it came through that some Moroccan Ghoum several hours previous had been the culprit.

I was chastised with accusing eyes as if at some war crimes tribu-nal. The stupor of my expression only enraged him further. Incredulously, I finally realized that a complaint was being regis-tered. What rotten irony that this mild inconvenience should call forth the very first civilian complaint since we landed in Oran long ago. In his self-pity was not one remote suggestion of any responsibil-ity for the German-delayed bomb at the Naples' post office set to go off at rush hour, for the cave massacre at Salerno, for the civilian slaughter at Grenoble, for the buzz bombs, for the Nuremberg Edicts, for the Jew and Gypsy genocide, for the horrors of Poland and the Ukraine. The utter self-righteousness of his accusing eyes turned me into a madman. Jerking out my pistol, I shouted an eye-witness account of German atrocities. Ultimately, I pointed to myself and screamed "Juden" until finally some hint of fright showed he understood. My rage was made the more intense by the fact that his expression never altered–except to reveal some fear and the smug realization that he was right all along about these shabby invaders of his homeland. It was just by a hair that I did not pull the trigger. Limp and shaking, I came downstairs and pulled my unit out in the darkness to find another home.

I had discarded my rifle for a Thompson 45 sub-machine gun, since it was clear that accuracy in returning fire was not as important as directing a stream of bullets so the opposing guy would go down. One day leaving a house at dusk, I saw a crouched body near our Jeep and heard a swish of air so I blasted that enemy. It turned out to be an adolescent German girl letting the air out of our tires. I was not elated at her death, neither was I distressed. The next morning Major Middleton said, "Sergeant, I'm recommending you for a commission, but you know what a rifle platoon leader is up against. How about it?" Reflecting but a second I replied, "Fine." After 22 days at Fountainbleau, I was a gentleman with gold bars on my lapels. It was February 1945, and I would soon be twenty-three years old.

6/ THE HERO SAM BALLEN

By THE SPRING OF 1945, the Second Infantry Regiment of the Fifth Infantry Division had pulled back to Rheims where France had surrendered in World War I. The European war was coming to an end, and our division was scheduled to make the beachhead invasion of Japan. During combat in the Vosges Mountains, I received a "Dear John" letter from Ethel saying that she was thinking of marrying a bland social worker I knew. This was a heavy blow. I wrote in reply that if she did, I would smash the 4-F son of a bitch when I returned. I expected I would be a survivor from the European Theatre of Operations, but as the days in combat dragged on I wasn't so sure. Ethel did not proceed with her engagement.

Taking advantage of the war's wind-down, I was able to run in to Paris for a free day or two by hopping on to a GI truck. It didn't take long for me to develop a close friendship with Danielle, a beautiful blond young salesgirl who lived not too far from Place Pigalle. One night in her sleep Danielle started talking German. Then the story came out that she was an army nurse from Germany but did not leave with the Wermacht when it pulled east from Paris. Henceforth, her name with me was the more Nordic Danny.

VE day had occurred and in early July we embarked from Cherbourg for New York Harbor. A hush came over us when we passed the Statue of Liberty, and tears were widespread when we thought of our comrades who would not be experiencing that moment. But then another somewhat angry hush came over us when we went through the narrows and saw civilian cars speeding by on the Brooklyn Belt Parkway. During all our time overseas, our families and friends had been writing how tough things were at home. There was rationing, and the highest priority was for the boys overseas. From North Africa to Italy to the Continent, we had in fact witnessed how civilians were low on the totem pole, and subconsciously we had reached a conclusion that similar deprivations were occurring at home. But in that instant of seeing the passenger cars racing by on the Belt Parkway, we felt that in a partial sense "we had been had."

51

The Fifth Infantry Division was one of the very first units to come back from the European Theater. We were told to dress up for a victory parade on Fifth Avenue, but instead, we were all marched to delousing showers. From Camp Campbell, Kentucky, we were given a 30-day furlough with the understanding that we would then leave immediately for the invasion of Japan. I subconsciously had the feeling that I would not be returning from the Far East, since Lady Luck had already given me a good quota of favors.

As soon as my mother and sister had calmed down after I walked into the apartment in the West Bronx with my duffel bag, I headed off to the East Bronx where Ethel lived in a two-story tenement owned by her family. It was not too far from that opening scene in the movie *Bonfire of the Vanities.* Well, I was swept off my feet at my first glimpse of her. Her virginal innocent purity was in stark contrast to the tarnished landscape we had grown accustomed to during the previous three years. It was normal in those days to accept marriage as the logical sequence of leaving adolescence, and anyway, deep in my bones, I did not think I would be returning on my own power from Japan. Maybe my 138 pounds in a brand-new Eisenhower officer's jacket had an enlightening effect on Ethel—before that visit was over, we had decided to get married in six days. The wedding was at the Grand Concourse Hotel, now I suppose an ethnic battle zone. However, things did not progress smoothly, even though Rabbi Klein of Free Synagogue would perform the ceremony at no charge since I was a GI.

The problem was that in two days when I went to the bathroom I noticed some skin eruptions on my male organ. They looked precisely like the rashes depicted on films shown to entering soldiers to frighten them into a chaste existence. I thought back to my good times with Danny in Paris and wondered if I would now pay the price of those frivolities. I immediately went down to the Army Headquarters at Whitehall Street and displayed myself before a doctor, who promptly stated, "Well, Lieutenant, you've got syphilis." "That's not possible. I have passed my Wasserman test in preparation for marriage." "Oh, that makes no difference. You've got some rare form of venereal disease. We will scratch your back with fifteen strains, and then we will know in the morning what you've got and how to treat it." After the nurse did exactly that, I wandered in a daze down to Battery Park and called Ethel all the way up in the East Bronx and asked if she could take the subway to see me since we needed a serious discussion. So the two of us sat on a bench in Battery Park and I told her of my predicament and asked if she wanted to call off the wedding. With a practicality that I have since come to expect as normal, she said we should proceed with the wedding and that I needed to cure myself as quickly as possible.

The next morning the doctor examined my back and said that all the scratches were negative. I was elated until the doctor continued. "Oh, no, you just have some really rare form of venereal disease. Go on up to the Navy Center on Nassau Street, and they will pinpoint it." After inspecting the rash, the doctor at the Navy Center confirmed that I indeed did have syphilis. He said that a specialist on these exotic forms would be coming in on a ship from the Orient after a fortnight. In the interim he essentially could do nothing. The fact that I was planning to get married in four days didn't seem to particularly concern him. In a most dejected state I walked back to Whitehall Street since I really didn't know what else to do. I then bumped into a medical captain, who asked, "What's wrong, Lieutenant? You sure have a long face." After I explained the situation, he had me unzip my trousers. Then he asked me to put out my hands and spread out my fingers. After a brief examination he said, "All you've got is scabies. There is no venereal disease." Of course I was ready to go on a rampage and could almost visualize the headlines: "LIEUTENANT GOES BERSERK! SHOOTS DOCTORS AT WHITEHALL AND NASSAU STREETS!"

During the first days of our marriage I had to take baths and apply ointment for the scabies, so you can imagine that our honeymoon was not exactly conventional. This may not have been the best introduction for Ethel into the physically romantic side of marriage. While we were on our honeymoon at Lake Champlain, the bombs were dropped at Hiroshima and Nagasaki and we spent more of our honeymoon discussing the permanence of our partnership than making love. Ethel was still a virgin when I left to go to Camp Campbell to be discharged almost immediately because of my service accumulations on a point scoring system. While I was there, Ethel told me on the telephone that she had scabies.

I had never been happy with the distorted Germanic roots of our family name, nor with its comic intonations. While still in the army, I adopted the name of Ballen from a medieval rabbi. I did not then realize its Sephardic connections. When our daughter Panina taught school at Eagle Pass, Texas, I learned there is a famous Ballen ranching family prominent in the Catholic Church across the Rio Grande at Piedras Negras. They probably abandoned their Jewish background centuries ago.

In early 1947 I met my cousin Sam who had just been rescued from Germany by my father and uncle. My cousin Sam was very proud of me and my military experience, and he adopted my name. He was the only survivor of his family in Poland; his brothers, sisters and parents were all murdered by the Germans. After the invasion of Poland, each member of the family had scattered at the father's suggestion. They believed that their chances of survival would be easier if they were by themselves. My cousin Sam went east to Russia, where he was conscripted into the Red Army. After a while he realized that he would not survive in front-line combat and managed opportunistically to become a political commissar in his division. At the end of the war he felt that the Soviet system might have merit for some of its citizens but not for him, so he escaped to Western Germany where he survived by pursuing the black market. He was sponsored by my father to come to the United States where he ultimately married a girl in New Jersey, had a successful marriage for 33 years, owned his own home and raised a family.

Unfortunately, he had picked up some enduring destructive characteristics. He would have nothing whatsoever to do with Jewish ladies who had survived the Holocaust, feeling that they were soiled merchandise. He really wanted to go to Texas and work for me, but I never extended the invitation. He commenced selling copies of the New Testament door to door to Blacks in Newark's ghetto. The downpayment would cover the cost, and then there would be an additional dollar to be paid every month till payout. He also offered an option whereby a priest would bless the volume at a premium price. Sadly, he never was able to free his mind of what he had experienced in Eastern Europe; he ended up taking his own life about a decade ago. But he is survived by several attractive children and a grandson named Sam Ballen.

My first private time with him was at Candlewood Lake in upstate New York where Ethel and I shared a weekend cabin with two other couples. My cousin was curious about my combat experiences. When I mentioned that we didn't invade Japan because the atomic bomb brought the war to a close, he immediately objected: "I'm surprised at you believing your government's fable. The Japanese surrendered two days after Russia declared war. Americans spent four years fighting the Japanese, but as soon as they knew they would be contending with the Soviets, they threw in the towel." I could not convince him otherwise.

It's a fact that large numbers of intelligent people from all walks of life swallow the myths of their governments or their churches or their synagogues.

7/ WALL STREET AT ITS BEST

AFTER GRADUATION FROM CCNY IN JUNE 1942, I circulated an employment application letter similar to the one sent in his job search by Robert Young, who ultimately ended up as president of the large investment trust, Allegheny Corporation. Back in the spring of 1942, the Dow Jones hit a low, if I recall correctly, of 103 and it was a rare day when the volume on the stock exchange reached 1,000,000 shares. There had been no real recovery in the employed population on Wall Street since the crash of 1929. There was a total generation gap on the Street. I received two interviews, one of which was at Lehman Brothers, then in the absolutely top tier of respected firms and housed in a distinguished building of its own at 1 William Street. I was hired in the Investment Advisory Service at $25 per week in June and remained until October, when I went into the Army. My department head was Stuart M. Shotwell, a perfect example of the figure one imagined typified the investment fraternity. He was over six feet tall, handsome, intelligent; he wore Seville Row suits and sported a Homburg on his daily commute back and forth from New Jersey to New York. My CCNY professors must have said some spectacular things to Shotwell for me to be hired in those sparse times.

When I returned from the war in November 1945, Shotwell assigned me to Amthor S. Welter as a research aide. He told Welter how lucky he was to have a *summa cum laude* assistant. Since my college grades were not that commendable, I was at a loss for words at this introduction but as the conversation progressed, it was not opportune for me to interject a correction and then time flowed by. However, when Ethel and I went up to Damariscotta, Maine in 1971 for a final visit with Am, who was dying of cancer, I reminded him of this flattery. Jokingly, Am said that I took ten years off of his life. He feared his junior aide and had to stretch to the cutting edge of his own intellectual powers.

Amthor really did not belong in Wall Street. He was highly literate and would have made a great theatre critic or book reviewer, but essentially he did not know what the crass side of Wall Street was all

57

about. Rolf Steffan, a physicist from Switzerland now living in Tesuque, told me that he had taken his doctorate under the supercritical Nobel theoretician Wolfgang Pauli, and one day he asked Pauli how he knew that a certain announced experiment was wrong. Pauli replied, "I knew in my urine that the description was in error." * The problem with endearing Amthor is that he never really knew in his urine what the field of investments was all about. He spent his time instead preparing investment reports consisting of beautiful compositions in precise English. He missed a great opportunity when he interviewed the president of American Express in the late 1940s and warned him about the size of the salad oil inventories they were financing in Jersey City. But Am did not follow up on this and was only a spectator when the great scandal erupted involving a crook named Di Angelis, who perpetrated a Mafia scam involving nonexistent salad oil inventories and including all of the other accoutrements of bimbo secretaries and private guards. Nevertheless, being assistant to somebody like Am was a valuable transition since I learned of the dignity of cordial relations amongst security analysts on Wall Street and also the purity of clear and honest thinking.

I must have impressed Stuart M. Shotwell in these first few months because I was then offered an outstanding opportunity for a young man in Wall Street, namely to become the assistant to Edwin L. Kennedy, the oil expert for both Lehman Brothers and Lehman Corporation. In the earlier days of Lehman Brothers its principal investments were in merchandising stocks and department store mergers and then later in motion picture stocks and Hollywood conglomerations. But by the end of World War II and in the immediate post-war years, the partners of Lehman had the foresight to recognize the importance of energy, and their largest portfolio had become the petroleum industry. Edwin L. Kennedy was recognized throughout the United States as the outstanding oil and gas security analyst, and I was the envy of other young men returning as veterans from World War II and entering employment on Wall Street when I was made the only assistant to Ed Kennedy. My father asked me if there were Christians working down at Lehman Brothers, and I told him that by far most of the people down there were Christians. My father's follow-up question was whether my boss was a Christian. After I replied in the affirmative, he asked whether my boss was smart.

---

*Pauli once said, "The Nobel Prize enhances some but other recipients honor the Nobel."

Yes, my boss was very, very smart. After some moments of reflection my dad said, "Well, the goyim here must be different from Poland."

Ed Kennedy was an organized, hard-working, factual security analyst who hailed from the Midwest and from modest circumstances. He traveled extensively throughout the oil patch and kept impressive notes of all of his interviews. He was completely fair with me and spent many, many hours introducing me to the economics and the flair of the oil business and to his contacts. I essentially got my entire foundation in oil and gas securities from Ed Kennedy.

To further my understanding I studied geology in the evening at Columbia University but had the misfortune to have the famous Dr. Coryell as professor. He was a learned pedantic who announced to the class that there were 800,000 classified fossils and he knew the names of 200,000 of them. He then proceeded for the next two semesters to prove he possessed this knowledge. I had previously studied metallurgy in the evening at Manhattan College, and that helped somewhat in later understanding the technological processes of drilling for oil. Ed Kennedy was courteous and loyal to his contacts in the oil industry, yet as much as I admired him, I recognized his trick of resorting to esoteric language whenever he was examined acutely in reporting to the selection committee of the Investment Advisory Service. If the questions about the worth of a stock became too penetrating, Ed would start to talk about the silurian formation or connate water or a thrust fault. Back in those days people in Wall Street were pretty ignorant about the oil business. Ed Kennedy might as well have been talking Greek. But in addition, Ed was a good example of someone missing the forest because of the trees. It is un-questioned that he was the most penetrating and informed oil and gas analyst in the entire country, yet he did not go on to the great heights that were captured, for instance, by someone like Mark Millard at Carl M. Loeb Rhoades, who could see the big picture yet knew nothing of the details, but capitalized on great movements in oil securities and oil and gas mergers. Millard shared his dealings with Howard Marshall, the general counsel of the Petroleum Administra-tor of War and former president of Signal Oil. (Now Marshall, at 90, is marrying a former stripper and busty model for Guess Jeans.) But Ed Kennedy tried to teach me a fundamental error: "Sam, you are not paid to not answer a question. When the Committee grills you, you better have an answer and not say I don't know."

It was my good fortune, and one that rarely comes to assistants, to play host to my former boss at Fiesta 1979. My family was all in costume and we were lunching at La Fonda's La Plazuela when Ed and his wife entered. I went up to his table, and he gasped at my jeans and bolo and said, "Why, what is Sam Ballen doing at La Fonda?" But I told the maitre d', Monty Chavez, to send him some wine and sign my name for the lunch.

On my very first day at Lehman Brothers I was tapped on the shoulder by the fellow sitting behind me, Joe Olmstead, a five-goal polo player, who said the secret of this business is that a stock is not a woman and you should not fall in love with it. And he then followed up by saying, "In this business, it's shit to shit and gold to gold." When I returned to Lehman after World War II, my salary was doubled to $50 per week. By 1948 my salary reached $4,000 per annum to which was added a Christmas bonus of about 20 percent. The first Christmas, a distinguished gentleman made the rounds shaking each employee's hand. I said, "I'm Sam Ballen." "I'm Robert Lehman," he replied. In no time at all this yarn went through the house.

Everything about Lehman was grand, running all the way from the intelligent and calm security analysts who managed complex investment proposals to the private elevator operator who greeted everyone by name each morning, and including the daily visits by the Italian shoeshiner who would do a brush-up only for twenty-five cents but would do a more thorough job if needed and would then receive an extra dime. This was a far cry from what used to be known as a "ferry boat shine." The latter could be obtained on the Staten Island Ferry to Wall Street and then cost only a nickel. The shoeshine operator would merely put his cloth on the shoe and would rock with the boat adding very little independent motion of his own. Robert Lehman was the active head of the firm and a flawless example of *noblesse oblige*. He was a dignified and handsome captain, still carrying the charm of the southern roots of his family. His cousin Herbert had been governor of New York State and then U.S. Senator; his other cousin, Allan, was a passive spectator at the firm, playing a somewhat quiet anchor role at Lehman Brothers as did Neils Bohr at Los Alamos during the war. Allan had some romantic episodes with a Broadway starlet and then voluntarily made a $4,000,000 settlement with his wife. This was a record in those days. After I left Lehman, Allan told Eddie Hilson I was the upcoming Monroe Gutman, the theoretician partner at Lehman Corporation. This was a surprise to me.

Each of the partners of Lehman had something special to offer and were not concerned with trivia. There is just no resemblance whatsoever to the greedy slaughterhouse that subsequently became the norm for Lehman Brothers and most of the other houses on Wall Street. One of the partners had the misfortune to execute commodity orders for Truman's aide, General Vaughan, who was acting on the basis of advance crop reports from the Agriculture Department. Since this Lehman partner noticed that every one of his client's long or short orders turned out to be profitable, he started to piggy-back the orders for himself, but when this scandal of advance crop reports became public, the partner was removed from Lehman Brothers within twenty-four hours. It was *de riguer* that one could not trade securities for one's own account until four days after the recommendation had gone out to clients. The *aviso* took the form of a night wire, which was a discounted Western Union telegram delivered by hand the next morning. Clients who were paying for advice in the Investment Advisory Service could use their own brokers for executing orders and they really were not propositioned to have Lehman retain the sales commission. Once we recommended Mission Oil, but the broker loaded on Mission Corp. When we learned this six weeks later we prepared to ridicule the broker. However, a clerk pointed out that Mission Oil had declined 15 percent while Mission Corp. had gone up 20 percent.

Lehman was one of the first few firms to have its own dining room reserved for partners and their guests. The scale of operation bears no resemblance to what is going on today. A good-sized Investment Advisory account would run to maybe $600,000, and a major account would run to just over seven figures. Public mutual funds were just getting under way, and organizations such as Keystone were purchasing research from Lehman Brothers. It was the most respected firm on the street.

After Ed Kennedy had gained confidence that I had learned something from his numerous private lectures, he assigned me primary responsibility for the natural gas industry, which was only then emerging. I lit on a roll, which was almost like shooting fish in a rain barrel. Back in those times natural gas was a waste product that only complicated the production and gathering of crude oil. The natural gas that was marketed was often sold at step-down rates. This meant that the price would be five cents per MCF, but when the volume increased, the price decreased to four cents per MCF, and possibly even lower than that. But at the end of World War II, the Big and Little Inch lines, which had been built as wartime projects to carry oil from the Gulf Coast to the East Coast to offset the numerous sinkings of tankers by German submarines, were converted to carrying natural gas into the New York area. Thus, Texas Eastern Transmission Company came into existence. I made a basic study of the pipeline industry and ended with very bullish conclusions, so Lehman participated in underwriting the numerous interstate gas pipelines that were promoted in the late 1940s.

There were critics of these investments at that time based on the fact that the Natural Gas Act of 1938 limited the earnings of an interstate pipeline to its net original cost of plant investment. Since annually there was a depreciation charge, the critics asserted that earnings would immediately reach a plateau and, henceforth, would be regulated downward. Today it seems obvious that in an expanding industry and through goldplating the pipeline because of advancing technology or safety requirements, the investment would in fact continuously increase. The allowed earnings would be on the total capitalization, so that it would be possible to trade on the equity, as the saying went, and get generous returns on the common stock. Most of my recommendations, or perhaps all of them, proved to be correct, but this was no great accomplishment since I was riding a wave on a new industry. The greatest British theoretical physicist since Maxwell, P.M. Dirac, said, "In 1925 second-rate men did first-rate work," and that is how it felt in the euphoria surrounding natural gas in the late 1940s. About that time, Sally Alley, an ingenious young lady who had worked with the Federal Power Commission, started putting out an FPC newsletter from Washington. Although the newsletter enabled one to keep abreast of developments, surprisingly, few people in Wall Street subscribed to it. We were the very first.

About 1947 there was a big to-do in Congress about overruling a disastrous decision by the U.S. Supreme Court in the Phillips case. This ill-conceived decision enabled the Federal Power Commission to regulate the well-head price of natural gas owned by pipeline companies even though the preamble of the Natural Gas Act of 1938 states that nothing in the act would pertain to the production or gathering of gas. Congress authorized a grand investigation of this situation called the G580 investigation under a distinguished civil servant named Burton Behling. Just before the investigators issued their report, President Truman nominated Burton Behling as commissioner in the FPC. Behling would have been the very first career civil servant to receive such an honor. However, when the G580 Report recommended that this price-fixing power be taken away from the Federal

Power Commission, President Truman withdrew the nomination of Burton Behling–politics over merit.

Going down to Washington with some regularity, I got a glimpse of the sordid structure of the legislative process. At hearings held in large rooms, proponents and opponents (of any proposed new pipeline) appeared and testified before an FPC examiner. The room would be packed with attorneys representing all conceivable lobbies; the railroads, barge companies, and trucking companies as a matter of course opposed every new natural gas pipeline and so would the trade unions in those industries. At the examiner's desk the key attorneys would be testifying, while in the back of the room the other attorneys would be playing cards, reading newspapers, or picking their noses, or just dozing off, but then periodically one of the attorneys would jump up, rush forward to the stenographer, and shout out his comment, which would go into the written record. Subsequently, his client would receive copies and be content. Since the natural gas investment portfolio had grown, Lehman Corporation at this time hired its own analyst, Larry Schmidt, to handle the natural gas pipelines. He and I ended up in disagreement when it came to Transcontinental Gas Pipeline. I felt Transco had ridden the crest of popularity and had gone the limit on capitalization rates, take-or-pay-for gas supply contacts, and all of the other ingredients that make up promoting a new company. I held my ground in my disagreement with him even though he was a more mature and respected analyst, and it did me no harm that I turned out to be correct.

The Investment Advisory people were talking about next year's earnings of United Gas when Allan Lehman asked, "What will the earnings be in ten years?" "We don't know because no analyst has ever been able to interview their tyrant president, N.C. McGowan." Said Allan, "Well, Calder is Chairman of Electric Bond & Share, which owns most of United Gas, and he is on Lehman Corp's Board so arrange for Ballen to go down to Shreveport and interview McGowan." I was astonished at Calder's letter to McGowan with an open copy to me. It sort of went, "Do you think you might possibly find time to permit this fellow from Lehman to interview you and I'm sorry to interfere with your busy schedule."

Just as most motel executives came out of Holiday Inn and just as Fred Harvey could have had a leg up on post-war hotel expansions, so practically all the operating executives of all the gas pipelines being organized came out of United Gas. With a different management philosophy, they could have ended up as the IBM of the pipeline industry, but McGowan was a close-to-the-vest operator. Two of his comments during the interview stand out:

1. Any man who lets his wife work doesn't belong in our family. Lots of these secretaries don't report their new married names. But I have a special inspector in the mailroom at Christmas and when we spot a strange name in incoming or outgoing cards, we trace them down and fire the offending lady.

2. You say we are committing too strongly on take-or-pay contracts and won't be able to meet obligations during a recession to pay for industrial gas without "taking" same. Well, that is true, but when the producer sues us for nonperformance, we will tie up the complaint in court for ten years and by then the economy will be in a prosperity cycle and we will have the funds to pay what we have lost at trial. (This was sort of a prescient forecast of the take-or-pay-for pitfall which plagued the industry in the 1980s.)

These two comments were not insignificant and were typical of an old-line nonprogressive management. United Gas missed the opportunities in the dramatic emergence of the interstate natural gas business and went on to a desultory history.

This Calder was the biggest man in New York although he kept a low, low profile. He was head of numerous social and corporate organizations, but most people never knew of his stature or power: head of the Metropolitan Opera and the Beekman Hospital, on the boards of the Tri-Continental and Lehman Corporation, and so forth. I crossed his path before and after the United Gas incident. I was the very first vet to return to Lehman after World War II, but one month later a new employee, Gordon Calder, was assigned a desk behind me. Gordon was a just-discharged marine. At noon I invited him to lunch, and we went to a low-down funky Puerto Rican place. Since I was so experienced (!) and was working on utilities, he asked what I thought of Electric Bond & Share stock. I said I thought the management was not sufficiently aggressive and I didn't like the stock. "You mean the operating management?" "No, the top management. Why do you ask?" "Well, my father is chairman." The remainder of the lunch was quietly contemplative. Then in 1955 I was at a party in Dallas and was introduced to the handsome president of Horizon Oil, Bruce Calder, Gordon's brother, and he said, "Oh, you're the one who likes Puerto Rican beans but doesn't like Electric Bond & Share." Well, Bruce and I became good friends; he was very successful in all avenues except his choice of wives but I think number five is a winner.

While I was still very new to the game, I interviewed the president of U.S. Steel Limited, which was a Canadian Corporation headquartered at Rockefeller Center. The president really told me nothing and midway through the interview asked rather angrily why I was not taking notes. When I finally wrote up the report, it created quite a stir throughout Lehman Brothers. There were readers who were not too careful and thought instead that I had broken a barrier and was interviewing the head man of United States Steel, which had always been closed-mouthed to security analysts. New Jersey Zinc was another company with a closed door for analyst visits, but they made an exception for Lehman's metal expert, Monte Zinc.

One of my home runs managed to scrape by with some divine protection. With the passage of the Natural Gas Act of 1938 and the growing bureaucratic strength of the Federal Power Commission, there was divergent philosophy on how to handle the FPC. Merriam of Northern Natural Gas decided to cooperate with the FPC while the truculent John McGuire of Panhandle Eastern Pipeline fought them tooth and nail. Symonds of Tennessee Gas would switch tactics in an opportunistic way, which apparently was occasionally strengthened by some wire-tapping. With the implementation of the ill-conceived Phillips decision, pipelines who owned their own gas reserves were limited to a utility rate of return on gas production. Since the liquids stripped out of the gas, such as propane and butane, were treated for accounting purposes as a credit to operating expenses, when propane reached a high price in the 1940s, Panhandle Eastern Pipeline lost something from a regulated allowable point of view every time they produced a unit of their own gas. After much strategic maneuvering, its gas reserves were conveyed to a new company called Hugoton Production, which was then distributed as a dividend to Panhandle's stockholders. I wrote the first analytical report on Hugoton and recommended the stock strongly by pointing out one could be buying gas reserves at six mills per MCF at the then price of the stock. While there were regulatory clouds, the upside potential could be enormous.

Ed Kennedy was very proud of my report and sent a copy to the dean of the Oil Department at the Chase National Bank, a dignified and experienced and clever expert named Lyon Terry. One day I received a call from Terry suggesting that I come over for a visit, which I immediately did. He began, "Now, Sam, this little discussion is just between you and me and will not involve anybody else." With that he proceeded to show me that in one of my calculations of British thermal units, I had ignored three decimal places. After I turned ghostly white, he then said that in another calculation of dekatherms I had ignored three decimal places in the opposite direction so the end result was neutral. Lyon Terry was a little bit jealous of the reputation Ed Kennedy had developed for himself and of the wealth that Ed Kennedy was accumulating. In those days a commercial banker's salary was not too generous. If Terry had exposed my error, the damage would have sloughed off onto Ed Kennedy, but Lyon Terry remained true to his word and never breathed a word of this paradox to anybody else. I guess his kindness had some permanent influence as in my later career I managed to forgive some serious errors in others. I was pleased decades later to learn from physicist Robert Serber that the A-bomb designers also made an up-and-down error in neutron cross section calculations that cancelled out.

I was sent out to counsel with some of Lehman's clients and in that way met Senator Prescott Bush, the former president's father. My only surviving recollection is of a man of reasonableness and character, but I wonder whether these qualities were diluted within his son. Most of these experiences were pleasant and ego inflating, but one of them was almost a crucifixion. I was sent to see Henry Moses, a powerful Wall Street attorney, and had the job of explaining to him some of his oil investments, which included Barber Oil. But I did not know that Moses was representing some litigants and knew infinitely more of Barber Oil even though I was supposed to be answering his questions. He quizzed me unmercifully. At that time Barber Oil was headed by Cap Rieber, who at one point was made president of Texas Company, and his first act was to call in all of the Texaco executives from around the world to a ballroom in New York City in a meeting which ended almost as soon as it started. He announced, "Every large corporation needs a son of a bitch. In the Texas Company that's me. Meeting adjourned."

Probably my most enjoyable visit was a lengthy one at the office of Henry Morganthau, former Secretary of Treasury and a neighbor friend of Franklin Delano Roosevelt up the Hudson River. All the time that I was explaining his oil investments to Mr. Morganthau, he looked at me quizzically. Finally he could contain himself no longer and asked where I was born, where I went to school, and where I had learned about the oil business. He correctly concluded that I was a native New Yorker who had never even seen an oil well. Nevertheless, he seemed to be satisfied with my answers and with my explanation of the dynamics of his oil investments. Just before I left he said, "You are indeed a boy wonder."

There was not an ounce of snobbery within the house of Lehman, yet Bobby knew that he had the most elegant shop in the entire investment community and he fostered the notion that everyone who worked for him was automatically the best. That ran from the secretaries to the runners, from his partners to his attorneys, and of course, to himself. The result was that some high captains of industry had to swallow their pride. When Bill Wildes, president of Republic National Gas from Dallas, came up to Lehman to explain the attractive things happening in his company, I was asked at my young age, in front of Mr. Wildes, whether what he said was an accurate summary of the facts. But obviously there was a firm streak underneath Bobby's relaxed charm. When the majority of his institutional securities salesmen came to him and averred that they should be receiving a larger percentage of the sales commission, he thanked them for the time that they had worked for Lehman and wished them the best. He then called in the remaining senior institutional salesmen, Marvin Levy and some others, and told them to divide up the accounts of those departing. The result was that Marvin Levy could not afford to accept the partnership in the firm when it was offered to him.

However, I could not ignore a distressful incident with the noble Stuart M. Shotwell, which preyed on me and led to my decision to plan to be self-employed and not dependent on others for my livelihood. Apparently, Shotwell had offended some of the clients, thereby upsetting the senior partners and causing his removal as head of the Investment Advisory Service. The wise and soft-spoken Paul Manheim was put in his place. Now no one in Lehman was ever fired other than for ethical violations. That applied to Stuart Shotwell, who would not resign no matter what the humiliation, because of his lengthy service, which mattered greatly in the formula for his annual profit-sharing allocation. The result was that Shotwell's enormous desk was moved from the large conference room where he formerly held forth into a conventionally sized office where it left virtually no room for anyone else to enter. But Shotwell just stoically maintained his composed, dignified stance.

The transformation of elegant, honest, moderate Lehman Brothers into a greedy caricature is typical of the Reagan era of excesses that conquered the Street. Peter Peterson saved the firm from one internal hemorrhage but then was "couped" out with a fine-diamond parachute. When my friend Al Friedman decided to forfeit his partnership at Lehman and join Dillon Read, the first colleague he called was Peterson, who was, surprisingly, of Greek parentage. The two commiserated with each other and then Friedman said, "It's a Greek tragedy." "No," said Peterson, "it's a Jewish tragedy." It is a fine testimonial to our democracy that a bloodstain of anti-Semitism has not erupted from the panorama of Levines, Boeskys, Milkens, etc. After all, there was some truth to the wag's "Irish men sing at bars and Italian men at the Opera and Jewish men at the SEC." After World War II a number of sociopsychologists investigated the behavior of the German populace and concluded that an "authoritarian" background was responsible. Maybe a similar inquiry needs to be made of these current Wall Street speculators but certainly not by the Camino del Monte Sol author, who is a talented writer on entrepreneur personalities but has been condemned locally for his elaborate charitable pledges not translated into subsequent contributions.

A distressful interview was with the mysterious Sergei Rubenstein, president of Panhandle Producing and Refining. A favorite of society columnists for his choice of women, he was ultimately murdered in his Central Park South suite. Throughout my interview with him he continued to receive a manicure from a classically beautiful blond.

The Lehman Brothers I knew in the late '40s was an unsurpassed, gentile center of excellence.

8/ SELF-SERVICE

IN THOSE EARLY DAYS the lowest professional caste on Wall Street was made up of security analysts who frequently were called statisticians. It actually was a mark of prestige not to belong to the New York Society of Security Analysts or attend its luncheons on the second floor of Oscar's. Today there are, in contrast, analysts earning seven figures. In early 1946 an expert on treasury bills was the scheduled speaker at Oscar's. On the morning before the luncheon meeting, he left Washington on the early train to New York. After opening remarks he noticed that his audience was squirming as he explained that the Fed's discount rate would rise. He had not read the morning paper's report that the rate had been reduced.

Companies did not expect or welcome visits from analysts, and it took some massaging to gain entrance. This also applied to annual meetings where it was rare for shareholders or analysts to show up. In early 1946 I went down to Wilmington for the annual meeting of Worthington Pump and Machinery. One other outsider was present. That attendee said, "Mr. Chairman, my name is Gilbert. Make note of it. I have returned from the war and will make it a point to attend these meetings and oversee the improprieties of management and protect the rights of stockholders." And that is just what the Gilbert brothers proceeded to do to the distress of entrenched managements.

In the fall of 1946 I attended the annual meeting of Socony Vacuum in its building down near Battery Park. It was held in a small meeting room with the officers at a desk. All the seats were taken, and about a dozen spectators were standing. I think a Vice President Nickerson presided and apologized that they were not prepared for such a large turnout. But he was interrupted by a swarthy fellow with a thick Dutch accent: "I have just returned from Jakarta where I was interned during the war. It is a lousy shame that I, a stockholder, am standing and you, Nickerson, an employee, is sitting. It is a lousy shame that you have paid yourself bonuses and my dividend remains the same. It is a lousy disgrace that you don't think of the stockholders who employ you before you think of yourselves." Nickerson was nonplused but spoke to his attorney and then promised the board would consider a supplement to the dividend. Said the Dutchman, "It better not be a lousy ten cents extra."

About mid 1948 we learned that Uhlrich Brothers in the Los Angeles basin had trouble disposing of gasoline from their refinery and pioneered self-service marketing with attendants in bikinis on rollerskates. They offered a four-cent reduction on regular gas with a five-cent reduction on ethyl and the same on super ethyl, with the latter two pumps connected to the same supply tank. The major oil marketers were frightened and tried to harass Uhlrich with claims of a fire hazard since automatic shutoff dispensers were not then on the market. But the major executives concluded the self-service appeal was limited to the peculiar transients of Los Angeles. The reception from Los Angeles motorists—the densest gasoline market in the world— was spectacular. I discussed this with a friend of mine, and we agreed to give our employers notice and attempt this innovation in Florida since we did not think motorists would get out of their cars in winter conditions to pump gas. Although I felt there could not be any better place to work than Lehman Brothers, I was impatient for monetary success and also wanted a hands-on work environment rather than securities research. In hindsight I sense that communication and genuine intimacy in my marriage were missing and I needed to "do my thing." The Lehman folks could not have been more supportive and said there was a place for me in the Investment Advisory Service if my entrepreneurial venture did not pan out. On the day scheduled to be the last, my partner, who had a wife and child, said he was sorry but he could not leave the security of his job with a fine Wall Street firm. This did not fill me with joy, but I was not consumed by anger and Ethel's support for my independence did not waiver. Years later this person apologized convincingly to me, and as far as I was concerned, I was not bothered by past history since both he and I went on to definite success.

With Ethel providing living money from her job at Quackenbush, I drove down to Florida and first thought of St. Petersburg or Tampa but was disillusioned by the unconcealed anti-Semitism of St. Petersburg, where a bridge carried a sign "No dogs or Jews welcome." Anyway I felt there were too many seniors for a novel marketing concept. By now I had copyrighted the name Gas-O-Mat. The major oil companies would not serve me, but finally Arkansas Fuel Oil said they would do so surreptitiously. I secured an option on a location on 36th Street, then the north end of Miami. Ethel's uncle, Sam Blackman, spent the winters in Miami Beach and he was a good leaning post for me. He was a very successful wholesale plumbing supply dealer in Long Island and moved in the big time although lacking any formal schooling. One of his theories has proved itself time and time again. I once asked him what he thought of a friend, and he replied he didn't know. When I protested that he had known his friend for more than thirty years, he replied, "Yes, but I've never done business with him."

Blackman referred me to his attorney, an appealing and bright Irish local who ecstatically called me one afternoon with the news that he had secured a business license for me at the 36th Street location. He added, "Oh, by the way, the fire marshall will be your partner." "Fine, how much will he invest?" "He will invest nothing, schmuck." "Well, I may end up a whore, but I am not starting that way." The attorney was furious. "You jerk, I have maneuvered this to success and you have wasted my time. I didn't realize I was dealing with a stupid school boy." So I packed my bags and drove back to New York City and let the Gas-O-Mat copyright lapse. Now I only grin with satisfaction when I pass the Gas-O-Mat station on the south side of Española or the Gas-O-Mat in Gallup or the thousands of self-service stations across the country.

Some of my friends have attributed to me the discovery of self-service gasoline dispensing but that would be self-serving since Uhlrich Brothers in Los Angeles had the original idea.

Since I had five years of Lehman experience under my belt, job offers were very easy to come by. Shotwell asked me to return, but I felt I wanted to try new territory. J. Robert Oppenheimer put it more elegantly when asked why he didn't return to Los Alamos. He said, "You can only fry an omelet once." The McNamara team of statisticians at Ford made an interesting proposal, but I turned it down after consultation with my warm friend Eli Black, a co-worker at Lehman. Eli had married into the affluent Lubbell family with clothing manufacturing interests in the East and oil interests in Tulsa managed by one of their sons. Eli was a most decent person and perhaps the most talented businessman I ever met. He went on to become chairman of United Fruit and explored novel labor relations with Cesar Chavez. Amongst his other activities he became Chairman of the Board of Trustees of *Commentary* at a time when it was true to its roots and had not gone Park Avenue under the dubious title of "neoconservative." But his success was tearing at Eli's insides. He put together a fabulously successful deal in Dallas, Long Mile Rubber, but had a forlorn look on his face when he saw our family getting ready for a camping trip to the Navajo Country.

At one of my tight cash moments when I was on my own in Dallas, I called him in New York and offered to sell him $10,000 of oil royalty I owned. After he had his analyst review pertinent factors with me, he asked why he should buy it. "Because I need the money." "Well, why didn't you say that–the check will be mailed today." About three weeks before his final crisis, I spoke to him on the phone. He sounded different and tense, and I was tempted to urge him to come to Santa Fe for a rest but I didn't. He jumped to his death from his office in the Pan Am Building when word leaked that United Fruit had paid a million-dollar bribe to the President of Honduras. Obviously, Eli was emotionally distraught because he was a smart enough businessman to know how to pay a bribe that escaped scrutiny. Eli's estate was plagued with suits, and family friends no longer called. His widow, Shirley, occupied their large house in Connecticut but had no money to bring in fuel oil. She spent a week at our house in Santa Fe and joined a School of American Research field trip to Chaco Canyon. She turned out to be a trooper rather than a spoiled Fifth Avenue complainer. Eli's son, Leon, ended up as co-manager of Mergers and Acquisitions at Drexel Burnham and walked away with a bundle and no indictments. It was good to see this because Eli was a most honest, civic-minded, involved citizen and altogether a sensitive and decent businessman despite this Honduras error of judgment. He had strong loyalties to Israel and never could understand my defense of the more primitive, pastoral way of life of the Arabs.

At Eli's urging I seriously considered two of the most admired and capital-rich Wall Street private firms: Allen & Company and Wertheim & Company. I concentrated on the latter because of its reputation for shrewdness, which did not compromise its integrity. By today's yardsticks, it is hard to believe that its $20 million of capital was among the largest in the entire investment community. Since I had been Ed Kennedy's assistant they wanted me without hesitation. I was interviewed by five partners and offered a job. One of the partners, Joseph Klingenstein, stood out as different, powerful, opinionated, and lacking any pretense. They told me to start the following Monday. As I was leaving the small conference room I stopped in surprise and asked, "What will I be earning?" They looked at each other with a little confusion since it was now apparent that compensation hadn't been discussed and then asked, "Will $8,000 be all right?"

"Yes, I can start with that."

9/ THE LEGACY OF NEDICKS

THE THREE PRINCIPAL PARTNERS of Wertheim and Company were Maurice Wertheim, Joseph Klingenstein, and Eddie Hilson. An outsider would be shocked to learn that these three totally different individuals were partners. Their basically different characteristics and uninhibited interchange were among the secrets of their success. The firm was started by Maurice Wertheim, who was elegant, cultured, and a supreme egotist. His father, Jake Wertheim, had been in the tobacco business but had also made early investments in what became General Motors and Sears Roebuck. Maurice graduated from Harvard and had a very colorful life, which included a grand art collection, a second trophy wife, a bird preserve in Scotland, a fishing preserve on the Gaspe Peninsula, and sponsorship of the American-Soviet Chess Team. During the Depression he offered charitable assistance to the Theater Guild, which then went on to produce "Oklahoma," among other plays. It was completely characteristic of Maurice when I concluded a lengthy discourse on a stock recommendation by saying that there was very little risk involved that he replied, "Young man, I never accept any risk."

Shortly after joining the firm, I gained a private relation with him when an inquiry went out to discover whether anyone in the firm could translate English to French and vice versa. I offered my amateurish assistance. It turned out that natives on the Gaspe Peninsula would periodically write to him for monetary assistance–to pay for a gall bladder operation or to provide support for unemployment, terminal cancer, or some other family catastrophe. Maurice had a male secretary who could not handle the incoming French or translate Maurice's dictated replies, and this function drifted into my corner. Invariably, Maurice would accommodate the request or veiled threat. If the supplicant asked for $50, he would send $50. In one case, there was a plea for $2,000 because the lady was at the end of her rope and threatened suicide for herself and her children if she could not surmount the described crisis. That was precisely the amount that Maurice sent to her. When I asked him about it, he said he really didn't want any rejections to be on his conscience.

If Lehman Brothers was equivalent to a serene country club, then Wertheim and Company was comparable to an intense but honorable think tank populated by very shrewd but virtuous professionals. Maurice's bloodlines included the Lehmans and the Loebs, and within him there was an attractive melange of "our crowd." His good genes did not end with his death; his daughter was Barbara Tuchman, the successful author and the envy of trained historians, and his granddaughter is Jessica Matthews, the skilled environmentalist who writes with regularity for *The Washington Post.**

Since Maurice was rarely in the shop, the second-ranking partner, Joseph Klingenstein, actually managed the firm although Maurice demonstrated veto power with an abrupt hand. Several of us in his absence, had worked out an interesting deal with Panhandle Eastern Pipeline. It was explained to him upon his return by J.K., but Wertheim bluntly buried all of our good work saying, "That McGuire is a crook and we will have nothing to do with Panhandle." J.K. was a phenomenal trader of securities, known and respected by all the insiders of Wall Street, but he was a nonentity outside of Wall Street until he endowed the Esther Klingenstein Psychiatric Center in honor of his mother. J.K. was a kind man with no affectations whatsoever and a workaholic who rarely took vacations. An investment to him would mean holding a security for maybe three months. Whenever other firms got hung up on underwriting positions that they were unable to move, and that included the big leaguers like Smith Barney and Morgan Stanley, they would approach J.K. and he had the courage of a lion in bidding for their positions at a discount. He was proud of his Depression time purchase of Superior Oil at $7 per share, which he still held after it passed $2,000. I recognized that he was something

---

* When Jessica Matthews was the 1991 J. Robert Oppenheimer Memorial lecturer at Los Alamos, I mentioned my last encounter with her grandfather, but Ethel tells me that Ms. Matthews did not appreciate the anecdote. Shortly before his death Mr. Wertheim asked me to investigate Amerada Petroleum and I ended up providing him with a written report. One Friday afternoon I bumped into him at the elevator bank on the 33rd floor of the Equitable office building and just before he entered the down elevator he said, "Your report on Amerada Petroleum." "Yes, Sir." "Think about it." The door of the elevator then closed behind him. I was crestfallen since that was his method of telling me that my report was not equal to his expectations and had not probed to whatever core he had in mind. The following morning, on Saturday, Maurice Wertheim had a fatal heart attack. His funeral was at his Fifth Avenue apartment on Monday. The immediate thought that ran through my mind was "I won't have to think about it."

special after I wrote a bullish report on Atlantic Refining and all of the accounts started loading up on the stock and at the same time the stock progressively sank lower and lower. When it finally reached the bottom, I had a call to come in to see J.K. Needless to say, I was quite nervous. "Ballen, what is your feeling now about Atlantic Refining?" "All the fundamentals that I described in my report are still valid, so therefore I have to recommend the stock, which can go no lower." "You mean aside from tomorrow and the day after?" And he then dismissed me and proceeded to load up on Atlantic Refining at what turned out to be its low.

Actually, he and I did not talk the same language since he was an in-and-out speculator in securities and most of the situations that I worked on were investments requiring a couple of years to work out. Consequently, J.K. did not participate in some of the most successful deals I sponsored. But I learned a great deal from him. It was his practice to hand out the bonus check at Christmas to each employee. When I came in, he gave me the following lecture: "You know, they tell me that my brother, who is a surgeon, is a genius and my son, who is an electrical engineer, they tell me is a genius, but I want to tell you there are no geniuses on Wall Street. Here is your bonus. We would like for you to think in terms of Wertheim as a permanent career, but I remind you, there are no geniuses in Wall Street." Another time this most honorable and noble family man wanted to get a point over to me with the following story. "You know, the Spiegel son from the mail-order family in Chicago came home from college and kept describing investment situations to his father, but after each presentation explained an ethical problem that consequently cancelled the recommendation, and finally his father said to him, 'Modie, make money honestly, but honestly or not, make money.'"

J.K. did not have the flair or taste of Maurice Wertheim, but he was a trading speculator par excellence. Maurice's style shone when he announced the very first outside financing done for Hershey Corporation, which was a preferred stock issue arranged by Wertheim's firm. Instead of the typical tombstone ad in the financial sections that list the investment firm, the issuing firm, the type of security, the price and the participating distributing firms, Maurice insisted that this tombstone ad simply carry two lines: on top, Hershey Corporation, and on bottom, Wertheim and Company.

I think, however, that J.K. did reluctantly gain some respect for me when he took me over to the old-line firm, Ladenberg Thalman, whose staff was putting together a large deal in the Sprayberry formation in Upton County, Texas. The deal had been assembled for them by the Ted Weiner oil promoters in Ft. Worth. One of Ladenberg's senior partners, a distinguished economist who had played a prominent role at the Dumbarton Oaks conference, described this investment. But it was obvious that he really knew nothing about the oil business and was being led down the primrose path by some talented Texas artist without full recognition of the risks involved. I vehemently argued against Wertheim's participation to the point where J.K. urged me to calm down. But I was successful in keeping Wertheim out of this watered deal. Unfortunately, my impressions were correct, and a few years later Ladenburg got into real trouble, embarrassing some old-line partners who were using basic capital they were not prepared to lose when the bubble finally burst.

The third major partner, Edwin I. Hilson, could not have been more different from his two colleagues. Hilson was a fun-loving, people-oriented impetuous deal-maker who produced more than his own share of profitability for the firm, but did so carrying a degree of risk well appreciated by the others. He had gotten into financial trouble during the Depression but survived with his confidence and charm intact. He moved in fancy social sets. His widow, Mildred, became the Perle Mesta of upper-crust New York, which included the social greeting for Richard Nixon after his denouement and hosting the marriage party for Henry Kissinger and Nancy. Hilson commented to me about Wertheim's fabulous reputation for fabulous deals, "We've had our share of lemons but we don't broadcast them."

On the north side of 120 Broadway was one of those narrow streets of downtown Manhattan. Each morning around 10:00, Hilson would drive to the side entrance to the building, get out of his car with all the other cars behind him honking their horns, ride up the elevator to the 33rd floor, and give his keys to his male secretary who would then go down and drive the car to a garage. Of course, Hilson must have had private arrangements with the downtown police, who overlooked this selfish conduct. Within the premises of Wertheim and Company, Hilson, who was about eighty-five percent bald, built a private barber shop about eight feet by ten feet into which none of the other partners would be permitted since they had not contributed to its construction. Each day for about ten minutes he would have a manicurist and a barber come up from the basement Terminal Barber Shop to improve his appearance. Hilson spent each winter down at the Hotel Nacionale in Havana, Cuba, in which Wertheim had a very important stock position. He also became president of the Havana Yacht Club. Each day during the nasty New York winters he would call from the poolside of the Hotel Nacionale and ask how things were going. But there was never a season that he did not come back with some attractive investment deal that he had engineered with one of the guests of the hotel at its pool or at the Yacht Club.

Wertheim also had an important stock position in Cuban American Sugar, which was managed by the father of John Crosby, the creator of the Santa Fe Opera. Ultimately, Wertheim's presence in Cuba paid off, since they "permitted themselves" to lose out and be bought out on proxy fights in both the hotel and the sugar operation about four months before Castro came to power. Although everything was happy and rosy on the surface with Eddie Hilson, there must have been some tense undercurrents–he died relatively young at the Republican Convention that nominated Eisenhower. His daughter committed suicide and his son, John, also died at a relatively young age from cancer. John had gone to the Los Alamos Ranch School, but that experience never took with him since he abhorred anything that had to do with hiking or camping or horses. John had many friends in Wall Street, and over 2,000 mourners attended his funeral at Temple Emmanuel in New York City.

Eddie Hilson told Lawrence Crosby, a Sullivan & Cromwell partner who was representing Wertheim as president of Cuban American Sugar, to buy the defunct bonds of Hotel Nacionale, but Crosby protested that World War II was coming on and he had two boys entering college. But Hilson insisted, so Crosby bought $2,000 of bonds and gave $1,000 to his wife and $500 to each of his sons. When twenty years later John Crosby was ready to buy a ranch and create the Santa Fe Opera, he used those bonds, then worth $40,000, to close the deal. My mentor Hilson also guided the young Bob Linton into Wall Street. Linton was enormously successful and resigned as chairman of Drexel Burnham at the right time. While his former partners were going to jail or into bankruptcy, only Linton fortunately escaped as a Teflon chairman and actually received cash for the front portion of his equity position. But unlike Johnny Hilson, Linton loved the Southwest and the outdoors and became a champion senior skier.

A fourth partner, Henry Hottinger, was really an undistinguished individual with a rabbit's paw of good luck. He had been Maurice Wertheim's secretary, and when the firm was organized, Maurice knew he would be away quite a bit, so he made his secretary a partner with some kind of overview of the other prima donnas. He never dreamed the firm would become as financially successful as it did. Hottinger used his wealth to assemble a world-class collection of over a dozen Stradivari violins. He looked askance at his other partners, who were trading in and out of securities. Hottinger's philosophy was never to sell anything, and in the great inflationary times of the post-war decades, his pattern of investments probably turned out to be just as successful as that of his more talented confreres. Another partner with whom I had dealings was A.C. Pete DuBois, whose function was to handle the over-the-counter regional brokerage firms and also to play customer golf at conventions of one sort or another. Sitting behind me in the non-air-conditioned Equitable office building was the prototype of a Wall Street analyst named Walter Neal, who in times previous had been the editor of *Moody's Railroad Manual.* Even in the depths of the summer, Walter Neal would finish his commute from New Jersey wearing a wool suit with vest and never a bead of perspiration on him. This only added to my discomfort from the heat and humidity since every day I recalled the luxury of Lehman's air-conditioned premises.

I kept telling Ethel that there was something peculiar going on down at Wertheim. Everybody was just treating me too nice and with too much respect, and this even included the junior partners. The answer came about six months later when one of their senior analysts, Bob Bach, and I journeyed down to New Orleans to interview the frenetic attorney, Joseph Jones, in connection with a study of Southdown Sugar. Bach and I were sharing the same motel room when we went out to Avery Island, owned by a fabulously wealthy family that included Senator Joseph Clark from Pennsylvania. Its oil royalty of 4,000 barrels per day was duplicated by the income that came from a deep salt mine on the property as well as their Tabasco sauce. Avery Island met its civic responsibility with an egret preserve. As we retired for the evening, Bach asked me, "How's Rose?" "Who's Rose?" And then it turned out that Rose Ballen was J.K.'s sister, and some of the more junior members of the firm had assumed that I was part of the "royal family."

After joining Wertheim I took a three-week fling through the oil patch and interviewed about thirty oil companies. Then in an intense fortnight I authored "Outlook for Oil Securities," which the firm printed and distributed to favored clients. Ten years later I met a bank president at a cocktail party in San Francisco who said, "Oh, you're the analyst who wrote the great study on oil securities." "Well, thanks, but my essential conclusions were wrong." "That makes no difference; the logic and format were impressive." At the time I thought his response was ironic, but now I subscribe to the supremacy of such methodology since Bohr said, "Predictions are difficult, especially of the future." But the Wertheim folks wanted to know what my top stock recommendation was. This was troubling since I was not carried away by anything I had seen except for the unusual architecture of the new four-story office building of Honolulu Oil in Midland, Texas. It would take a Jungian to analyze what it was that caused me to champion Honolulu Oil stock to Wertheim's partners. But shortly afterwards Honolulu made an unusual wildcat discovery in the Cambrian formation, and the stock doubled overnight. So my entry to Wertheim was now on solid ground.

The Wertheim partners took a plunge and hired four graduates of the Harvard School of Business. The prize was Henry Brandt, who was number one in its most famous class. Arthur Rock was briefly assigned to me to assist in a study I was making of relative movements between integrated oil stocks and producer oil stocks. I then committed a most derogatory evaluation. I really was not impressed by Arthur Rock. A year or two later on one of my visits from Dallas to New York I offered a taxi ride to him, and he explained to me that he was investing in some analog computer companies with no book value and no earnings. I truly felt sorry for him and wondered if he would be approaching me for some grub money. Well, of course, Arthur Rock proved to be the most prescient and successful private financier of newly emerging technological concerns in the whole country. He assisted such enterprises as Intel, Scientific Data Systems, Genentec, Apple Computing, and other comparable start-ups. He proved to have a prophetic talent of hearing ten presentations involving ten black boxes and successfully selecting the one that was real in the marketplace. Many years later when he was featured on the cover of Time Magazine, I wrote him a congratulatory note admitting that I should have been listening to him rather than lecturing, but no response was forthcoming.

Early in my Wertheim career I hit a grand home run, but a good part of the credit must rest with lucky timing and the assistance of some of the specialists at American Securities Corp., which was owned by William Rosenwald. W.R. was one of the heirs of the Sears Roebuck fortune, and very much introverted. He had followed his long-time psychiatrist in a move from Philadelphia to New York. He was the principal philanthropist to the United Jewish Appeal, but quixotically his brother, Lessing, was the principal financial backer of the anti-Zionist American Council for Judaism. Fortunately, the two remained loving brothers, even though they were at opposite political poles. The successful investment I am referring to involved a half-interest in some gas wells in the Rio Vista field northeast of San Francisco. They were half-owned by D.D. "Tex" Feldman of Dallas with the other half owned by Brazos Oil and Gas, the petroleum arm of Dow Chemical. The chief geologist of Dow was a unique and talented opportunist named Basil Zavoico, who acted as broker for "Tex" Feldman. The investment proved spectacularly successful because it was leveraged with several classes of debt and preferred stock. The natural gas was sold to Pacific Gas and Electric with a price tied directly to the price of Bunker C Fuel Oil in the San Francisco Harbor. During the Korean War the price of fuel oil doubled. Then the wildcat acreage to the east proved productive with two extension structures. This was the start of my own petite net worth since Wertheim's partners permitted me to buy twelve shares of the stock with a very thin common stock capitalization at $1.00 per share. The ultimate value worked out to five figures.

During the summer of my first year at Wertheim, I asked for a leave of absence with no pay to go to Oklahoma University to take three courses in petroleum engineering and one in oil and gas law. The day I left the firm Eddie Hilson called me in and said they would continue to pay my salary while I was at the school and they hoped I would come back even though they would respect me as a free agent. When I mumbled my appreciation Hilson cut me short and said, "Cut out that crap. You can get a job anywhere you want in Wall Street, but I don't think you can do better than coming back with us."

The two months Ethel and I and our daughter Nina spent in Norman were an eyeopener. This was our first experience with a soft friendship with the citizens and our first realization that for us this was a better way of life than the rat race in New York. One evening at about midnight the phone rang. It was Pete DuBois in New York, who asked what I thought about the River Island extension well. When I said I didn't know anything about it, he then shouted, "Good God, man, don't you know you're rich?" I was at a loss for words but went in and woke up Ethel. I said, "Ethel, we're rich." She promptly went back to sleep. Later, when I returned to Wertheim, I asked Henry Hottinger to let me see the electric log on the River Islands number one well. I did some reservoir analysis and concluded that the area would make some profit, but it was anything but a bonanza. When I explained this to Hottinger, he said he realized that; he didn't try to correct his partners because they would learn the reality soon enough.

Professor Cloud at Oklahoma University, who taught the oil and gas law course, was famous for discouraging coeds from enrolling in his class, and I have no insight as to why. But one girl did enroll in our class, and Professor Cloud proceeded to become more and more vulgar and more and more pornographic. Finally, by the third session, she quit. It did not occur to me or anyone else to protest this treatment or come to the lady's defense; rather, all of us chuckled with satisfaction at Cloud's successful performance.

It was at the end of the semester that our good friend Don Dietrich called from Santa Fe where he was spending the summer with the Japanese artist Chuzo Tamotsu and suggested that on our way home we carry some of his possessions from Norman out to Santa Fe. When he insisted that I would not regret the reverse excursion, we did in fact drive out to Santa Fe, where we spent several nights on the lawn of the house now next to Snooky Blakemore on East Garcia. That was our very first introduction to the tranquil way of life in Santa Fe, so different from anything else we had experienced.

The investment in the Rio Vista gas field was named Vistario Corporation. And if that was successful, then in a private transaction I seemingly played a key role in a disaster. Wertheim employed a private auditor named Goodkin, who possibly was related to the successful and vivacious Santa Fe realtor Pat French. Goodkin's son approached me on one of my visits up from Dallas to look into Venezuelan Petroleum, which was selling for eighty-seven and a half cents per share on the American Stock Exchange. Venezuelan Pete had assets in the Maracaibo Basin in Venezuela and was about 70 percent owned by Sinclair Petroleum. I went up to Rockefeller Center and interviewed their management. There patently was nothing of interest in the company or the stock, and that is what I reported to young Goodkin. About a year later I bumped into him in the hallway of the Equitable Building. He looked at me as if I were Adolf Eichmann and screamed, "You cost me a million dollars!" and turned and ran. I was stunned but then thought back to Venezuelan Petroleum and looked in the papers, and lo and behold, it was selling for over $100 per share. Sinclair was on a buying spree, trying to get over 90 percent of the stock for accounting consolidation purposes. In hindsight, Goodkin must have had some clients who were Sinclair executives, and he must have noticed that they were loading up on Venezuelan Pete stock.

While still in New York, I joined John Van Deusen from the closed-end Tri-Continental Fund and Peter Vermilye of J.P. Morgan on a two-week trip to the newly discovered Alberta oil fields. We were the first Wall Street analysts up there. The three of us went together to interview oil company executives, and we were showing our precociousness by asking minuscule questions. One of the executives stopped us and said, "Boys, this thing up here is big, big. Just forget your detailed questions." John Van Deusen beat me each night at chess, but that did not discourage our easy intimacy. While lunching with him one day at the Palliser Hotel in Calgary, I suggested that when we got back to New York we should organize an oil analysts club and invite about a dozen of the recognized oil analysts on the Street to join. This became what is now the prestigious National Association of Petroleum Investment Analysts. Last year they put out a booklet describing the history of the organization, correctly attributing its genesis.

Ethel and I were in agreement after we returned to New York that we preferred the Southwest, but we did not know how to arrange an affordable relocation. Fortunately this came about from Eddie Hilson, who was so thrilled at the success of Vistario Corporation that he tenderly asked me if I would object to moving to the Southwest and opening a petroleum office for Wertheim. I hesitated with my response and did not want to reveal my elation. We selected Dallas because the only person I knew west of the Hudson River was Frank Jacobson of Buffalo Oil, whom I had met in an unsuccessful negotiation to acquire some of Buffalo's properties in the Panhandle oil field. So in 1950 we pulled up stakes, and I drove our two-door Studebaker down to Dallas while Ethel and Nina flew down. We moved into a simple apartment in Oak Cliff and managed finally with some difficulty to share an office in the Mercantile Securities Building with Clardy and Barnett, since prime office space was then very tight.

There was always resistance to some of the suggested private investments in Wertheim because of its experience with Nedicks, which was a chain of fast-order food counters throughout New York City. During the Depression this bankrupt and losing operation was sold at auction. Maurice was intrigued by its real estate leases throughout Manhattan, and Wertheim was the successful bidder at $25,000. A few years later with a partial recovery from the Depression, Wertheim sold this for $4,000,000. Any time an investment proposition was brought to their attention, they instinctively wondered if it was as good as Nedicks. And in this way they subsequently passed up many great opportunities because at first blush they did not compare analogously to that happy experience with Nedicks!

10/ *"BIG D"*

DALLAS IN THE FIFTIES was emerging from a pleasant oil, banking, and cotton town of 300,000 into an avant-garde dynamic city in the forefront of oil-payment financing and leveraged conglomerate buyouts. A typical anecdote had Clint Murchison Sr.'s lieutenant explaining to him that a $6,000,000 proposed purchase was at a standstill because of a $10,000 obstacle. Clint gushed, "Gosh, you're not letting $10,000 stand in the way of a $6,000,000 deal." "But Mr. Murchison, that's $10,000 cash." At the same time there were primitive relics side by side with the innovative entrepreneurism. There was essentially no residential air-conditioning, absolutely no auto air-conditioning—only the Mercantile Bank and Mercantile Securities Buildings could ease the oppressive semiannual heat waves. Brown bags concealing whiskey were the norm in downtown Dallas, but in more than half of Dallas' square miles no alcohol of any form was sold. Jim Crowism was harsh and overt with a patina of anti-Semitism in the oil industry expressed in subtle covert forms. Yet an all-encompassing friendliness and concern for your neighbor was felt throughout the city.

A month after I opened my office in Dallas, the manager of Harris Upham took me down to see Neely Landrum, a real estate mogul and head of a large savings and loan institution. "Ballen, I've heard about you. Some of our best people are from New York. It takes six years for them to discard their Eastern ways but then they become excellent citizens." I learned subsequently that he was correct in his timing.

The old-line Jewish community had French Alsatian or German roots and was now being challenged by newcomers from the eastern seaboard with Polish-Russian heritage. Thus developed a deep internal dialogue on how to handle the first intellectual anti-Semite in the United States, a professor at Southern Methodist University named John Beatty, who wrote *The Iron Curtain Over America*. Beatty was a good historian and a colonel in the Army Intelligence Reserve. There was a trace of accuracy in his arguments. He claimed that the ancestors of most American Jews were converts from the pagan Khazzars of Russia. Examples were David Dubinsky and Julius Rosenberg—unlike the olive skinned *People of the Book* like Bernard Baruch. His next conclusion was that all the troubles in America came from the Khazzars masquerading as Jews. He claimed, consequently, that he was anti-Khazzar but couldn't be accused of being anti-Semitic. *The New York Times* refused to review his book which was published by a Dallas printer. Stores would not carry it until the Jewish-managed Foleys in Houston stocked it out of concern for First Amendment loyalties. Beatty was not reticent in preaching his theories in his classes—to the discomfort of his few Jewish students. The Jewish newcomers to the Dallas scene wanted to storm the barricades and make Beatty's tenure an open vocal issue. The well-motivated president of SMU, Willis Tate, advised the old-timers that the conservative Methodist trustees, with their strong Wichita Falls contingent, would not abandon Dr. Beatty. Fortunately, this evil intellectual rogue died before the debate tore the small Jewish community apart.

There were wonderful characters more than tolerated in the downtown establishment. The leading attorney was Tom Knight of Thompson, Knight, Simmons and Weisberg. His genius bordered on insanity, and he ultimately crossed the line and spent his final decades institutionalized *non compos mentis*. He called his daughter Ugh and always referred to his second wife by her former married name. Jim Cleaver accompanied Tom Knight to New York to close a big deal for General American Oil. With a few hours to spare, they journeyed up to the Metropolitan Museum of Art and squeezed into a packed elevator. When the operator called, "Floors, please," and Tom shouted, "Take us to the tits and butts," Cleaver cringed. My client S.R. Baker from Worcester, Massachusetts, went into an oil deal in which he felt he was being cheated by Sam Boren, an attorney with the Thompson, Knight law firm. He flew down to Dallas to explain the situation to Knight, who said, "Why, that's awful—you should sue the sons of bitches."

Then there was the immaculate attorney who underwent a complete change of wardrobe twice a day after a private shower in his office. Added to the eccentricities was the Little Mothers club in the Downtown Dallas Athletic Club. Entry was restricted to Doug Forbes, Buddy Fogelson, and Sylvester Daysant, who had paid one of the DAC mortgage payments in the Depression. When Ben Jack Cage was jailed for selling unregistered stock, he sold shares to his jailers.

But no one was more flamboyant than the brilliant eccentric

wildcatter Billy Duke Rudman, known in his youth as the Osage Jew. He grew up in eastern Oklahoma, where his dad had a clothing store and his only playmates were Osage Indians. He was the very first to forbid smoking in his elegant offices, whose restrooms featured gold fixtures shaped like genitalia. It was no surprise that when a new oil province in North Dakota was opened on the Nessan Anticline, Duke Rudman owned the underlying royalty. Shortly after we arrived in Dallas I received a card from Billy on which was a picture of himself naked in a tub and attended by a huge black masseuse. The legend read, "If you would like a smooth skin like the Duke's, this card entitles you to one treatment in Madam Safhia's House in Texarkana." Today the Duke carries around a copy of the $23 million check he sent to the IRS when he sold his oil properties to the Lewis oil syndicate of Denver just at the very peak of oil prices. At that time the Duke and a friend found themselves in a top Parisian restaurant and noticed the American at the next table could handle the menu. "Good buddy, could you order for us?" Duke asked. At the end of the meal the Duke insisted the American join their tour through France, but the American said he had to get back to New York. "You don't understand...I will make it worth your while." Still only a polite declination was forthcoming. "Well, when you get to Dallas, please let me entertain you. Here's my card." The return card bore the name David Rockefeller.

Previously the sale of oil reserves had been frowned upon, although now such financial sophistication was admired. At a famous dinner party in the nineteen-fifties, an East Texas wildcatter got into a verbal brouhaha with a more elegant Dallas oil man and the East Texan finally bellowed out, "I may have married a whore but I've never sold production."

What about ethics? Well, there were both responses. When Bob Strauss' partner, Dick Gump was president of the Oil Well Drilling Contractors Association, a motion introduced at its convention at the Statler-Hilton to condemn kickbacks on drilling contracts died for lack of a second. And when Rhodes scholar Critchell Parsons was caught by his wife in a prominent club with a fancy redhead, she clobbered them both with a loaded purse. But when I had the unenviable task of liquidating Chem-Ag Product Inc. for Commercial Solvents at fifteen cents on the dollar, Sam Wimpy said he was entitled to $25,000 from Christian fairness rather than the $5,000 we offered. He refused to accept the lower figure and got nothing. There was also Candy Barr, the sensational stripteaser, who openly offended the church auxiliaries. They railroaded her to a stiff prison term with two marijuana cigarettes planted in her bra. When my office partner was low on cash, he brokered some oil royalty to a bank's employee pension fund but the respected petroleum engineer who was a trustee insisted on a kickback of one-third of the commission. My office partner was in a quandary. I advised, "Well, I wouldn't do it. But you are up against the wall, and anyway if you go along with him, you will know where to bring your future offerings."

The Blacks knew that their mission in life was to soothe the days of the better-situated Whites, and of course, many warm, loving relations developed between maid and household. The first voice to speak out against segregation was Rabbi Levi Olan when Temple Emanuel was in South Dallas. He almost lost his congregation for expressing his views. It was understood that young men at Texas A&M would "have to change their luck" with a black woman before becoming solid alumni. Carl Brannin, the Unitarian liberal, started the picket line at Green's across from the Mercantile National Bank to integrate the lunch counter; fortunately there was no violence. Of course the police were deeply racist. A black motorist who had driven into the back of our vehicle at a traffic light was ticketed. Three weeks later our phone rang at 6 a.m.: "Ballen, get your ass down to the Courthouse today at nine o'clock." I shot back, "Who the hell are you and how dare you call me at this hour." After a long pause, "Ballen, are you White?" You know the rest of the story as the officer apologized to me. When I was Chairman of Electrical Log Services Inc. I inquired one day of the very decent Arch Pennington, who was president of the company, about the whereabouts of the black janitor, whom I hadn't seen in a while. "Oh, he retired on social security." "What does his pension with Southwestern Life pay him?" After a long pause, Arch asked, "Well, you didn't intend for him to be covered in the company pension plan?" It took some doing, but Southwestern Life acknowledged its error and placed the black retiree on its pension rolls.

The very first meeting of the NAACP in Dallas was at Fair Park. Ethel and I were among a small handful of whites to hear Martin Luther King give his standard speech, which was repeated the rest of his days. But when Ethel invited a black doctor and his family to our house for dinner, I argued for gradualism until the doctor asked, "How do I gradually sit down at a lunch counter?" Of course, we had to conceal our NAACP membership from our bankers.

The anti-Zionist American Council for Judaism was very strong in Dallas. The Executive Director, Joe Frank, one day invited a black friend to the YMCA cafeteria. When he got back to his office, he was summoned to the office of my partner, Jerome K. Crossman. Frank resigned that afternoon. But this was a blessing in disguise. He became a revered professor at the prep school in Carbondale, Colorado, before succumbing to a fatal heart attack on the ski slopes. Yet Crossman, too, was a most respected and decent man. He convened a luncheon of insurance company presidents in a private room at the Baker Hotel, locked the door, and said, "You guys are not leaving until you agree on how to provide home mortgages for upper-income Blacks." That is how Hamilton Park near Loop 12 and Central Expressway came into being.

The Petroleum Engineers Club usually met for lunch at the Baker and the Geologic Society at the Adolphus. The meetings would start with the most filthy stories, generally involving black genitalia with the white-gloved black waitresses going about their business. This was followed by far-out Texas Aggie jokes. But one day Hank Gruy exploded when one of Southwest Life Insurance Company's engineers told an Aggie tale. Gruy rose and pledged to cancel his firm's pension plan with SW Life and Harold Dunn, President of Shamrock Oil & Gas and an Aggie, had to come down from Amarillo to preserve the account.

But all that I've recited was secondary to the warmth of Dallasites and to the excitement of these talented young men fresh from World War II entering the forefront of industry and finance and putting their rural backgrounds behind when they moved to the cultural center of Texas. Those whom we today would call Yuppies were a small grouping, and we knew each other and greeted each other warmly when we walked Elm or Commerce or Main. It was us against the stuffed shirts of New York and Chicago, and we knew we were ahead of them in the novel techniques of finance. Every home run hit by a local boy was cheered by each of us. We all basked in the success of Bob Bradley in oil or Jim Ling in electronics or Fred Florence in banking or Glenn Turner in law and, of course, Stanley Marcus in merchandising.

The most powerful oil company was Magnolia Petroleum, a subsidiary of Socony, with its flying red horse atop its downtown "skyscraper." Slats Latimer was Magnolia's chief and on the board of everything important in Dallas. Magnolia had done such a great job exploring for oil domestically that it was widely recognized as the treasure chest of Socony. When Raleigh Warner became head of

Socony he knew he had a problem in the arrogant egotism of the Magnolia gang and addressed it by having a team of Socony officers invite Latimer to meet them at Love Field on a Sunday morning. Latimer then learned that Socony's board had met on Saturday to liquidate the Magnolia subsidiary. He had been dethroned in absentia.

The Dallas Morning News with its essayist Bill Ruggles set the pattern for very conservative positions that were accepted thoughout the establishment. What would Bill Ruggles say when his intelligent and independent daughter hiked the northern New Mexico highlands alone, married the respected legal scholar Alan Bromberg, and instructed her carpenter to build a ledge on their swimming pool for "making love"? But the real idealogue of conservative bent was the talented, charismatic, and revered Reverend Criswell, pastor of the largest and wealthiest Southern Baptist Church in the world. I became an occasional paddleball opponent of Reverend Criswell at the downtown Dallas YMCA, where the game had been invented. When the story of changed attitudes in the South is finally written, due credit will have to be given to Senior Pastor Criswell. For years he was the theological supporter of segregation, saying God wanted the separation of the races. But then suddenly he changed and acknowledged from the pulpit that he had been in error. It was Criswell and not LBJ who carried the South to enlightened practices. Some years ago I found in my desk some 1950 blotters from Criswell welcoming people to lunchtime prayer meetings. How thrilling it was to receive the following letter from him:

August 12, 1991

Mr. Samuel B. Ballen, Chairman
La Fonda Santa Fe, New Mexico 87501

Dear old friend, Samuel Ballen:

You are kind and thoughtful beyond compare to write this letter to me and to enclose these Pre-Easter blotters. I can't believe that I was ever that young! I will celebrate my 82nd birthday in December this year.

It blessed my heart to hear from you after these many, many years. I still go to the "Y" every day of my life. It enables me to maintain my very active and busy schedule as Senior Pastor of our dear First Baptist Church and as Chancellor of our wonderful preacher's school. I teach a class there two mornings a week.

Thank you again for your kindness. May God in heaven reward you for it and bless you forever and ever.

Devotedly and faithfully,
your old friend,
William A. Criswell

Early in my days in Dallas I purchased for Wertheim a large block of royalty in the Sprayberry formation. Wertheim then called me to New York to join at luncheon with Algur Meadows, the smooth dean of property acquisitions with his nearly 50 percent of General American Oil. I was concerned because it was now known that this Sprayberry production came from vugs rather than porosity and the pressure-decline curves were not encouraging. At lunch at the Hampshire House, Meadows said to my mentor, Hilson, "This was a great purchase at $250 per royalty acre. There are only a few times in one's life to capitalize on dramatic plays. The East Texas field was one, and this Sprayberry play is another." Well, Meadows was wrong, but Hilson was much impressed and confirmed in his high regard for me.

Hilson was also elated with a lease-buying program in the Rockies initiated by Tom Stroock, years later President Bush's ambassador to Guatemala. Stroock was smart, attractive, forward thinking, and wholesomely energetic. After Stroock's father died, Hilson took a liking to him and assisted Stroock in Bush's class at Yale. Stroock's grandfather was the Santa Fe merchant Spiegelberg, and his grandmother Flora Spiegelberg initiated in Santa Fe a literary salon that included Bishop Lamy. Like me, Stroock had a mind of his own. Despite the responsibility for his lovely wife Marta and young daughter he quit Stanolind in Casper, Wyoming, after a run-in with his superior. Stroock spent his first night in Dallas at the YMCA and convinced me to advance $50,000 for a lease-buying program of federal and state leases. Times were different then, both in IRS regulations and in accepted compliance. A federal acre cost fifty cents, a sum that covered delay rentals for three years and all of which could be expensed. Then if the lease was sold at a profit, statutory depletion could be deducted. Although there were restrictions on the number of acres that could be held per state, it was accepted practice to use the names of secretaries as nominees and no one gave a damn. Hilson inquired whether the percentage allocated to Stroock was fair, which I confirmed "Considering his age of 26." "What's his age got to do with it? You're twenty-eight and maybe we should remember that at Christmas bonus time," replied Hilson.

In the fifties Dallas was the banking center of the Southwest and the top of the line was Fred Florence, president of the Republic National Bank. He was without question the most impressive commercial banker I've ever met. I believe Fred started as a sweep-up boy at a bank in Galveston and came to Dallas to operate a day-and-night storefront bank. His talents were recognized by Karl Hoblitzelle, who made him president despite his Jewish roots. There was an unmatched combination in him of clear forward thinking and a dynamism that all of Texas was proud of. When he finally was gripped by a fatal illness, a close friend did not recognize him at the hospital; he had aged thirty years in three days when he learned he faced a problem he could not lick.

Morris Jaffe, senior partner of Wynne, Jaffe and Tinsely, mentioned that his father sold used pipe to borderline wildcatters, including Dad Joiner, who discovered the prolific East Texas oil field. But the junk-tubing firm was overextended and the Republic would not renew its promissory note. "Now," father Jaffe said to John Scott, "that will destroy my family business." "Sorry, Mr. Jaffe, but we have our own problems here in the bank." "Well, at least let me talk to Fred Florence." But Florence said only that he was sorry. As they walked out of the president's office, Jaffe patted Florence on the shoulder and thanked him for the audience. Then he went over to John Scott and said, "See, Mr. Florence said to renew my note for 100 days." And that's what they did. Of course, the Republic was fit to be tied when they learned of the deception, but by then Jaffe had made some assets liquid. Unlike today, each loan officer had a dollar limit for lending and didn't know about committees. When I needed $300,000 to try to buy control of Dallas Capital Corp., Florence spoke to me for five minutes, then called in Orin Hite and said, "We're giving Ballen a $300,000 commitment. Work out the details."

A turn for the worse in my fortunes came when Wertheim partner Hottinger asked me to explain something about some wells we were drilling with Bill Shriver. I sent Hottinger's letter on to Shriver, asking him to reply and commenting, "Bear in mind that Hottinger is not too sophisticated about oil operations." Well, the next time I was in New York, Hottinger was squirming in his seat and finally pulled out the letter with my notation, which Shriver had enclosed with his reply. The balance of that conversation was not exactly serenity, but

I felt honesty was the best tactic and insisted Hottinger had to face up to the accuracy of my warning.

In 1952 Eddie Hilson had a fatal heart attack, and Klingenstein was now the undisputed head of Wertheim. He was a man I much respected, but we did not talk the same language. Said shrewd JK: "Ballen, I don't understand oil, and I'll only have confidence in you after you've made your fortune. Mark Millard at Loeb Rhoades has done just that. What about making your office joint with them?" This sounded appealing to me. I would represent two of the most imaginative and successful firms on the Street. Millard was enthused by the idea and said Loeb Rhoades would, of course, pay half the costs of the Dallas office. Replied JK, "Oh no, I didn't invite you to save money. Wertheim will pay all the expenses." So the proposition died! By 1955 JK insisted I come back to New York. When I preferred Dallas, JK gave me a one year consulting contract and enabled me to take over Wertheim's Dallas office. Simultaneously, Joe Downer, my assistant, moved into my spot and returned to New York.

The most talented person I knew in Dallas was Hy Yellin. He came down from Connecticut as an aeronautic engineer and then became an oil pipeline engineer. He opened Sony's first repair center for its electronic toys. Yellin was a superb chef and a talented piano player and then got involved in a women's dress shop. But invariably he would fail financially in these endeavors. He correctly attributed this to guilt feelings about success gleaned from his mother who remained a committed communist and Yiddish poet to the very end. When he married Baptist Kathleen Fox from Center, Texas, her father would not make the trip to Dallas and I filled the gap and gave away the bride. So that was how gorgeous, sparkling, talented Kathleen became one of our family's closest friends, an attachement continuing to today.

Many of our friends were immigrant scientists with the Graduate Research Center. Adam Dziewanski, a geophysicist from Poland, was on temporary tour in Dallas. He did not want to return to Poland— nor did he want to be a defector. He solved that problem by falling in love with a splendid girl from Oklahoma with part Indian heritage. Adam said I was the first capitalist he met and since I wasn't too bad a sort, it conditioned him to be receptive to the ways of the West. Adam ended up as Chairman of the Geophysics Dept. at Harvard and the pioneer of seismic tomography.

11/ SERENDIPITY

IT WAS SHORTLY AFTER WE ARRIVED in Dallas and I had sublet an office with the oil producers Clardy & Barnett that I received a call from Frank Schoetz. He was seeing some activity in Franco Wyoming Oil Company stock and thought I should take a look at it. Schoetz, a German refugee who ran the Foreign Trading Post at Wertheim, was a man of absolute honesty and an unwavering workaholic, lacking any traces of humor. I had learned never to overlook or take his suggestions lightly. He had previously asked me to look at Hudson's Bay because of its exposure to the developing Western Canadian oil play. I had spent days looking in all of the available manuals and was unable to locate any reference to Hudson's Bay. This was a puzzle since it was a popular name in the folklore of Western Canada, and the leading department stores in the prairie states were the Hudson's Bay stores. Finally, I discovered that it was organized in 1670 by King Charles II as *Honorable Company of ADVENTURERS OF ENGLAND TRADING IN HUDSON'S BAY LTD.* With this lead I was able to determine that, along with Calgary and Edmonton, Hudson's Bay had the largest exposure of privately owned feelands in Alberta and Saskatchewan. It was an ideal method to safely participate in the oil play that caught on after the discoveries at Leduc and Red Water.

But to get back to Franco Wyoming, this became more and more interesting as I ascertained that it was incorporated in Delaware but held its annual meeting in Cheyenne, Wyoming. It was controlled by Louis Gaillochet, who resided in Paris, France, and its U.S. investment banker was Carl Pforzheimer. Pforzheimer & Company was a respected Wall Street firm specializing in oil stocks. It had become fabulously wealthy after the breakup of the Standard of New Jersey monopoly. Pforzheimer had been the Jersey specialist on the New York Stock Exchange. It had insider insight of values of the numerous companies that were distributed to the parent-company stockholders out of the breakup. This was before any SEC regulations fostering full disclosure of accounting data. Pforzheimer was one of the few investors who knew which stocks to buy and which to sell.

95

It soon became apparent to me that Franco Wyoming was a holding company with its essential assets other than cash and marketable securities residing in three subsidiaries: McElroy Ranch Company, Franco Western Oil Company, and Franco Central Oil Company. Since McElroy had its home office in Ft. Worth, this seemed to be a good place to start an investigation, so I called Ed Brooks, the president of McElroy Ranch Company. "Good morning, Mr. Brooks, I am associated with Wertheim & Company, who make an over-the-counter market* in the stock of Franco Wyoming and I'd like to ask some questions about your operations." His immediate response was, "Well this is something you had better ask the president in Paris." "Could you at least confirm that the McElroy Ranch in Upton County is under lease to Gulf Oil, who are drilling a well there, and what are the terms of the lease to Gulf?" Brooks replied, "The Ranch is leased to Gulf but I can't tell you anything about its terms." "Now, Mr. Brooks, the lease is undoubtedly recorded in the county seat and won't you save me a trip out there?" "No, I'm sorry but I'm not permitted to give out that information."

So Ethel and I and our engaging Nina got into our two-door Studebaker and commenced our first trip out to West Texas. We arrived in Midland unaware that all the lodging facilities were taken up by oil-lease hounds scampering about after the reef discovery in Scurry County. Finally, we went to the city police and asked if they had any lodging suggestion. The result was that a questionable "Inn" across from the Scharbauer Hotel cleaned out one of its broom closets and put a cot in there on which the three of us spent a rather sleepless night. The next morning we drove down to Rankin but barely made it because I had no idea that there was only open range between the two cities. There was no commercial facility or service station whatsoever until we limped into Rankin, the county seat of Upton County. We checked into the only motel, which had wooden sidewalks elevated from the adjacent dusty street. After we signed the guest register with a Dallas address, the country lady behind the front desk exclaimed, "Oh, big city folk." Ethel asked where we could get fresh milk for our daughter, and we then learned that there was no fresh milk in Rankin. However, the proprietress would help out by giving us some condensed milk.

I went over to the county courthouse and had no difficulty locat-

---

* This is the unlisted market, on neither the New York or American stock exchanges.

ing the recorded lease between McElroy Ranch Company and Gulf Oil and then had two pleasant surprises. First, the lease required Gulf to drill five deep tests to the deep Ellenberger formation and second, the royalty to McElroy Ranch would be 20 percent. Back in those days the standard royalty was 12½ percent with maybe a kicker of a sixteenth, so 20 percent was really a lush premium. The daily drilling column in the Midland Paper revealed the first of these deep tests was now actually under way. Feeling that the trip was indeed worthwhile, we came back home via the southern route and passed the Big Lake oil field, which had been the major property of Plymouth Oil Company. The field was discovered by the wildcatter Mike Benedum. I used to read about the field back in New York and now actually saw it.

The investigation of Franco Wyoming started to get more interesting when I undertook to translate its Annual Report, which was in French. Slowly it dawned on me, with some uncertainty, that Franco Wyoming was reporting results on an unconsolidated basis. The parent company was reporting only earnings that were passed up from the operating subsidiaries. This was unheard of—essentially all publicly owned companies would report their balance sheet and profit-and-loss statements on a consolidated basis. This meant that the segments in the Moody and Standard & Poor manuals were worthless. But I still could not believe that what I had uncovered could be true. At this point, my friendship with Tom Beckett came in handy.

Tom Beckett together with two of his cronies in the navy organized First Southwest Company as a municipal bond firm in Dallas when the three of them got out of World War II service. Beckett's father owned a successful manufacturing operation, and Tom was a pioneer Texas graduate of the Harvard Business School. He handled himself with some hauteur rather than as a beer-drinking good old boy. Tom was tall and handsome and totally bald. He was married to a beautiful and vivacious Texas belle named Hazel, and they lived in a socially appropriate home in Highland Park. In every respect, Tom was a worthy citizen, but the cross he bore was a hearty appetite for alcohol. He ultimately died from this affliction, and I was honored to serve as one of his pallbearers. As new Yankee immigrants to Dallas, we were privileged periodically to be invited by Tom and Hazel to the leading upper-crust steak house, Arthurs. The final incidents of that evening out were invariably the same. First, Tom would drunkenly stagger out to the front door after being stopped on the way in turn by each of the black waiters, whether they had served us or not.

At each stop, Tom would grasp for his wallet and make a presentation to each of them. Second, he would manage to drive back to his house, somehow or other missing light poles, pedestrians, and other cars.

Tom and I developed a close friendship right off. He was intrigued by my "scholarly" background and at one point stated with great conviction that after J.K., the senior partner of Wertheim, passed on, I was the logical successor to take the helm. I doubt if anyone else at Wertheim had any such rash notion. Tom knew of my uncertainties in translating a French Annual Report and told me that Hazel had majored in French at Southern Methodist University. So one night Hazel and I, French dictionary readily at hand, poured over the French report together and confirmed that Franco Wyoming was issuing its financial statements on a nonconsolidated basis and thereby obscuring the true value of the company. By now I knew that I was on to something really juicy. I let Frank Schoetz know that it was going to take me a while to write my report but that Franco Wyoming stock was a steal. The stock was selling for $17 at a time when it had cash and marketable securities, such as Standard of Indiana Common, equal to $21 per share without even considering its real assets of the McElroy Ranch Company and a host of operating properties in California, Kansas, and Wyoming.

To add some delicious frosting, while I was writing my report and after Wertheim had already accumulated a good block of Franco Wyoming at under $20, Gulf reported a discovery in the Ellenberger on the McElroy Ranch. Investor interest was sparked everywhere. First Southwest was going joint on the position with Wertheim but Tom Beckett individually loaded up on the stock. My report came out shortly thereafter and made quite a sensation. Analysts had to take my findings on faith since not too many of them could handle French text. About three months after my report had been privately circulated, an ad appeared in the *Wall Street Journal* that John S. Harold, Inc. had a report available on Franco Wyoming for something like $75. John S. Harold was a much admired oil security evaluation firm, and I respected its principals. Tom Beckett asked if I would be interested in buying a copy of the report and I said no, since I doubted if they knew any more than I did. But Tom went ahead and purchased a copy. To our shock, we saw that it was a plagiarized version of my report, including one entire paragraph without a syllable changed. All we did was laugh and wonder if the principals knew what one of their analysts was doing.

Now my mentor, Eddie Hilson, back in New York was getting a

real charge about this and licking his chops since he was the one who had championed the unorthodox notion of sending me to the Southwest and it had paid off. On top of that, he was not by nature a "passive" investor. Some years previous, he had held stock in Tiffany's and was chagrined at its poor performance, which he felt could be attributed to inefficient management. He found out that McKenzie & Company was willing to make a management study of Tiffany's for $25,000. Hilson told the Tiffany president that he himself would pay the $25,000 provided the president pledged he would read the report.

Hilson urged me to go up to the annual meeting in May in Cheyenne, Wyoming. Ethel and I and Nina took the two-door Studebaker to make the 1,000-mile drive. We stopped at one of the mountain parks in Colorado and had a memorable picnic, which included a photograph of our happy Nina on one of the picnic tables. Then one afternoon we drove into Cheyenne. On its main street a lady ran out and said, "Call operator 51 New York." She then ran back to her office. I must have been out of character for the locale or she was quick to note our Texas auto plates or my secretary Phyllis Bledsoe had told her to watch for a green Studebaker. In any case, I immediately called and reached Eddie Hilson. He was absolutely livid and lit into me with instructions on how I should handle myself at the annual meeting: "Who do you think you are, not checking in for your phone messages?" Well, my egotism told me that I knew more about Franco Wyoming than anybody else. It never occurred to me that I should seek experienced instructions no matter how high or mighty.

The annual meeting was a bit hilarious. Ed Brooks was there together with Carl Pforzheimer, together with Louie Guillochet who had come in from Paris, together with their long-time Wyoming attorney who I believe was named O'Leary. This was the first time in the history of the company that any outsider had shown up at the annual meeting. I turned to Ed Brooks and said, "Now you are going to answer some questions without forcing me to search out a publicly recorded document." But Ed Brooks then professionally and openly answered my questions.* After the meeting we adjourned to the bar where Pforzheimer hosted friendly libations. I attended the next two

---

* Brooks and I subsequently became warm friends. At his retirement he told me that he received some award from the Colorado School of Mines but then he confided that he had completed his professional career as an exploration geologist without once making a discovery. However, his dry holes had proved up the subsurface contours so that others could drill successful producing wells.

annual meetings of Franco Wyoming and in subsequent years, Guillochet had printed remarks that started off, "We welcome Sam Ballen from Dallas, Texas."

Franco Wyoming worked out to over $100 per share. Back in Dallas an aura of respect surrounded me, and I was pointed out on the street as the genius oil analyst from New York. The Dallas Harvard School of Business Chapter asked me to referee a debate among some big shots, and the Petroleum Accountants Club asked me to make a speech, which wowed them. When Grady Vaughn asked me to go work for him, I politely declined. Cornelius Shields asked me to come up to New York and skirted around a job offer but once he understood the magnitude of running an oil operation, he backed off without trying to entice me. Hilson asked me how much stock I had bought. I told him that it might not have occurred to him, but that one needed funds in order to buy stock. And that is why I did not own a single share of stock. The whole thing was an intellectual exercise, and I had neither the greedy appetite to make money, or an effective appreciation of using personal credit. The big dividend I got from Franco Wyoming was to earn the warm friendship of Creston Funk, a charming over-the-counter securities man from San Antonio, who pumped me dry and ended up knowing everything that I knew about Franco.

12/ NINA TELSA

For Lois, Panina, Lee, Lenore, Marta, and Sara (July 1989)

Well, I have finally turned the material over to the accountants for my 1988 income tax return and can now get around to responding to three questions that surfaced in the condensed conversations we had about my contribution to the Temple. That has gone forward and enclosed is a letter from the president of the Temple. Probably sometime in the next bunch of months, when everyone is in town, it might be appropriate for us to have a private little gathering around the plaque. I categorized the three questions as what about Nina, what about the Temple, and what about your own mortgages. So here goes:

NINA TELSA WAS BORN at St. Vincent's Hospital in Manhattan on March 15, 1950. She was delivered by natural childbirth, which was very rare at that time. Ethel was on an emotional high and came walking down the hallway shortly after delivery to visit with me until the nuns took her back to her room. The senior nun said, "How lucky you are. Your daughter was born normal." It was only then that I realized how frequently the opposite occurred and the nuns had to inform the parents of a deformed child. We were living at 8 Stuyvesant Oval, about 16th Street on the east side of Manhattan, in a new project built by the Metropolitan Life Insurance Co. Because of the intense post-war housing shortage, apartments were allocated on the basis of numerical points for service in the military. Since I had been overseas nearly three years and had received many battle ribbons, we had a very high score and were granted one of the first apartments in that project. Nina was named after Ethel's mother's mother, whose name was Minna. She was a dignified Romanian Jew who lived with her husband in Brooklyn. She died a natural death of old age. I hardly knew her since she spoke only Yiddish. Telsa, Nina's middle name, was for my father's mother, whom I did not know. She had lived and died in Lodz, Poland. My father always had a very bitter opinion of his father but always spoke lovingly of his mother. Even though he never saw

101

her after he left Europe to come to the United States, he periodically wrote to her. In my father's last year of life he continually recalled the hardships his mother had lived through and how much he missed her.

Almost from her birth, Nina was an exciting and outgoing baby. She was able to stand erect when held by her feet when only a few months old and that is how I would play with her. She grew the long black hair of my own mother and had piercing and friendly eyes. When she was three months old, the three of us drove in our Studebaker to Norman, Oklahoma, where I took three courses in petroleum engineering and one course in oil and gas law at the University of Oklahoma. Ethel took a course in golf, but that was not the greatest success. We had a good time in Oklahoma. We were overwhelmed by the friendliness of the people and somehow managed to survive the heat. Although we did not then know Iris Herzfeld, we did meet her father who was on the faculty in the Architecture Department. He was introduced to us by our friends Don and Sue Dietrich. We knew the Dietrichs from Cornwall-on-the-Hudson in early 1946, when they rented us an apartment that we shared with the Krugmans in the quasi-basement of their home.

Don had transferred from CCNY to be a professor of psychology at Oklahoma University, but that particular summer, he and his wife Sue, together with their kids, Robin and Patty, were in Santa Fe and bunking at the house of Chuzo Tamotsu on Garcia Street. Toward the close of the summer session at OU, Don called and asked me to drop by Santa Fe on our way back to New York and to carry some furnishings for him. I said I didn't know what map he was looking at because Santa Fe was not on the way to New York. He replied, "Don't you concern yourself about that. The excursion will be interesting to you." We piled up the car with some of Don's possessions, so that Ethel and Nina could hardly fit in, and drove the 600 miles from Norman to Santa Fe and camped more or less on the lawn of Chuzo's house. Nina was in somewhat of a crying fit then, probably because of the travel and change of water, and we were irritable. Don said that you cannot love an infant too much. One day he took us with Sue to Bandelier for a picnic. The Dietrichs were always tight on money, and Sue had just used some extra funds to purchase a Western jacket at Cooper's on the Santa Fe Plaza. She was immensely proud of the garment. It was lying on the picnic table when, lo and behold, a skunk just more or less walked right up to the table. All of us quietly backed off while the skunk walked around. Sue was fearful that he would eject his scent. Finally, the skunk took off and we returned to finish our picnic.

I know that we left Santa Fe for the long drive back to New York City (there was no interstate highway system then) on August 4 because Don urged us to stay to go down to see an Indian dance at Santo Domingo. I had no concept then of what an electrifying experience that would be and shrugged it off, saying that I had to get back to Wall Street. I should have mentioned that we had a really narrow escape on the drive out to Oklahoma. Ethel and Nina were asleep in the car and I was driving through Indiana in a rainstorm, when suddenly the Studebaker went completely out of control, went off the highway into a wood, spun around several times, just missed being creamed by several trees, and finally came to rest. Ethel then woke up. Several of the other cars on the highway came to inspect our condition and reported that Indiana was using paraffin oil to surface its highways and the unstable condition in rain was notorious. But we survived.

Our first Dallas apartment was out in Wynnewood Village in southern Oak Cliff. Nina was an absolute joy and had the benefit of loving concentration that I guess belongs to every first-born. Ethel, of course, was nursing Nina. The Korean War had started, and I was afraid of being called up for service since I was still in the Infantry Reserve. While I had volunteered for combat in World War II, I had no enthusiasm for going to Korea. I also had to protect Ethel and Nina, so we went out and bought a home for $24,000 at 9831 Galway Drive, which I certainly could not afford. At that time my base was $9,000 per year but I had confidence in my potential. Our inducement to make such a purchase was that mortgage payments were suspended on a moratorium for soldiers who were called back into service.

For Labor Day, 1951, we went out to The Lodge at Cloudcroft, New Mexico, but to our amazement we were more or less the only guests and we were quite bored. We did "play" the golf course there, until we lost all three balls! On the veranda in front of the Lodge was a low wall on which Nina climbed. She walked about on it until we investigated and discovered, to our fright, that there was a very precipitous cliff and to fall off would have been no fun. Because we had no companions at the Lodge at Cloudcroft, we decided to drive back to Santa Fe, not realizing that it was Fiesta. Naturally, there were no rooms when we got into town. We went to the police station, whose staff found us a little room in the De Vargas Hotel. That night we were quite frightened when we saw a line of people marching with crosses and candles and wondered if we had fallen into a Ku Klux Klan rally.

Nina's Dallas home was a new subdivision east of White Rock Lake called Lake Park Estates. It was composed mainly of middle-income people from East Texas, but there was one Jewish couple down the block named Selikoff. The husband was a native Texan, and the wife was from Missouri. To the right of our house lived the Duncans, a very wholesome family from Paris, Texas, who were very devout Baptists. They had two young sons, and the wife's mother, "Missy" Hart, lived with them to help out since the father, Thomas Marshall, was incapacitated and in a wheelchair because of polio, which he had picked up in the service in World War II. They were a very down-to-earth, family-oriented couple and early on, Nina would play with Van, the younger of the boys. Van was not as spontaneously at ease or outgoing as the rest of the family. But genuine friendship and love came to Nina from Lois and Marshall and Tommy and "Missy."

To the left of our house lived an interesting couple, Dr. Dillon Garner and his wife Mae, and their two young boys, who did not get particularly involved with Nina. The Garners had moved from Paragould, Arkansas, because Dillon felt he had greater opportunities to open an office as a surgeon in expanding Dallas. Nina was a free-ranging spirit and did not confine herself to our fenced-in yard, but oftentimes would be found wandering with her German Shepherd pet, Lady, in a grassed island just in front of our home. In November 1951 Nina's sister Lois was born, but that did not come about with any particular advance planning. Down at work I had met Bernie Lucas, who was a customer representative at Harris Upham, through an introduction from Eddie Byer, who was the manager of the office and had migrated from the East shortly before me. I had never before met a Jew like Bernie Lucas. He was several generations a Southerner and quite conservative politically with a southern drawl that couldn't be cut with a pickax. He asked me to join Temple Emmanuel, and while I was surprised at the suggestion, we went ahead and did so. This was our very first religious affiliation, but then Lois was "blessed" there. Nina accepted Lois from the very inception. She often repeated "sweet baby, sweet baby" and never displayed any resentment or jealousy at a rival entering the family.

But in point of fact, things were not peaches and cream in our household. We were having difficulty adjusting to the totally different way of life from back east, Ethel was bogged down with motherhood, and I was gazing at the exotic secretarial corps that populated downtown Dallas. Its members found me appealing because I was so different from the run-of-the-mill Dallas men just then emerging into the securities business. I was the representative of Wertheim & Co., which was light-years more sophisticated and wealthy than the typical Dallas over-the-counter firm. At that time the highest position a Dallas girl could aim for was to be an executive secretary.

It was probably in early January 1952 that my mentor and boss, Edwin I. Hilson, made a trip down to the office from New York. Most things went poorly for me even though he took a liking to Ethel. We went out at night together with Tom and Hazel Beckett. Hilson was taken aback by our German Shepherd leaping on him, and then he was dismayed at the cream-colored sport jacket that I wore that night. We went to the famous steakhouse, Arthurs, where I drank much too much. Then we went over to the Becketts' in Highland Park, where I continued to drink too much and had to run out onto the front lawn to throw up. Ethel and I went home without saying good-bye, either to Hilson or the Becketts. In the morning I woke with a splitting hangover and called the Becketts to find out who had taken Hilson back to his hotel. When I described my predicament, Tom suggested that I drink some more scotch as the cure, which I did.

All of us were invited for lunch in the private dining room of Fred Florence, the president of the Republic National Bank of Dallas. Once again, I did not carry myself too well in the discussion and at one point prefaced my comments by saying, "Well, I am only a pipsqueak." When we left, Hilson chewed me out and said that as a representative of Wertheim I was in no way a pipsqueak. But when he left to return home, he peeled off a $100 bill and gave it to my secretary Phyllis Bledsoe and told her to buy a plant for us. Since $100 was a lot of money in those days, we bought a tree, which we planted in the front yard. Phyllis was the best of the best. She was senior secretary at Standard of Texas but took a salary cut to come with me with my assurance her sex would not limit her advancement. After three years she left to marry a VA doctor, who was an alcoholic, and her life became a tragedy. This unsuccessful visit with Hilson represented some malaise in my life, which was typified by confusion in my relation to family and confusion in adjusting to Dallas.

On Saturday, February 2, 1952, I came back home from some chore in the afternoon and started to do some work in the back yard. Ethel said that she would have to go out and do some shopping but that Lois was sleeping and Nina was next door playing with Van. After a while, I became curious as to where Nina and Van were and started to look around for them. By this time Ethel had come home, and I mentioned that I was going to make a more determined search for Nina and Van. I started walking around the several houses, calling out her name louder and louder. I heard nothing. Then I drifted to the back yard, which was fenced. Behind the fence was an alley that was used to pick up garbage, and on the other side of the alley was a neighboring home with the only swimming pool in the area. As I was walking around the back fenceline, shouting Nina's name, I finally heard a whimper.

By this time, Marshall Duncan had himself become concerned and had pushed himself in his wheelchair to his own back yard. He heard the whimper at the same time and said, "It is Van." Marshall became frantic because he could not get himself out of his wheelchair. My impression is that somehow I leaped over the back chain-linked fence, scratching my clothing, and ran through an open gate and saw in an instant that even though the pool had been drained for the winter, some shallow rain water had collected in the deep end. Nina was floating face down in this small pool and Van was in the dry opposite end whimpering. I grabbed Nina and put her on the ground alongside the pool and started to apply artificial respiration, which at that time was not the technique now fostered by CPR. I screamed for Ethel to call Dr. Garner. Ethel shouted, "Is it serious?" and I said, "Yes, it is." While I was performing artificial respiration, Marshall was screaming, "Is Van all right," and I said, "Yes, he is." By that time many neighbors had congregated around us. Dr. Garner arrived and took over the first aid attempt and Ethel came up and we held each other. The irony was that Nina looked 100 percent perfect, except, of course, that she was lifeless. By now, someone had called both the police and an ambulance; and while we could not get it through our heads that someone who didn't have a scratch on her could be in serious difficulty, I did hear one of the neighbors say, "It is hopeless." That was the first touch of deep despair I had.

The hospital orderlies put Nina into an ambulance, and Ethel and I and Dr. Garner rode down to the hospital on Gaston Avenue. I pleaded with Dr. Garner to give her some injection to restore her heartbeat, but he said, "Sam, there has been too much brain damage, and you really would not want me to do that." Of course, in those days no one knew of the possibility of preserving life after many minutes in cold water, but that probably would not have applied to our situation because we were having warm weather and the collected rain water would have been tepid. Rabbi Levi Olan met us at the hospital and tried to console us. Ethel and I were sobbing uncontrollably all that evening. I believe we got somebody to come in to babysit that night for Lois. Ethel and I clung to each other, wailing all night and knowing that we needed each other in order to survive. One of the hardest tasks was for me to call my mother and Ethel's mother that night with the news of our incredible loss.

We never did find out how Nina had gotten from the two fenced yards into the area in the back with the swimming pool. Van was barely three years old and was himself in shock. He had never been too communicative, and we could not ask him to tell us what happened. Nina's Memorial Service was at Sparkman Brand Funeral Home, and she was buried at Temple Emmanuel Cemetery. Her gravesite is immediately next to the grave of the great Rabbi David Lefkowitz and the even greater Rabbi Levi Olan. There was an enormous crowd of neighbors and friends who came to that funeral. One of the things Olan said at the memorial service was that we cannot predict what joy or sorrow might have been part of her future years. My mother came down for the funeral, but my father was too shook up to make the trip. Ethel's mother came down and then stayed for quite a while to help us. Subsequently, Dottie Krugman came down from New York and stayed with us for a while to be of help.

All of our adjoining neighbors flooded us with support. On the evening of the drowning the announcement was made on the Dallas radio, and Decker Jackson, who was head of First Southwest Company, came over with his wife to be of support. The property owner to the back came home that evening and naturally was quite upset. I told him it was an accident and there was no point in passing any guilt or blame around. He subsequently came over and asked if he could make a financial settlement with us. I told him to forget it, that there was no way we could enjoy any money derived from such a loss. During the next six months, they sold their house and moved away. They must have had that trauma on their conscience even though I never felt they really were to blame.

I truly was shaken to my depths and I don't believe a day has passed that I have not thought about Nina. At Don Dietrich's suggestion, I spent some time with a local psychiatrist, Dr. Charles Bloss, who was a practicing Baptist. He helped me a great deal. It was an enormous blow to learn, about 1980, from a visitor to Santa Fe that Dr. Bloss had committed suicide. Ethel ostensibly was holding up quite strongly and would not consent to any medical counseling, but about a year later it fell on her like a ton of bricks. Then she did go to see a German psychiatrist, Dr. Weisz, but I doubt if she permitted any intimacy and I doubt if he was of any real assistance to her.

We remained good friends with the Duncans and "Missy" helped with all our later girls. Marshall had a fatal heart attack while giving a speech in his wheelchair on a platform in Lubbock. Lois Duncan has visited twice in Santa Fe. About a month after Nina's death, Marshall met me one afternoon on my return home and said with a beaming face, "Don't grieve; Nina is on the lap of the Lord." But I never believed that.

About fifteen years ago, we contributed $30,000 in La Fonda debentures to the College of Santa Fe as a scholarship program for La Fonda employees and their children, named for Nina Telsa Ballen, but that has fallen into disuse and needs to be reactivated along more sensible lines. I would say that Nina seemed to possess the better part of me and the better part of Ethel and gave promise of being a loving and committed person, but she did not have the chance to experience *LIFE*...its grandeur and its sorrows.

So now what about the Temple? I think Ethel and I share the same feelings about religion, namely, we feel that faith is somewhat important, but we are not attracted to structured or revealed theology. For a while, we were members of the Unitarian Church in Dallas but then returned to Temple Emmanuel. Then for a while in Santa Fe we were members both of Temple Beth Shalom and the Unitarian Church but then ultimately gave up attendance at the latter institution. The plaque to be installed will say "May This Sanctuary Dedicated In Memory Of Nina Telsa Ballen Expand The Heart And Mind Of Each Worshiper," and that about summarizes our feelings toward all religion. Certainly many people are pointed in the right direction by their church or synagogue but we cannot forget Nobel Laureate Francois Jacob: "Do not venerate gods or men, not gods, cause there are no gods, not men, cause they are not gods."

I did accept the Chairmanship of the Santa Fe Temple Building Fund and got the drive off the ground, and at that time we made a significant cash contribution. Younger people later took over the solicitation and did an excellent job. They raised over $1 million which was a most impressive mining of a very small community of contributors, which included a fair number of Christians. They went into debt in order to add the classrooms and some other additions and woke up to find that they were spending their money on interest payments and not reducing the principal. So Gail Rapapport undertook a new effort to reduce the mortgage. I knew that, modest in our circumstances though we were, we could not ignore their appeal. Therefore Ethel and I decided to contribute another sum, which we borrowed from the bank and which we will be paying off over a three-year period. This response by us generated action by other people so that the mortgage has now been substantially reduced. We have not asked for any publicity on this, and we declined the invitation to have the Sanctuary named for Nina since we believe that the Sanctuary belongs to everybody and should not be named for any single individual. In this imperfect world, we believe that it is naive and immature to be a universalist and ignore one's own roots, and we do not believe that our dedication to humanity is diminished in any way whatsoever by acknowledging our pleasure with and responsibility to Jewry.

And now your own mortgages. There are two philosophies concerning accumulated savings. Warren Buffet, the phenomenal investor from Omaha, who is worth over a billion dollars, has publicly stated that he was leaving nothing to his children because he does not want to deprive them of the challenge and the thrill of striving that he had. I have seen an interview on television in which his thirty-five year old daughter said she is perfectly content with that because her real treasure is the education her father made possible. The other extreme is those people who feel an obligation and compulsion to accumulate a large estate to pass on to their heirs. Both philosophies have merit, but we are somewhat confused by the two poles. I guess that, like so many other things, moderation is the best solution. From early on, I have made it a practice to set aside something like 5 percent of my earnings to give to charitable causes each year, and that is periodically supplemented by digging in to past aggregations.

It is humiliating to witness those who suffer from the generosity of their parents and, as a result, never get committed to life and never, in an energetic way, use whatever talents they possess. Since each of you is fortunate to have good health and good intelligence, there is no need to smother you with trust funds. My immediate priorities are:

(A) to pay off our indebtedness, which can only be accomplished through after income tax surplus cash flow;

(B) to make contributions of securities to Sara to bring her up to the same position that you all enjoy;

(C) to provide Ethel with sufficient funds to take care of herself in later years in the event that she survives me as a widow; and

(D) to then perhaps provide each of you a modest increment and finally to devote any remaining surplus to other causes and friends.

You probably know that I decided twenty years ago not to devote concentrated energies in building wealth and that had something to do with leaving Dallas. If it should turn out that our investments prove bountiful, then it might be possible that each of you would find yourselves with an incremental inheritance. However, to predict and plan too strongly for a future based on unearned resources is very dangerous.

We do occasionally see the tragedy of children fighting among themselves over inheritances. Such may have been the case for the three children of my great uncle S and my great aunt L. Certainly, we do not want that to happen in our family, so we probably will make some provision in our will for there to be serious penalty if anyone is so greedy as to seek an attorney to "protect her rights."

If you use your inheritance to further your education or to advance in your profession so that you experience the joy of being self-reliant, then we will have earned enough dividends from providing a limited inheritance.

Well, this is the end of my lengthy monologue, which I hope provides some answers to your questions. I was wrong to have so abruptly sprung that Temple contribution on you, but then it made this deeper explanation possible.

Love,

Dad

ADDENDUM:

I wrote the portion about inheritances to encourage our daughters to do their own thing—to stand on their own feet and not just float in anticipation of largess from our estate. I say amen to the business of their doing their own thing because it would be hard to find more independent-minded children and that suits us fine.

After Nina's death we struggled toward sanity, and with the help of friends and neighbors and with the passing of time, we slowly became composed. But there is no question that Lois, then three months old, did not have spontaneous, caring parents. We left her for two weeks at a nearby nursery and went down to Acapulco, which then was home to only four hotels and not the rip-off tourist trap it is today. How wonderful that Lois is today a competent, secure nurse in

Santa Fe. She is taking her master's degree in midwifery and enjoys a splendid daughter and loving husband, who is a Doctor of Oriental Medicine. Tiny Lois has now climbed forty-two of the fifty-two Colorado mountains over 14,000 feet in height. She is admired far and wide.

In short order, just a year apart, came daughters Lee and Panina. We named them Joanne Lee and Paula Sue but their independent expressions dictated a change to their own selection. Lee is a beautiful ballet teacher and yoga instructor in northern California. Panina is a world-traveled linguist and elementary school teacher with a fine husband who is a math teacher and carpenter and a daughter still aggressively nursing at twenty-two months. They live in Albuquerque. Panina and husband Christopher, who is the grandson of the sculptor Una Hanberry, decided that a mother is more important to a child than a father so they named their daughter Eliana Kelley Ballen. Independent Panina was about fourteen when she hitchhiked with a boyfriend out to the Shalako dance at Zuni. She and Bob were stopped at Grants by the sheriff, who called our home, but they were left to continue when Lee told the officer their journey had our blessing. When we all got home, I lectured Bob, with my carbine at my side, "You have put my daughter at great risk. Everyone who is loose in the United States rides down US 66. I'm very angry at you and you can't see each other for two weeks." "Ok, Mr. Ballen, I am sorry. I didn't know about US 66. We will never hitchhike there again but how about US 285?"

So our hands were full with three infant girls when Ethel again became pregnant. After much soul-searching we decided on an abortion to preserve the tranquility of our home. A nurse we knew from Costa Rica refused to offer any assistance, so we ended up with a doctor who maneuvered the operation into a Dallas hospital. I paid him nothing but arranged for some sweetheart purchases and sales of private securities. Was Hillary's commodity trading success fortuitous?

Two years later came lovable Lenore who now has a master's degree in Creative Arts Therapy. She has been living the last ten years with an internist, who is our near son-in-law. They own a house together in Tucson. Then four years later came Marta, adventuresome from inception. Rabbi Levi Olan had just been named a trustee of the University of Texas when I bumped into him at the SMU Community Course. He said, "Sam, it's not a boy." My retort was, "Neither is it Harvard." That was the one and only time Olan did not have the final word.

Marta is involved in physical plant projects at the hotel but she is a professional endangered species hunter with contracts from the Forest Service and Indian Reservations. She is a vegetarian and a follower of Mother Amaghi from Kerala, India. Maybe in time she will appreciate I.I. Rabi's comment about J. Robert Oppenheimer, "He should have studied the Talmud instead of the Bhagavad-Gita." Marta lives in Santa Fe but periodically goes off to the Carson National Forest searching for spotted owls or to Bluff, Utah, looking for endangered ferrets.

Ethel was left to raise these five girls while I traveled about in the oil industry. After we moved to Santa Fe—which then had a daily nonstop jet to Dallas—Ethel asked, "Why don't we just buy those adjoining five acre lots selling for $8,000 instead of searching oil deals in the Permian Basin?" But I said, "What do you know about business?" Now those lots sell for $300,000. Ethel let our girls be themselves. She declined the invitation of Judge Harl Byrd's mother-in-law, the very proper Mrs. Chipman, to join a young ladies' etiquette club she was tutoring. But when Mrs. Chipman told me that her charming daughter, Corona, said I had a great sense of humor, I replied, "If you can make a woman laugh, you can seduce her." Mrs. Chipman loudly snorted, so maybe she didn't miss our five girls.

Our Fiftieth Wedding Celebration was admirably conducted by twelve-year-old granddaughter Sara at our home on July 29, 1995. Our renewal of vows was accompanied by a beautiful song created and sung by our daughters and their men.

13/ OLD LADY NAVAJO MOUNTAIN

On Sunday, November 17, 1991, Ethel and I left Mesa, Arizona, where Lisbeth Eubank is in a private home with five other senior ladies cared for by three attractive practical nurses. Unlike the other "tenants," Lisbeth is cheerful, talkative, alert, and commanding at eighty-six, but Ethel suspects she did not fully identify me because she kept asking where my home was. Our previous visit to her apartment in Phoenix ended with our discovery of the front cover of a 1946 issue of *Colliers Magazine* that showed Lisbeth instructing a kindergarten class at Navajo Mountain how to blow their noses. When we left, Lisbeth said goodbye: "I'll let you know when I die." But she didn't. Although Laura Gilpin acknowledged Lisbeth in *Enduring Navajo*, Lisbeth has somehow escaped the attention of historians. This is surprising since her accomplishments during a career of fifty years' service with the Bureau of Indian Affairs does not take second place to Anna's with the King of Siam. Seven years ago, when I could detect her memory starting to become unreliable and she modestly refused to dictate her memoirs, I proposed taking a month off to record on paper the fact that she knew more about the Navajo than any other Anglo. But I was diverted by business crises, and now it is too late.

Lisbeth came from a respected family in Virginia, graduated from college in West Virginia, and then entered the Cerrillos Road Indian School in Santa Fe as a teacher in the twenties. She became the first solid teacher at Navajo Mountain Boarding School, in the most remote corner of the contiguous 48 states with an awesome mailing address: San Juan County, Utah, via Tonalea, Arizona. The school was located near the trading post at the northeast corner of the mountain and just over the Utah state line. The Colorado and San Juan rivers and Cummings Mesa and Paiute Canyon made land travel from Utah impossible. The school consisted of three large, connected hogans: one for classes, one for kitchen and dining room and the third for living quarters for Lisbeth, who supervised its construction by Hopi carpenters. They did not plot out the circular structures on the ground but just proceeded to put up posts and vigas, and then miraculously it

113

all came together. In addition there were some sandstone dormitories. The students knew no English and had never seen running water or toilets, and there had to be segregated seating by maternal clan. By the time Lisbeth retired in the sixties, the first two Navajo college graduates were her students as was the first Navajo medical doctor. She was granted a homestead by the chapter for her retirement, but instead she went to Africa with the Peace Corps and never returned to Navajo Mountain. Her final lucid years were spent as a docent with the Heard Museum in Phoenix, but she needed an unlisted telephone number because any Navajo in trouble with the police would try to call her for protection.

As a school teacher in those early days, she also operated the shortwave radio and the electric generator, functioned as health officer, and supervised the helicopter drops of emergency food during the great post-war snow blizzard on the Rainbow Plateau. She felt viscerally that the Navajo were the most appealing group of people on earth and those at Navajo Mountain were the cream of the Navajo Nation. This admiration was reciprocated—she was admitted to ceremonies closed to Anglos. For one such ceremony she had to enter bare chested. Lisbeth married a fine Oklahoma Indian and then raised her son Randy as a widow. She knew something was wrong when Randy kept coming home late, but she said nothing. Finally one afternoon Randy rode up to the school with something on the back of his saddle. "Mom, we just have to take in this Navajo tot. He's an orphan. His father died in Korea. We just have to take him." So Lisbeth also raised a second "son," who became fire marshal of Tucson after he was formally adopted by Will Rogers' son in California.

My forty-year close friendship with her commenced when I was invited to join some Californians for a two-week initial exploration of Navajo Canyon complex. The leader was a physically and professionally powerful attorney, Carl Wheat, who, as a youngster, had accompanied Teddy Roosevelt to Rainbow Bridge. My invitation came from Charles Gooding, who knew how devastated I was by Nina's death. He was one of my early La Fonda investors. He subsequently willed his stock to the University of Chicago. But Jack Hecht, partner of Dempsey-Tegler stock traders, also was concerned about me and called me to come to a Town House lanai in Los Angeles. When I found there was no work assignment, he simply said, "Just loll around for four days; Wertheim can stand the expense."

The only way to Navajo Mountain was north from Flagstaff, across the Little Colorado on a suspension bridge, into the sand ruts to Tuba City, at Red Lake through another secondary diversion to Inscription House, across three miles of rocks in a two hour journey into the Rainbow Plateau, and finally on to the Navajo Mountain Trading Post. In the earliest years one had to dismantle a wagon at a tight defile to get through. The Richardsons improved the road when they built Rainbow Lodge at the west side of the mountain. On our 1952 trip we spent the night camping out just north of the Inscription House Trading Post and then arrived at Navajo Mountain at about 3 p.m. Although some sheltered liberals claimed the traders were price gouging the Navajos, I could sense only admiration for these isolated merchants. They could not accumulate any estate by improving the physical plant because the leases from the Navajo Tribe could be cancelled at whim and any assignment had to be approved by the BIA. The trader was a target of those few Navajo derelicts, needed to speak Navajo, and had to extend credit with the collateral of pawn jewelry governed by specific regulations. The trader's store was bank, post office, community center, Peace Corps, repository of hand-woven rugs, which were frequently purchased by the pound, and also the army enlistment center. And frequently the trader had to handle burials since death was a taboo to the traditionalists.

The store at Navajo Mountain had been established near a spring by Ben Wetherill. When I was there in 1952, it had just been purchased by Ralph and Madeline Cameron. All these traders were keen individualists, so camaraderie was offset by petty rivalry infused by contraband whisky so that periodically the traders would get "swacked." Ralph Cameron was an ex-truck driver making the run from Salt Lake City to Flagstaff and certainly no intellectual. Madeline's father, Dunn, had previously been the trader, and she needed someone handy with machinery and not afraid to stare down Navajo bucks, so she became Mrs. Cameron. I was one of the few who got along with Ralph. I appreciated what he had done to repair the trail to Rainbow Bridge without any Park Service or BIA subsidies. Everyone else considered him a varlet. Barry Goldwater had cut a landing strip on the southwest side of the mountain because he had a half-ownership in Rainbow Lodge, but then the BIA ploughed a better strip near the Indian School and put in a windsock. In the seventies when "prosperity" showed its face at the trading post Ralph got a simple plane which he soon crash landed, probably while flying intoxicated. Madeline ran the post with the assistance of the son of a

Czech housekeeper in Santa Fe (what a small world) who married a lovely Navajo from Shonto. The civilizing glue to this encampment, both Navajo and Anglo, was Lisbeth Eubank, but the patriarch was Segniyazibegay—son of Little Small Canyon—who even after his ninety-fifth birthday would still ride his horse across the plateau with a proud carriage, anticipating that he would be buried with all his jewelry.

What made these Navajos so special? Well, the plateau was first settled by White Man Killer and his relatives, who fled the Tuba City area after a run-in with a Mormon. Kit Carson's round-up of the Navajos during the Civil War and forcing them on the "Long Walk" to internment at Fort Sumner never touched these Navajos. They hid out in the numerous isolated canyons fingering out from the laccolith of Navajo Mountain, which, at 10,345 feet, was the dominant feature of the landscape. Our Anglo literature claims the "Long Walk" was retribution for the marauding young bucks raiding Spanish settlements. The Navajos suggest some gold discoveries at Monument Valley played a contributing role. The Navajos say their young girls were raped, and all the tall Navajo men were shot by U.S. Cavalry men.

Prehistorically, the area was more densely populated. Just northeast of Lisbeth's school, on a rise, was an Anasazi ruin that had been cannibalized by a pot hunter, and just south of the mountain on the plateau was a large surface ruin of red rocks. In an alcove at the base of the mountain above Rainbow Lodge were some storage bins and in the Navajo Canyon complex perhaps thirty good-sized dwellings, including one cantilevered out. All culminated in the grand Inscription House Ruin of the tributary Neetsin Canyon. While traversing a smooth sandstone slope to a cantilevered ruin in that same canyon with young Bob Malott, who went on to become president of Food Machinery Corp., I felt myself slide and gasped, "Bob, I'm a goner." Bob supplied the right medicine with an indecent laugh and told me to flatten against the rock. On Cummings Mesa to the west were numerous ancient dwellings as well as a multistoried cliff house in south Aztec Creek.

Lisbeth arranged the logistics of the 1952 exploration initiated by Carl Wheat, who was preparing six volumes of early mapping of the Rocky Mountain West. His work is now out of print and much sought after by collectors. There were seven Anglos, three Navajos, ten horses, and three mules. We had secured special permission from the Chapter House to spend the night on top of Navajo Mountain, which we climbed by way of War God Spring Canyon. On top we found the wooden-frame remnants of a heliograph survey party left the middle of the nineteenth century. Now there is a flashing beacon on top. Orthodox Navajos would have considered this fixture a blasphemy. I was giddy from the experience, looking north to the juncture of the San Juan and Colorado rivers and to the dissected country in between. Northeast one overlooked the Henry Mountains and to the east, Monument Valley and to the northwest Kaiparowitz Plateau.

It was cold and we built a roaring fire. Then I asked Ephraim Crank, the only English-speaking Navajo, why the Navajos were standing with their backs to the fire. Ephraim looked at us and replied, "How come the white men are standing facing the fire?" To the dismay of some of my California comrades I asked if the Navajo had made a mistake to sign a peace treaty with the Whites and after discussion among themselves, Ephraim said Chief Hoskinimy told the story of the billy goat who was chained to a tree but wanted to be free and bucked the tree until he killed himself. In my infantile giddiness I started to talk about developing the area with motels, shopping centers, and dude ranches whose guests could journey down to Rainbow Bridge, but Ephraim interjected, "We won't work for you."

The next two weeks, in Navajo Canyon, we came upon Joe Many Goats in a most isolated settlement with his two wives. Now we have a handsome pot made by one of Many Goats' nieces. Tom Dougi, the quiet wrangler, found a prehistoric pot which he gave to Wheat and which is now with the Museum of Northern Arizona in Flagstaff. Tom's grandfather was one of the guides on the first trip to Rainbow Bridge. Tom's son became a respected sculptor and his grandson, Iskhotin, is a student at the Art School in Santa Fe. The untaught sculptor Tomas Dougi made the cover of *Beyond Tradition* and had a part in the movie *Dances with Wolves.* He drawled, "Ah cannot come into Santa Fe without women wanting to get in bed with me. If ah did all that ah would lose myself." He was a ranger in Vietnam and a pretty good poet, with a physique you wouldn't want to challenge when he was sober. "Sam, you never thought someone from Navajo Mountain would be on the cover of *Beyond Tradition,* did you?" When he accompanied our Los Alamos friends to a campout on Hamilton Mesa, he built up Dottie Walker's controlled fire and then screamed, "You fuckin physicists don't appreciate fire—without fire we wouldn't have survived the glacier age. Let's pray to fire before the light which left the sun eight minutes ago goes down." A quick calculation showed his eight minutes was correct.* Before we concluded the 1952 excursion, we all chipped in and sent a large swing set to Lizbeth's school. It was the only play equipment then on the premises. "How do your students make out on IQ scores?" "Very poorly, but at Easter when I carefully hide the eggs, they find them all in no time." So much for the Bell Curve...Curse.

Over the next decade I spent at least two weeks a year at Navajo Mountain and after a while knew more about the area than most Navajos. Each year Buck Whitehat would be our guide, and even though he spoke no English and my Navajo did not exceed a dozen words, I think we had closer communication than can be imagined. The 1953 trip was also arranged by Carl Wheat with Lisbeth's assistance, and we beat out Doc Marston in discovering and measuring an insignificant arch, which we named Whitehat Arch and got us all admitted to the Explorers Club. Carl Wheat had the aggressive, dynamic posture admired in our society. Even though he tried to be respectful and even-handed with our Navajos, they just didn't cotton to his direct orders and floundered to accomplish what he had in mind. Carl was then about sixty years old, and Buck Whitehat was perhaps sixty-five. One day, Carl's horse, frightened by the height, would not take some steps to a lower ledge close to an awesome canyon. We all awkwardly waited while Carl tried to manipulate his horse. Finally, Whitehat nodded him down, mounted Carl's horse, spurred him with his deerskin moccasins down two ledges, and abruptly stopped with the mount's nose gazing over the abyss. Then Whitehat calmly handed the reins to Wheat, who was quiet for the rest of the day. Carl's son, Frank, became the leading securities attorney in California, a distinguished commissioner of the SEC, and a world-wide nature explorer. Someday I need to meet him and honor his father who changed my life.**

Quite definitely the most knowledgeable explorer in the region was a Californian, Doc Marston, who retired at an early age so he could use his vigorous years to wander that magnificent country. It was a real honor when he wrote to me inquiring how to climb the Octagon on Cummings Mesa, but I wasn't much help.

I introduced Ethel to Navajo County in the spring of 1955. She was captivated completely. We left Dallas and picked up Chuzo

---

* Alas, this talented self-made artist was killed in an auto crash February, 1996, with a seventy car caravan from a viewing at Tuba City to burial at his folk's orchard at Navajo Mountain.
** Fortunately that happened the summer of 1996 here in Santa Fe.

Tamotsu's Model A Ford in Santa Fe. We spent the night in the still-closed Los Alamos, to which my chemist cousin Jacob got us clearance. The next day we climbed into Valle Grande and then on progressively more primitive roads into Cuba. We limped into Chaco Canyon for the night after relying on the excellent Southern California Auto Club map of Indian Country. There was not a soul at Chaco Canyon. No rangers, no tourists, no Indians, no nothing other than a welcome water well spigot. The Model A used only molecules of gasoline, and nothing could go wrong mechanically. This proved a blessing when we got caught in a sandstorm crossing Chilchilbito Wash. I screamed for Ethel to jump out and push, and away we went. That night was a welcome one in the Goulding's hayloft in Monument Valley. There we met Goulding's son-in-law, Knee. Ten years later he used his sand buggy with DC-3 tires and twenty-seven gears to unstick us from a sand dune. After an hour and a half on the trail, I asked him, "how much", and he answered, "courtesy of the road," and drove away.

So, on to Lisbeth's at Navajo Mountain, where she arranged for Whitehat to lead us to Rainbow Bridge. We started out wearing prescription sunglasses. The unused trail was tough. Ten hours later we were in pitch black and trusting that the horses were surefooted in the up-and-down dry stream beds. When I first visited the Bridge in 1954, the register showed 2600 visitors (from the time of its discovery in 1909), but this time in 1957, visitors had numbered more than 8000. The next day we rode down Forbidden Canyon to the Colorado River. Whitehat needed no instructions to turn his eyes elsewhere when we went skinny-dipping in the chocolate-colored Colorado. Ethel was hooked.

Each year thereafter we visited the Rainbow Plateau with our children, and that included one Christmas when Lisbeth gave us the dining room hogan so we wouldn't have to camp in the cold. Our girls didn't protest and these early explorations of the wilderness had a lasting influence—each one of our daughters in her own way is addicted to the outdoors. Lisbeth wanted to spread our few dollars around, and in that way we got to know the calm, talented Isabel Onesalt, who worked at the school. When Isabel and Tony's first child fell off a wagon as a youngster, his head was run over by a wheel and he was left brain damaged. Barry Goldwater flew Isabel and her son into the hospital at Tuba City, but after a few days she borrowed a horse and rode the sixty miles back to Navajo Mountain with her son. When we met her, she had a charming eight-year-old daughter and this somnolent son. After leaving all our young daughters at Isabel's hogan one year, Tony and Ethel and I explored Cummings Mesa. Until last year I believed Ethel was the first Anglo woman on Cummings Mesa, but now I see where Gladwell Richardson makes that claim for his mother. This year we joined a Museum of Northern Arizona four-day backpack trip up Cummings Mesa, so I confidently claim Ethel is the oldest Anglo woman to hike up Cummings Mesa.

It was natural that by 1956 I was talking about leaving Dallas and reviving Rainbow Lodge and Ethel was offering no resistance. Lisbeth was excited and put us in touch with the Bill Wilsons, then retired and living on old-age assistance in Clarkdale, Arizona. Their story was a sad one. With great difficulty the Wilsons had completed beautiful Rainbow Lodge on the southwest flank of Navajo Mountain. The lodge featured an enormous picture window overlooking the plateau. They carried in all the topsoil for a flower and vegetable garden and piped down water from Indischee Spring on the 9,000-foot bench of the mountain. They built a corral for horses and started to build up a West Coast tourist following for three-day Bridge trips when along came World War II and gasoline rationing. To survive, they sold a half-interest to Barry Goldwater.

Although occupancy started to build in the late forties, a fire destroyed nearly everything, and, of course, there was no insurance.* So, after a quarter-century of struggles, the Wilsons went down to Clarkdale penniless but with dignity. We reached some sensible understandings to buy the Wilsons' half interest but never could pin Goldwater down. Negotiations continued and continued, and then we would be back to square one. I guess he just didn't want to sell—a decision which proved to be a mistake for him. He had been much revered by the plateau Navajos, and his autographed photo was in many hogans; however after he tried to be conciliatory in the Navajo-Hopi land dispute, they considered him a double-dealer. There was no way I could change Isabel's mind on this issue. The Navajos stripped the derelict lodge buildings of every two-by-four and one-by-six and the store that Myles Headrich tried to revive vanished like a ghost. It was lucky for me that Goldwater wouldn't trade because along came Lake Powell with luxury boat rides to the Bridge. Many current tourists object to walking the necessary 400 steps from the marina to the Bridge.

---

* Fires in Navajo Country can be the expression of some youth who feels he was mistreated by the white boss. This may have been the case at Rainbow Lodge. Quien sabe?

We had ten flat tires on the trip with the Model A, and every trading post helped us magnificently, but we had to limp into Gallup because the Christian Mission at Ganado wouldn't assist as it was Sunday! Late Monday afternoon we got to Santa Fe and left the car for service at Cecil Sherwood's on College Street. As we walked to La Fonda for our very first check-in, there was a loud chortle from under the grease rack. Every essential nut but one tying the body to the frame was gone, and the remaining one had two turns left on the bolt.

There was a black male schoolteacher at Inscription House and Lizbeth went out of her way to welcome him and overcome the prejudice of the Navajos, who felt the BIA was supplying second-rate stuff. Then when Lisbeth went off to Africa, her replacement was a black lady teacher who would have passed muster in most circumstances but could not fill the shoes of the saintly Lisbeth. Fortunately by then I was pretty much known in the territory and could survive without Lisbeth. Also the widow Madeline came around to feeding me and Ethel as friends and not paying guests. We started to pierce her protective exterior and we became warm friends until she sold the post to a hard-to-figure man from Utah and retired to Miami, Oklahoma. The best grub we ever tasted was July 4, 1976, when Ethel and I wandered out to Navajo Mountain. Everyone was gone to Flagstaff to celebrate the bicentennial parade except seven-year-old half-Navajo Shirley Folgeraitor. We needed gas and food, but the store was locked tight. Shirley said she would get the keys and turn on the pump. The youngster climbed around the shelves to sell us some basics. We told her we wanted to walk on Little Navajo Mountain. "When will you be back?" she asked. "Oh, in around three hours." Upon our return, we found this seven-year-old girl had baked us a cake "to celebrate July Fourth."

Lisbeth's prize student was Bert Tallsalt, and thirty-five years after our first meeting, we had become close buddies. He was a "code talker"* in the Pacific during World War II and wondered, after seeing the developed world, how he would adjust to returning home. "But when I passed Inscription House and saw the dome of Navajo Mountain I knew everything would be all right." He was the first veteran elected to the Tribal Council at Window Rock but much too honest and straightforward to make politics a career. Spirituality

---

* The Navajos conveyed critical dispatches in their native tongue, which code was never broken by the Japanese.

effused from him. When we both passed under Rainbow Bridge, he let me walk on so he could say his appropriate prayer. He was born in Nokai Canyon, the most isolated spot in the contiguous forty-eight states. He was called "boy" by his parents and was given the name Bert by a white teacher when he first went to school. One day, as a youngster herding sheep, he felt strange, that something was wrong. Twenty minutes later he saw the first Whites in his life, John Wetherill leading Charles Bernheimer's group on horses across Paiute Mesa to Oljeto. Bert ended up at Kayenta, where he leads a community center for senior citizens. I told him Aristotle said, "A gentleman does not ask for help unless he desperately is in need and then he does so quietly." Bert immediately commented, "The man who said that never needed help." Bert is a good photographer and a good student of the ethno-geology of the Rainbow Plateau. He saved me from a fruitless search for an overhang cliff ruin on the south flank of Paiute Mesa that Lisbeth in confidence revealed to me although she had not seen it. "Oh," said Bert, "around 1950 a group of ruffian Texan pothunters were spoiling some of the surface sites on the mesa and we told them about this fictitious cliff dwelling with original Anasazi artifacts. They four-wheeled it and spent the balance of their vacation in hopeless search." Bert claims an old Navajo at the mountain first told the Paiute Naja Begay how to get to Rainbow Bridge, but historic record says otherwise.

About 1983 Ethel and I found Whitehat much crippled by arthritis. He was lying on his back in his hogan with his wife and her sister attending to him. He was whittling on a piece of piñon, and I instinctively presented him with a handsome knife I had just purchased at Sears. His look of gratitude was worth a thousand times the cost. Then about 1987 Bert Tallsalt led me and Bob Walker, a great physicist and outdoorsman, to Whitehat's bed, where he lay terminally ill. He was blind, but I feel he knew me when I spoke to him. He grasped my fingers and sucked on them. Two months later he died, one of the bravest and simplest and proudest men anywhere.

Now there is electricity at Navajo Mountain and a great steel and glass school at Rainbow City, a marina at the San Juan River and a paved road snaking ten miles north from Inscription House. This "progress" is nothing compared to the time of the squaw dance near Keith Holiday's hogan or the time no one locked a door at the Rainbow Plateau or when Jim Madman returned after fifteen years in Los Angeles and explained to me, "I no crazy, just mad." Now there is no Old Lady Navajo Mountain, the name Lisbeth gave herself as her tenure at the school came to a close. And now there is extensive locoweed, and the leach field under the chapter house is undergoing critical review by the tribe's environmentalists. Water is critical at Navajo Mountain. After an Anglo lady assigned to Navajo Health Services failed in three exploratory water tests at a cost of close to $300,000, she transferred out of the agency in disgust.

Of course, it is dangerous to glamorize any group of people. There are saints and wastrels at Navajo Mountain. They are generous in adopting orphans, but selfish, petty bickering is not unknown. Unfortunately, alcohol increasingly takes its toll. Crime is not absent from outsiders who tried to break into the old Navajo Mountain Trading Post and did break into a Shiprock Post. A few teenagers at nearby Bryant's Post strangled a Navajo Policeman after a failed break-in but were caught. Ethel and I are trying to be of assistance in reactivating the Navajo Mountain Trading Post, and the chapter has given us use of a house with electricity, a propane range, and two wall heaters. There are as many govermental agencies in Window Rock as in Washington, and all sorts of certificates are necessary. But we haven't given up hope, even though a few bureaucrats haven't realized their role is to help people rather than flaunt authority through the enforcement of onerous regulations.

In late 1968 some friends from New York, Dr. Herbert Krugman, Manager of Public Opinion Research for General Electric, and Dr. Dorothy Krugman, specialist in IQ testing of infants, said they would visit the Southwest and wanted me to arrange something. I figured nothing would be better than a horse trip to Rainbow Bridge but my good intentions went asunder. I flew to Farmington and rented a Ford. I then drove to Navajo Mountain, which I had not visited for seven years. I ventured up a trail to the base of the mountain to experience its spirituality. When I got ready to leave, the battery was dead. Inspection showed it was bone dry.

Telling myself not to panic, I walked several miles and found Isabel Onesalt who was shearing her sheep. After thirty minutes she looked up, and said, "You rich now." After her son in his pickup jumped my car to life, Isabel and I sat down to talk about my forthcoming trip, for which we would need nine saddled horses and two pack animals.

I was surprised to learn that times had changed and horses were now rationed at the Rainbow Plateau. But Isabel said she could arrange for the animals from neighbors. So the Krugmans, the Ballens, the Aamodts from Los Alamos, Sig Forman and young Josh Schloss, and

Paula plus Lois and a girlfriend from St. Johns College, who were going to walk in, arrived at Navajo Mountain and met the Austin daughter from Shonto plus wranglers and animals who had come in from Betatakin, thirty-five miles away.

The Navajos had never been to Rainbow Bridge and had no enthusiasm for the trip. But I said I would guide them, and off we went. The disasters were many and varied, Paula's saddle was loose, and she fell off. Herb's legs were too long for his stirrups. The Navajos weren't carrying water and soon borrowed excessively from our canteens. Some dread gripped me when we came to the first and second springs, which were dry, but I didn't say anything to our riders. Soon the New York Ph.D.s started to bitch, "how much further." The *coup de grace* was when we got to Red Bud Pass and found that torrential rains had washed away the stone footings. The Navajos said we had to turn back. In a rage I started to beat the horses—lamely explaining to the Aamodts and Krugmans that the Navajos treated their animals quite brutally.

After thirty minutes of rolling substitute rocks into the defile, we finally made it through the pass and into Echo campground. Rainbow Bridge was just around a bend, and we would see it in the morning. Alarmingly, there was no evidence of Lois and her friend. Worried about them, I tossed and turned all night. But in the morning we saw she had signed the register with a note that a ranger in his Lake Powell outboard had taken them in for the night. Herb was too exhausted and too angry to walk the one-quarter mile to view the Bridge, and he never did. The trip back ran better, and the group was able to spell themselves while climbing Cliff Canyon.

Back at our originating campsite I asked the Navajo leader, Miss Austin, what we owed and keeled over on hearing the astronomical sum she mentioned. "But we never paid anything like that." "Oh, yes, you cheat us before." What a slap in the face! When I reported the insult to Lee Aamodt, he provided the appropriate retort: "But the question is, who is doing it to whom now?" In the end, I had to strip the wallets of each of us to make up the ransom. We then headed for home. Deeply troubled, I wrote Isabel Onesalt that if in years past there had been failure of communication, she should let me know as we surely didn't want to cheat her. No answer. After five months I wrote to her again, this time including a stamped, self-addressed envelope back to Santa Fe. Again, no answer. I repeated this four months later but still no reply. About 1989 Lisbeth Eubank showed up in Santa Fe with her friend, the Canyon Road artist Webb Young.

When I asked her for an explanation, she said, "Sam, that letter means a lot to you." "You bet." "Well, it doesn't to Isabel."

There are magnificent qualities of the folk in Navajo Mountain, but I can't say I am always totally on their wavelength of communication. The background culture is so different between the traditionalists and the moderns. But I am not alone. Al Packard's father, who created the great jewelry store across from La Fonda, said that after a lifetime of trading arts and crafts with Santo Domingo Indians, he did not confidently believe that he had fully registered what was in their minds.

14/ THE PURE AND THE HUMBLE

In the post war years two of the most powerful oil companies operating in Texas were Pure Oil and Humble Oil. Neither corporate entity is now in existence. There used to be a favorite yarn that when a Baptist preacher in Beaumont told his congregation, "God Bless the Pure and the Humble," one of the congregants shouted back, "What About Shell?" This little yarn is a reminder that I and my colleague, Jay Nuland, were too pure and too humble to capitalize when we had the very first practical idea of what is now known as a leveraged, unfriendly buyout.

Toward late 1955 I happened to do some brief investigation of Pure Oil and noticed that the value of its oil reserves was three times what the stock was selling for. In addition, there were its substantial refineries, service stations, and pipelines. How could a stock sell at such a discount from value? There is a school originated by a University of Chicago Professor, Jim Laurie, who now resides in Santa Fe, convinced that the stock market is perfect. According to this school, the mass of professional investors digest all the pertinent information about a stock, which, as a result of their decisions, then sells at the proper or efficient price. My own experience is just the reverse: the stock market, in fact, is a stylish business. Stocks sell for more or less than true value in the manner described by Graham-Dodd's textbook, which is the bible of security analysis.

At first I imagined that the steep concession in Pure's stock price was academic: it was generally understood that the Dawes family in Chicago, buttressed by the Rockfellers in New York, owned a sufficient amount of stock to do whatever they wanted with the company. A little further research through proxy statements indicated that the Chicago and New York principals, backed by their powerful Houston general counsel, Judge Elkins, actually owned less than five percent of the stock. Of course, it was possible that allied friendly shareholders were secreted in other trust company names. But I was encouraged to pursue the situation a bit further and once again struck apparent pay dirt. The company was incorporated in Ohio, which permitted a fifty percent vote for dissolution of the company. Further, they had a preferred stock issue outstanding, which had the right to vote dollar for dollar on issues of liquidation.

In those days, Wall Street private capital would not assume any extreme risk, even involving as little as $10 million. For any locked-in investment, there had to be a definable plan for gaining liquidity. This was best exemplified when Eddie Hilson mentioned that "both in sex and in business, the most discouraging situation is a partial insertion." But the existence of this preferred stock issue meant that the risk could be minimized by buying up the preferred stock, accumulating some common stock, and then making a tender offer and being able to easily liquidate Pure and sell its reserves to other companies. One could visualize an immediate profit of about $500 million, which in those days was quite a pile of change. And even though we had never heard of "golden parachutes," I promptly thought of the possibility of carving out $25 or $50 million as a retirement bonus for the senior officers of Pure in order to earn their quietude in such a reorganization.

I reflected quietly on this but was at a loss on how to proceed. My youth alone would cause the New York Wertheim parties to question such a novel recommendation. It happened that I was called down to Houston for a meeting with Dow Chemical and decided to stay at the Shamrock Hotel out on South Main. The Shamrock Hotel was a legend throughout the oil patch. It had been conceived and constructed by Glen McCarthy, a dynamic local wildcatter who had become fabulously rich from several discoveries in salt domes on the Gulf Coast. He was really not a nice person. Several times at New York bars he had physically beaten up selected patrons. He even lacked the courtesy to conceal his extensive romantic interests from his loyal wife. The daughter of an established Houston family, she had eloped with this roughneck without her parents' consent. But Glen McCarthy was ingenious. He had built the Shamrock Hotel as a tribute to his Irish background and insisted that every color in the hotel be a shade of green; thus almost 1,000 shades of green were displayed.

The grand opening of the hotel turned into an intemperate brawl. One hundred starlets from Hollywood were flown in, and each received lavish and personalized gifts. During the opening banquet, which was broadcast on the local radio station, several of the microphones were inadvertently turned on. Over the airwaves went some of the dueling between notables and these starlets. But this was not an unusual tactic of McCarthy. Several years later, when he got into trouble with a petrochemical plant, he needed to get financing from the Equitable Insurance Company. It was rather reliably rumored that the Equitable's loan officer who was sent down to investigate spent three days but never left the hotel to visit the plant because of more enticing opportunities right at hand. Yet McCarthy had his own charm, which was widely appreciated, even during the days when he subsequently went bankrupt and never made a significant comeback. The Monday morning after the opening, a reporter bumped into the local commercial banker, Jesse Jones, and asked, "Were you at the opening?" "No, but I'll be there at the closing." When the Hilton purchased the property from the Equitable, it took only one day for Glen McCarthy's portrait at the main elevator landing to come down and for Conrad Hilton's to go up.

In late afternoon, after I had finished my business, I returned to the Shamrock for a quiet drink. However, my plans changed when I bumped into Jay Nuland, who was working for Carl M. Loeb Rhoades out of New York. Together, we accosted one of the newest oil analysts for Lehman Brothers, a man who was part of a fancy Northshore Long Island social set. The latter chap invited us to be his guests for dinner in the Shamrock's principal restaurant, and we readily accepted. I had high regard for Jay Nuland, who was about my age, had graduated from the Harvard School of Business, and was the son of a longtime officer in the Pacific for Cal-Tex. This was a joint marketing entity of Standard of California and the Texas Company. Jay was a fine oil analyst with good fundamentals; he also had a touch of imagination and *joie de vivre*. His wife, Ky, moved in an impressive circle of Catholic bigshots.

When Jay and I appeared for dinner, we found our host had invited three lovely and not-too-distant young Houstonions, which made the dinner party a pleasant event with the best wines and topped off the evening with good champagne. I know I could never have swindled my expense account to cover such a bill, but fortunately our host stood by his earlier invitation that we were his guests. The next morning, when Jay and I met for breakfast, we were a bit freer than usual with each other because of the frivolity of the previous evening. Jay asked me what I was doing. "Jay, I've uncovered a highly undervalued integrated oil company that is a sitting duck for a take-over." He replied that he had just uncovered the same thing. I said that my company was north of the Ohio River; he said that his company was headquartered west of the Hudson River (Pure's corporate headquarters were in Chicago). I said that despite popular impression it appeared that the insiders owned very little stock. He said that the risk could be minimized by purchasing securities senior to the common. We looked at each other long and hard. I then said, "Jay, it looks like you and I are riding the same horse and if so, it's better that we join forces than be competitors." He agreed and suggested that we each write the name of our target on a folded slip of paper and that we would honor each other if by chance our candidates were different. And so I wrote "Pure" on a piece of paper, folded it, and handed it to him. When I opened his piece of paper, it also said "Pure."

This was the beginning of our problems. We both knew that, in accordance with the psychology of the times, the principals of our firms would likely not take us seriously because we were only in our early thirties. We agreed that he would speak to the seniors at Carl M. Loeb Rhoades and I would talk to the seniors at Wertheim & Co. Each of them said the same thing: "We do not want to get involved with an unfriendly deal. However, if you can find an oil person of unquestioned reputation to head up such a program, then we would back him as silent participants."

Jay and I divided up our assignments. I would undertake to get an outstanding Texas oilman enthused about the project, and Jay would try to get an outstanding Wall Street law firm to research the various Bylaws and Articles of Incorporation and domicility regulations, preferably on a contingent-fee basis. Jay was successful with Wendell Wilke's law firm. This was a notable achievement because, in those days, such top-line Wall Street firms did not accept contingent-fee cases. The Wilke firm assigned a brilliant, introverted corporate tax attorney who, after several months of investigation, reported that our early impressions were correct. All the balls would fall into the required slots. Essential to the reorganization and a key factor that supported our appraisal scheme was what was then called the A-B-C method of oil financing. This technique eliminated corporate income tax on conveyance of oil reserves to third parties.

Many bankers, including Rushton Ardrey of the Republic in Dallas, Hugo Anderson (father of R. O. Anderson in Roswell) at the First National in Chicago, and Eugene McElvaney with the First National in Dallas, claimed they originated this simple method. If an oil lease has a market value of $100 and is owned by A, he could sell it to B for ten dollars less a reserved oil payment of ninety dollars payable out of eighty-five percent of the gross oil income plus eight percent interest. At the same time that A sells the lease for ten dollars, he sells the oil payment for ninety dollars to an intermediary C, who borrows ninety dollars at seven and a half percent interest and earns one-half percent for acting as a conduit. The ninety dollars becomes free of tax since C can amortize a dollar of revenue for each dollar of cost. This was a sweetheart arrangement for everyone except the IRS, which decades later changed the law to close this loophole. Many individuals specialized in acting as C; they included the brother of Fred Florence, the president of the Republic National Bank, whose Indian Oil Company did lots of business with the Republic, to its great profit. It turned out that this very prestigious Wall Street attorney did not understand A-B-C financing. I had to explain it to him, and he finally caught on. This is a good illustration of how young people can grasp novel ideas way ahead of their seniors. I sadly recognized thirty-five years later that I was playing the role of the dull senior and not able to follow my juniors when they spoke of chaos theory or parallel computing.

My end of the assignment did not develop as successfully as Jay's. I approached Jake Hamon, an attractive, independent oilman in Dallas who had previously been president of the American Petroleum Institute when that slot was generally reserved for major company brass. Jake Hamon was not the run-of-the-mill oilman. He was an immensely wealthy independent producer who had literary interests. He was married to a vivacious lady from south Texas, now a leading supporter of the arts in Dallas. He walked in several different camps in Texas and was welcomed in each of them. I explained the Pure situation to him. He caught on immediately and needed no explanation about the ramifications of A-B-C financing. He thought for quite a while and then said, "Your ideas are sound and the profit criteria are reasonable, but I just can't get involved in this. I have played too many rounds of golf with the Pure executives. They will not willingly agree to forfeiture of their empire, and I just don't want to get involved in any adversary arrangement. But have no fear, Sam. I will protect your confidence absolutely, and no one outside this room will ever hear of this." I believed him.

It was then necessary for me to go to New York and discuss the next step with Jay Nuland. In those days that meant taking an American Airlines DC-6 out of Love Field—and who should sit next to me but Tex Feldman. I asked, "How come you're flying like the rest of us, Tex, and not on your own plane?" He replied, "My ship is in for repairs. My limousine will be waiting at La Guardia to take me down to my suite at the Sherry Netherlands. Can I give you a lift and what are you up to?" Without mentioning the name of the company, I explained to him in generalities the situation I had found. I was feeling a bit dejected, since we really had not yet received any support from our respective employers. Tex asked what we wanted, if he was to grab hold of the deal and run with it. I said five percent of the profit but I would first have to check with my associate. Tex's limousine took me down to my hotel, the Wertheim-owned Madison. He and I arranged that I would check with him if we wanted to pursue our discussions. Jay and I were obviously not too experienced in this, but we got the Wilke attorney to draw up a four-sentence letter protecting us for five percent of the profit and that would of course accrue to Loeb Rhoades and Wertheim because we were still employees. So the next evening Nuland and I went up to Tex's suite in the Sherry Netherlands and told him he would first have to execute that letter before we divulged the name of the company. Tex said that he didn't like to sign what lawyers drew up. He walked over to his desk, took out a blank sheet of paper, studied our letter, and slowly commenced writing. He ended up writing precisely the text our attorney had prepared, word for word, and then signed it.

He marveled when we revealed it was Pure Oil and explained all the ramifications. He quickly stated that we would need a meeting in Dallas the next week at his luxurious offices in the Republic Bank, together with his attorney, the respected and pompous Paul Jackson, who used to be general counsel for the IRS in Washington. The Wilke attorney came down for a luncheon meeting in Tex's private dining room. Jackson just would not listen to me because the profit was so large and kept throwing cold water on the concept. Finally, Tex Feldman said he was intrigued, but he would only go into the deal with the consent of Judge Elkins. I gasped, "How can you reveal this to Judge Elkins, he is general counsel for Pure and he will blow the lid for sure." Feldman responded, "Don't you worry about me and the Judge; I know how to handle him." Gosh, what leverage did Tex secretly have with the Judge? And so in our naivete we consented to his approaching Judge Elkins and trying to arrange a friendly deal. Two weeks later, Nuland called from New York and said Feldman had gone in to see Judge Elkins that morning. I never did inquire how he knew and still don't know. But three weeks later Pure announced an emergency meeting of shareholders to call in its preferred stock. That action effectively removed the safety element of our proposition.

Well, of course, Feldman had double-crossed us. Pure, in some manner or another, must have made it worth his while. Several years later, Loeb Rhoades acted as financial advisor in the sale of Pure Oil to one of the West Coast integrated companies, but sufficient time had gone by that neither Jay nor I felt there was anything improper, nor did we claim any participation in their fee. We were just too pure and too humble to have ever successfully consummated our creative concept.

15/ ELSI, THE CASH COW

DURING WORLD WAR I, the Alsatian engineer Marcel Schlumberger, was conducting electrical experiments in the Pechelbronn oil fields to assist the pinpointing of German artillery. He noticed that when an electrical emitter was lowered down a borehole, the readings of electrical resistivity would vary, depending on the stratigraphy of the rocks. The resistance would be affected if the pore spaces between the grains contained water or oil, and the anomaly in measured resistance would indicate whether the formation was sandstone or shale or limestone. From this applied research the Schlumberger family developed a new discipline called oil well logging, and the billion-dollar firm of Schlumberger Ltd. became a fixture on the New York Stock Exchange.

Marcel's son Pierre brought the firm to prominence by developing a whole series of intricate down-hole logging tools. Although a Protestant, he married an assimilated wealthy Alsatian Jew, Claire, and then moved his family to Houston to be at the heart of the overseas oil industry. Because their culinary tastes went beyond Texas barbecue and Gulf Coast catfish and "aase tee," Pierre and Claire sponsored a Parisian restaurateur, Emil Berman, to open Maxim's in downtown Houston across from the Bank of Southwest Building. Shortly thereafter, Maxim's distinguished itself as the finest eatery in Houston. Unlike the curvy, eye-shadowed waitresses of most other establishments, his staff were typically 40-year-old ladies who knew they could not get a better spot, thus the service at Maxim's was the most attentive. Still, when poor Berman arranged a date for a visiting oil geologist, the vice squad filed pandering charges against him.

Pierre became a leading supporter of the arts in Houston and was well encrusted in Houston's social life. However, he experienced a personal tragedy when depression drove his wife to suicide at the tender age of forty-five.

The end product of Schlumberger's process was a strip chart, similar to a cardiogram printout with several curves correlated to the depth of the subsurface formations. There were radioactivity logs, sonic logs, gamma ray-neutron logs, self-potential logs, and so forth.

Professional well-log analysts joined the geologists and reservoir engineers in the community of specialists guiding oil exploration activities. Naturally, these logs were eagerly sought after by companies owning adjacent leases or, in the case of virgin basins, by operators contemplating wildcat entry. In early times those logs were treasured by the operators or, in the case of "tight" holes (those kept secret), were guarded as the most confidential of records. Eventually, operators on federal or state lands were required, after varying periods of time, to release their logs for public inspection.

The brother-in-law of Antoine Peissell, one of Schlumberger's senior executives from Lyon, was an honest self-effacing east Texan, R.I. Seale, who ran the first log in the Rockies and the first log in Alberta. To accommodate those who wanted extra copies of released logs, and wanted them in reduced scale to fit into file cabinets, Bob Seale arranged for a blueprint shop to reproduce them on half-scale and they would then be manually folded to eight inch lengths. When the demand overwhelmed him, he turned to a fishing buddy in Dallas, Lee Pierce, to help him carry forward with the concept. Bob Seale did not want to sever his employment with Schlumberger to pursue this activity full time. Eventually, though, he had to decide between being a logging engineer or an affluent small businessman. Lee Pierce had a hard time meeting the demand even after his wife pitched in and they turned their bedroom into a folding arena day and night. Lee Pierce, a New York orphan, was upright, had no airs and was an excellent, penny-pinching, hands-on, small businessman. He was not like the self-made man who worshiped his creator. Before long, this service started to assume even larger dimensions. The Pierce-Seale partnership was covering north Texas and the Panhandle out of Dallas, but the big province was the Permian Basin with Midland as the white-collar center. Lee Pierce sold an interest to Max David, a geologist with Phillips. David opened an office in Midland and it became the largest district office. The business was coining money.

The partners (Pierce, David, and Seale) could not believe that their prosperity would last. Pierce and David had negotiated a sale to the people who had initiated this service in Calgary, where most minerals were owned by the provinces and practically all logs were deposited in public files. When Seale did not want to go along with the sale, Pierce approached me for a solution to their conflict. At the same time, Seale approached First Southwest for financial support. Pierce was dedicated to honorable conduct, but now he found that although he had shaken hands with Arvil Minor, the president of

Rileys in Calgary, he was having to accommodate Bob Seale and sell to Ballen and First Southwest. Arvil Minor's associates, Jim Fouts and Jimmie Neale, were furious and asked for a meeting before suing us. Minimum research identified Neale as a pipeline contractor whose principal client was Tennessee Gas Transmission. Bill Smallwood of First Southwest was a good friend of Gardner Symonds, president of Tennessee Gas Transmission. We posted an autographed photo of Gardner Symonds in a prominent location of our meeting room, and Neale calmed down instantly. The chemistry between me and Fouts worked well that day in 1956, and from then until now he and I have been business partners. Our families have supported each other in the periodic crises surrounding our children and our bank accounts.

The gilding of the lily on our purchase from Pierce *et al.* was securing an IRS Determination Letter, which cannot be obtained today. The IRS permitted us to assign practically all of the capitalized purchase cost to films of half-scaled logs at nine dollars per unit to be amortized twenty-five percent per annum of the declining balance. Then we were permitted to expense immediately the cost of making new films. We set up a thin corporation with most of the capital in debt securities we owned ourselves and the same with a class of preferred stock. Few dollars were allocated to the common stock. Decker Jackson, the absolute head of First Southwest, became distressed at the amount of time Smallwood was spending with the log service, so I corralled a group of investors to buy out First Southwest, and Smallwood resigned as president. I then made a fortuitous selection of a senior clerk as president. With no college under his belt and no pretense of grandeur, Arch Pennington showed exceptional common-sense leadership. After seeing him handle many a tense crisis or business relocation, I made the statement publicly that Arch Pennington could run Ford Motor. I feel he could have done better than all those "big three" chiefs who lost touch with reality before sharp market-share loss forced them to their senses.

We named our concern Electrical Log Services, Inc. One of our directors prepared a logo consisting of a Bohr-type image of the hydrogen atom. Our registered acronym was ELSI. We convinced most oil companies to release their logs to us as a matter of course against our delivery of three reduced copies at no charge. Then we convinced most operators to instruct Schlumberger and Lane Wells and Welex to automatically deliver a copy of their log to us simultaneous with delivery to the client operator. In order to avoid any possible question of improper use of confidential data, I ceased all activities in oil exploration.

ELSI's integrity was accepted throughout the oil patch, and we soon became dominant in our geographic areas. We secured some mortgage financing from Prudential and retired our own debt. The commercial bankers were surprised that we were able to obtain ten-year financing on such obscure assets. By then, most blueprint shops were offering competing products in the local oil towns. We knew that if we bought them out, we would really be buying customer lists although we ostensibly assigned the purchase price to their film libraries, which were duplicates of our own. In hindsight this was a possible violation of the Sherman Anti-Trust Act, but our attorneys in those more accommodating days advised that the risk of the U.S. Justice Department slapping our wrists was minimal. So we purchased the log services in Tyler, Wichita Falls, Abilene, Amarillo, Durango, Denver, Salt Lake City, Billings, Casper, and Austin. With over a million films in our vault, we now had a "monopoly." We set the price of new logs low to discourage competition and added a fifty cent premium to logs more than thirty days old when they came out of our vault. Things were going very beautifully indeed. We were selling 4,000 copies of logs per day with a profit margin of more than forty percent. After trying all forms of shipment from Dallas to our regional offices, we found the most reliable transport was by Greyhound bus. This mode enabled us to have personal interface with the bus driver and ensure on-time delivery.

Our manager in Abilene was Ted Strickland, a clean-cut young man with no children but with a pert wife whose hobby was collecting glass figurines. When we moved him to Denver and agreed to pay moving expenses, I learned about those glass figurines from the bills of the freight-packing firm. One day Strickland asked me whether he could run for the Colorado state legislature. Not giving it a second thought, I answered affirmatively and mentioned some folderol about each citizen's responsibilities in a democracy. He won that election, showed a real talent for politics, and became majority Republican leader of the state's senate. However, when he ran for governor, he was buried in a post-Watergate deluge. He is now a powerful, accomplished statesman for the oil industry.

District offices of oil companies open and close as the wave of exploration changes. Now, with improved telecommunication instruments that even permit transmission of electric log stripes over radio waves, district offices have been centralized. We had an office in Durango, but the Four Corners Pictured Cliffs and Mesa Verde natural gas play had run out of steam and most district offices were pulled back to Denver. Finally, I could delay the inevitable no longer and flew to Durango to close the office. When I arrived, the door was closed and Ken Henson was nowhere to be seen. In some confusion I walked down to the Strater Hotel and found Ken behind the bar. I said, "I'll have a beer, and please come over to my table when you have a moment." "Oh, golly, Mr. Ballen, the business just died and I would have gone out of my mind waiting in the office." "Yeah, I can understand that but you should have mentioned it to someone." I asked Ken if he wanted severance settlement or preferred that we move him back home to Sweetwater where he would find a place in the Midland office. He selected the latter.

Two years later Ken and Roy Cunningham left to open a competing shop in Midland. When our executives met, I said, "I'm no Churchill, but what comes to mind is his challenge after the loss of the Hood: 'Sink the Bismark.'" We sent Frank Morris out from Dallas to Midland to supervise our counterattack. He leased a room at the Scharbauer Hotel. One day he called and said, "You know my room looks down the alley behind Henson's shop. They put out their trash every day at 6 p.m. It wouldn't take much for me to go through the cans before the sanitation truck shows up." Ethical standards change, but back in 1962 it didn't take much to give Frank Morris the green light. Soon we knew their pricing strategy and who their customers were, and it didn't take long for them to fold. Their meat-marketer money-backer in Odessa committed suicide.

Civilians found it hard to believe that oil operators concluded that everyone would be more efficient in finding oil by releasing these logs. If an adjacent lease owner really wanted a log, it could be secured tediously by financing a dinner or fishing trip or by providing a passionate redhead. But it was not unusual for the chief of geophysics of, say, Sun Oil to call me with something like, "Ah...do you guys ever have...uh...logs released...oh, that show the...er...velocity of formation in (long pause) Upton County?" "Oh yes, last week's release sheet included Sun's sonic log #1 Wasson." The gasp of surprise that followed sounded like the immediate response of the most liberal journalist of the Texas Observer who couldn't believe oil men could be above board.

In addition to a weekly list of releases for each territory we covered, we also published every eighteen months a catalogue of older logs with their assigned numbers. Our principal telephone order taker, Corrine Brandenburg, was as phenomenal as an idiot savant in handling our catalogues. She sat outside my office after the production plant moved from Dallas to Midland, and I would catch the following conversation: "No, Bob Foree, you don't want N3721984, you want, I'm sure, N4721984." We found it more efficient in those days to manually produce these catalogues using flex-o-print cards, which were then alphabetized by hand. One year Hughes Electronics signed a contract to do the West Texas catalogue by computer for $45,000 with eight months delivery. We got the catalogues in fourteen months and were led to believe that it cost them over $180,000! But we were also using handicapped persons to custom-fold to eight or twelve or sixteen inches. We resisted offers from Pitney-Bowes to design an automatic selection folding machine because it would abolish the jobs of these handicapped people. But an engineer in Garland with Varo Industries, the nighttime vision people, insisted on an advance with delivery of a machine promised in six months. Rather out of curiosity we succumbed, but he never was able to develop such a machine.

In the mid-sixties there was discussion of digitizing these analog curves and running analytical equations by computer from top to bottom. Bob Broding of Century Geophysical in Tulsa, an electrical engineering professor from Texas Christian University, and I joined to write the very first paper ever on "Computer Analysis of Well Logs." The *Oil and Gas Journal* published it with a front-cover lead. I concluded that the technology was not then equal to the task, because the curves crossed each other, but a firm named III from California developed an automatic curve follower. One was sold to Mobil for $1,000,000, but before long it went into storage in the basement. A bright professor at the University of Illinois at Urbana, Vladimir Tuman, did some interesting experimentation with computers and down-hole logs, but I don't think he achieved any practical success. Tuman was a Christian from Iran and a designated executive in the post-Mossadegh Consortium. But he wasn't trusted by the Western companies because he was an Iranian, and he wasn't trusted by the Moslems because he was a Christian. So he ended up being sojourned for three months at a crack at all the US companies' laboratories. He emerged as the best-trained petroleum professional in the United States. One day my friend Natasha Voshinin told me she had translated my *Oil and Gas Journal* article from Russian into English: it had been translated from English into Russian in one of the Russian journals. She told me that the reviewer had criticized our article for concentrating on individual wells rather than on basins. "Natalie, I would like to see your translation." "Oh, this is a confidential project for Mobil and I can't show it to you."

Our principal competitor was Jack Riley, who had initiated many libraries of logs but was forced to sell them one by one to pour funds into a plant to convert Navion airplanes and add ten miles per hour to the manufacturer's specifications. The last log office he retained was in Oklahoma City, and we tried unsuccessfully many times to buy it. One day he appeared at my office in the Southland Center and said he would sell for $600,000 cash. Arch Pennington and I stepped outside and I said: "Arch, let's buy it; we can merge with Amarillo and it will be a thirty month payout for us." Arch said, "Oh, Sam, you don't know Riley like I do. If he is asking $600,000 he will take $250,000, so let's offer $275,000." " But Arch, what difference about his economics, it's a thirty-month payout for us. Let's not pass up this opportunity." But Pennington, whose judgment I always respected, insisted that Riley would come down so we went back into my office and offered him $350,000 cash. He said, "Thank you" and walked out. Two years later when I was in Ft. Lauderdale, I went up to Riley's aviation plant where we spent three hours negotiating. He finally said he would think about it. I learned later that two weeks after our first visit, he had sold Oklahoma City to Rizely Trucking in Denver.

Things were going so beautifully that I felt my family could move to Santa Fe. I would supervise the business by telephone and mail, and Trans Texas Air had a daily non-stop jet from Santa Fe to Dallas. Way back in the sixties we had secured a predecessor of the fax machine, then made by Magnavox and later sold to Xerox. The process worked fairly well unless it rained; then there would be interfering influences on the lines. Eighteen months after moving to Santa Fe I committed the worst blunder of my business career, an almost unbelievable piece of stupidity. I surely was affected by the cultural adjustment. It started with a call from Bob McCord, a cerebral reservoir engineer graduate of Rice who had worked with Creole in Venezuela. We became mutual-admiration friends, and he purchased some stock early on in ELSI. He was married to an equally smart ultra-conservative wife, Glenna, and it was always a heady intellectual experience to be with them. Bob had sold McCord and Associates to University Computing Company for their stock and had gone on UCC's Board of Directors.

The guiding light of UCC was Sam Wyly, a former powerful salesman for Honeywell in Dallas, who was then talked of in the same breath as Ross Perot. McCord told me UCC was anxious to expand into energy lines that could be exploited by computer savvy and if I would consider selling to them, the man to contact was John Larcade. UCC stock on the New York Exchange had settled from a frothy 160 to 75, so it seemed worth pursuing. I had no real confidence in UCC stock, in part because I did not understand computers and could not incisively analyze UCC's reports, its prospectus, or its listing statements on the New York Stock Exchange. So a trade was negotiated whereby certain UCC shares were received at closing and then incremental UCC shares would be received in each of three years *at the price they sold in each such anniversary* if our earnings met certain targets in each future year. The tax laws of such "pooling of interest" permitted us to sell fifteen percent of the shares we received at closing at capital gains rates. The Dallas attorney we used was (and still is) a good friend of mine and a skilled practitioner. I was surprised that he did not change one syllable in the draft contract prepared by UCC's attorneys. Forty days after our closing, for reasons having nothing to do with ELSI business, he was carted off to a mental institution suffering from a complete nervous breakdown. He did not exit for four months.

There was an unrelated but foreboding incident the afternoon of closing when we bumped into R. H. in the elevator foyer and he revealed he had just been hired as UCC's officer in charge of finance. I had admired H. for more than a decade, ever since Jim Cleaver and I had organized the Dallas Association of Investment Analysts and H. was part of the founder group. But over the years I noticed a cloud of disaster followed him. When he became Financial Vice President of Stekholl Petroleum, I aired my concern to Ethel. It took only nine months for Stekholl to go belly up. After seeing H. outside the elevators, I turned to Arch Pennington and poured out my fears. "Arch, my stomach just fell down that elevator shaft."

While Ethel and I were in Italy later in 1970, we finally managed to get a copy of the *International Herald Tribune* and UCC was listed— not at sixty, but at six. While we were enjoying an aperitif at a sidewalk cafe in Rome, Ethel asked me what UCC was selling for and I answered, "There's a typographical error in the paper." But the same error appeared in the next day's paper—UCC was at five and a half! My concern surely showed because a waitress commented to another, "facia bruta," or ugly face. By the time we got home, the stock was down to two dollars and then went even lower. At first, I thought we were protected by the insurance of supplemental payments of UCC stock valued at the anniversary prices. Then the roof fell in: an IRS regulation limited the number of future increments of stock not to exceed the number of initial shares. That was included in a sentence in our closing contract on which I had not focused. Not only had our fortune evaporated, but the stock we had given to valuable ELSI employees had shrunk embarrassingly.

The loyal group of investors who had demonstrated their confidence in me now had to divide their portfolio value by an order of magnitude. I could not sleep at night. I tossed and turned in wondrous anger at how I had fallen into such a trap when everyone praised me as the soberest of shrewd investors. I immediately informed my bankers of this difficulty. Bill Vernon, president of the Santa Fe National Bank, inquired if his bank was in trouble. "No, Bill, you are not in trouble, I am. If it ever gets to the point where you are in jeopardy, you will hear first from me, but that is not your condition now." I was tied in emotional knots until one night it dawned on me that Einstein had experienced a class A blunder with his cosmological constant, Fermi had overlooked the obvious when he did not realize he had split the uranium atom, Oppenheimer had let his talents come out second best in jousting with Roger Robb, and Alexander Alexandrovich Friedmann had missed a Nobel when he failed to extend his equations to an expanding universe. If these millennium-class brains had suffered from really significant errors, then I had to accept that I was human and not superman and could only learn from the experience. I had my health and the love of my wife, and only two of my shareholders took me to task. I never again had anything to do with them. Jim Fouts stood by me in that low moment and so did Audrey Seale. I am eternally grateful to them both.

But the pressure on me was not over and not just because UCC fired me when I tried to negotiate a settlement with them. During a civil trial we at last learned what UCC's scam was all about. It was just pure white-collar crime. UCC's management, Arthur Young's accountants, and the lawyers Wynne Jaffe and Tinsley had been swept up in Wyly's enthusiasm. Their prospectus included a footnote to the effect that three transactions had above-normal profit margins. When they finally were compelled by Judge Bob Hill to produce applicable documents, we immediately discovered the fraud. UCC would organize a subsidiary and sell software to it for a promissory note. The subsidiary would sell equivalent computer time to another sub against a promissory note. Then the second sub would sell equivalent computer time to a quasi-sub against a non- recourse promissory note.

UCC could decide in September how much profit they had to create to meet year-end targets and then issue the marching orders. All the subsidiaries ultimately went bankrupt, and the promissory notes were not serviced. Revenues that should have been eliminated in a consolidated statement as a sale and leaseback were shown as profits by Arthur Young even though their field-audit notes raised the obvious red flag.

UCC offered $400,000 in settlement, this was a fraction of what we were reasonably entitled to. I needed the money but knew our stockholders should probably reject it and just let a jury decide. But besides my needing the money for La Fonda, I felt that UCC would certainly go down the tube and a large judgment might never be collectable. Thus the directors accepted the settlement. I was the only witness for our side because we could not afford to hire expert witnesses. Later, Judge Bob Hill said I was the most brilliant witness to appear in his court. That compliment did not assuage my grief. I knew that the hubris of my self-confidence had led to this disaster by not having a strong outsider review the transaction from the beginning. Judge Hill then became a member of the New Orleans Federal Appeals Court. When he and his wife were returning from a vacation in Kenya and changed at Paris to a non-stop flight to Dallas, he complained in mid-Atlantic of his asthma, and his wife went forward for an oxygen bottle. By the time she got back to their row, Judge Hill was dead.

ELSI stayed with UCC until the parent company became pressed for cash. ELSI was sold to A. C. Neilson just in time to coin heaps of money during the oil boom of the seventies. But as the price of oil slipped from forty dollars per barrel to eighteen dollars and the number of domestic drilling rigs from 4,000 to 650, ELSI itself ran into hard times. It became a division of Petroleum Information, only a fraction of its former grandeur.

While I was still CEO of ELSI and shortly after we moved to Santa Fe, ELSI purchased the historic, centrally located La Fonda hotel in Santa Fe using a wholly owned subsidiary, Corporacion de La Fonda, Inc. When the sale to UCC was negotiated, UCC declined to include La Fonda among its acquired assets. When ELSI was liquidated after the sale to UCC was completed, the stock of Corporacion was distributed to the shareholders of ELSI as a non-taxable distribution. We planned to use our installment payments to come from UCC to remodel this world-famous hotel at the end of the Santa Fe Trail. Little did we anticipate what fate had in store for us.

16/ CANADIAN ON THE CANADIAN

EVEN MOST TEXANS ARE SURPRISED to learn there is a lovely city in the northeast corner of the Texas Panhandle named Canadian—the "River City on the Rise" as the Chamber of Commerce boasts. It borders the Canadian River, which originates just north of New Mexico near the Vermejo Ranch. Some of the friendliest folks in all the Southwest live there but many of their customs are hard to relate to in 1995.

- Around noon people go to "dinner" and then at night sit down to "supper."
- Until only a few years ago, if you wanted to go to the movies, you had to drive 45 miles west to Pampa.
- The area is spotted with large cattle ranches, and to own one you either are born into or marry into the acreage—you cannot buy one of the spreads.
- The largest building in town is the Women's Christian Temperance Union Hall.
- Canadian is only 25 miles from the eastern border with Oklahoma, yet it is called West Texas.
- The main freight line of the Santa Fe Railroad goes right through Canadian with thirty stretched trains a day, none of which stops in Canadian.
- The city council official meeting commences each session with a prayer "in Jesus' name," and no one suspects that there's a more appropriate way to conduct public business.
- There are many good churches and auxiliaries in town around which life rotates; there is no other way to socialize other than as part of your church's evening programs.
- The leading citizen in town was the wealthy, charitable Maloof Abraham, respectfully called by everyone "Ooffie." He had Lebanese roots but became a committed Presbyterian. A more down-to-earth contributor to the area cannot be imagined.

Unlike the typical flat Panhandle landscape, Canadian is bordered by breaks and mesas, beautiful in their own way but quite dissimilar from those in New Mexico. The countryside exudes *POWER* from

145

the well-maintained fence lines and the healthy cattle and the Christmas trees atop the 9,000 feet deep oil and gas wells. Fine but unostentatious ranch homes dot the landscape. The hand wave greeting as one pickup passes another and the courtesy as one vehicle swings wide in passing so as not to press his neighbor into a bar ditch are typical. The following gag could have originated in Canadian: "How do you get a one-armed Aggie out of a tree?…You wave to him."

I was touched by Canadian for thirty years, and this chapter was started three hours after the funeral service for Virginia Whipple at the First Methodist Church when 300 mourners of a population of 3600 packed the sanctuary and in unison sang "The Old Rugged Cross." The great unprepossessing mayor of Dallas, R.L. Thornton, used to say in the fifties, "Dallas is a good place to live in and a good place to die in." Canadian is certainly a good place to die in—unlike Santa Fe, where so many Anglo drifters pass to the great beyond almost unnoticed. In the seventies the husband of a decent lady who worked at La Fonda's front desk was a stable employee at the *Santa Fe New Mexican*. His hobby each annual vacation was to retrace the Continental Divide on horse and foot from the Canadian border south. In a fit of depression he parked on the shoulder of US 66 just east of Gallup on the Continental Divide and shot himself. Other than his wife and a brother from the Midwest, Ethel and I were the only witnesses to his funeral service and that scenario can, sadly, be repeated for some Anglo newcomers.

Virginia Whipple was in charge of bookkeeping for High Plains Natural Gas for almost twenty years, and a more loyal employee could not be found. Unfortunately, she could not become computer literate—neither could I—and her position became untenable when Carol Story was hired after she returned home to the Panhandle from Houston. There are many stories to tell of Carol's expertise as an accountant with computers. After overlooking the obvious for several years, I finally convinced Virginia to retire with some financial incentives, and this evolved pleasantly since she was not consumed with resentment.

Canadian is the county seat of Hemphill County and adjacent to Ochiltree County, where Virginia was born. Ochiltree was listed by *US News and World Report* as the No. 1 county in the nation in per capita wealth some years ago when wheat and oil were priced respectably. The irony is that during dust-bowl days Ochiltree County was a disaster area with many "grapes of wrath" refugees to California, but this was before the Ogallala aquifer was drilled for irrigation.

Although Virginia was no intellectual giant, she had a quiet dignity that had to be respected. In 1972 we were involved in a vituperative rate case before the Railroad Commission in Austin and Virginia was our expert on our books of account. Able, acerbic attorney Bob Lemon for the City of Perryton tried and tried again to get Virginia to answer his questions as he wished—but all to no avail. Completely exasperated, Lemon rephrased his chief question, and simple Virginia cried out, "Oh, Bob, is that what you mean?" But she again turned his question to our advantage. Of course, Virginia knew nothing but the truth and could not conceive of double-crossing any of nature's creatures. J.B. Whigham, city manager of Perryton, was our dedicated opponent and a key witness for Perryton at that hearing, but he testified completely truthfully even when his answers injured his city's position.

The origin of my involvement with Canadian dates back to 1962 when my office partner, Bud Mandell, presented the toughest intellectual puzzle ever in our business dealings. In 1927 Keystone Pipe and Supply of Butler, Pennsylvania had supplied pipe for a gas transmission line through the five northeastern counties of the Texas Panhandle and the adjoining two counties in the Oklahoma Panhandle. They seized control of Public Service Corporation of Texas when the promoters defaulted in payment as the Depression affected everything. Now thirty-five years later, the diminutive, honest, but dictatorial manager, I.E. Horwitz, in Fort Worth, knew he was up in years and wanted to sell, but he wanted original cost even though the system was ninety percent depreciated. Public Service Corporation of Texas was under FPC jurisdiction, and the FPC restricted profit to net original cost. Numerous potential buyers had walked away from the challenge. But I worked out a complicated leveraged buyout, to use today's lingo, and received the blessing of all the appropriate divisions of the FPC. Bud and I then borrowed $100,000 as a forfeiture deposit on the deal, signed contracts, and made what we believed would be perfunctory filings with the FPC. But then the revered Chief of Accounts with the FPC, Russell Rainwater, called and said, "Ballen, I see what you're trying to do but I insist the acquisition adjustment (the difference between the sales price and the net book value) be written off the day you close." I responded, "But that will give us a negative debt/equity ratio." "Correct, and your deal won't roll." "But,

Mr. Rainwater, your division chiefs approved our plan and we have deposited $100,000 forfeiture money." Rainwater ended with, "Ballen, my people are idiots, but I am not."

It didn't register with me that Rainwater must have Indian heritage, nor did I check to learn that he would be retiring in three months. Instead, with his cooperation, we worked out a more complicated plan involving three corporations, two of which would be liquidated the day of closing, with an "S" corporation surviving. But then the SEC said that even for that one day we would be in violation of the Public Utility Holding Company Act. They orally agreed to let it roll. On the date of closing we taped a conversation (questionably admissible in court) in which the SEC chief confirmed what they would allow us to do that day. The closing procedures were so complicated that while driving back from Ft. Worth on the Turnpike, I jerked to a gasp with the realization that the promissory note kept by the sellers was from our shell subsidiary with no assets and there was nothing to keep us from milking its earnings. Finally, Bud Mandell recognized that what dawned on me was true and asked what we should do. The seller's attorney was Henry Simon, also attorney for the Gurleys who owned Vermejo Ranch. "Bud, let's do nothing for the time being. It's Friday and by Monday morning Simon will awake with a sweat and we'll hear from him." It was Saturday morning when I received a pleading call from Ft. Worth. I told him to relax and told Simon to prepare the necessary amendments to get himself back on track. I mentioned there was no need to inform his client. But when the IRS audited the transaction together with all the volumes of documents, they overlooked the implications of recapture of depreciation. This was a new concept in tax law. Since the regulations had not been issued, Ernst & Ernst felt it was acceptable for us to run the risk of not reporting the recapture. The IRS got lost in the paperwork and never wised-up to the recapture which was a significant liability.

Among our fifteen investors were former Texas Governor Allan Shivers and his partner, Gary Morrison. But right off troubles really started. The city of Perryton, our largest customer, had a contract fixing the price of gas at $0.25/MCF unless it was "in the public interest" to go higher and now the price of gas was moving past $0.40. Perryton had verbally agreed to adjust its price to market conditions but now claimed we had misinterpreted the city's position. Our attorneys, Fulbright and Jaworski, said the argument was moot since the Texas Supreme Court decision in the City of Alvin case left ratemaking authority with the Railroad Commission, which had to set rates on "fair value." Fulbright's legal knowledge got a grade of A; its common sense got a grade of F. It took us five years to win our point through the Supreme Court, but, clandestinely, our legal expenses were insured by Oscar Wyatt's Coastal States. He stood by his word, and we managed to keep these payments off our books. But when we were fighting this docket before the Railroad Commission, our stockholder, Gary Morrison, called me: "Sam, you're going about this thing dead wrong." I said, "Well we've got excellent attorneys, and they say we will prevail." "Damn, I can settle this in an afternoon on the golf course with the commissioners." I was stunned and at a loss for words and said I needed to think about it. When I called him the next day and said we would abide by the legal process, he said I wasn't astute enough to be president and hung up. Oh, yes, we lost before the Railroad Commission.

Canadian is surrounded by Indian lore. To the south is the town of Mobeetie, which was surveyed by Sam Houston's son Temple Houston and which was protected by a contingent of black soldiers at Ft. Elliott. Around 1879 a commissary wagon train was proceeding from Ft. Supply in Oklahoma to replenish Ft. Elliott when the advance guard was attacked by Comanche deserters from the reservation. The U.S. troopers took refuge for two rainy days in some depressions. This event is labeled in the history books as the "Battle of Buffalo Wallow." Captain Arrington of the Texas Rangers came in to "pacify" the area and then settled in on a local ranch. His grandson, George Arrington, an enormous hunk of a man, served as mayor of Canadian in the late seventies. When he left to go to Oklahoma A&M instead of Texas A&M, it was said at his departure banquet that when George Arrington left for Oklahoma, he raised the average IQ of two states.

To the southeast of Canadian is the town of Cheyenne, Oklahoma, where General Custer and his 7th Cavalry massacred women and children and Chief Black Kettle in the Battle of the Washita. Custer wired the War Department what a great military victory he had won. But the word passed north on the Indian grapevine as the 7th Cavalry marched to Montana to get that son of a bitch. To the northwest of Canadian occurred the last pitched encounter with the Plains Indians at the Battle of Adobe Walls, where the famous Ute Chief, Buckskin Charley, was a participant.

When we organized High Plains Natural Gas in 1963, we knew that our predecessor had fought three times in the courts with the city of Perryton. I announced to our staff: "Perryton is our biggest customer, and we are going to get along with each other and forget about the adversary history." Within ten years we were in court with them four times, including twice before the Texas Supreme Court. But that is all past history now and we get along with each other just fine. Finally, there is mutual respect, and realistic cooperation, and a dose of common sense accepted by all the parties.

One of the hardest decisions I ever had to make occurred in the seventies in a frigid winter when the wind rushed down from the front range of the Rockies and dropped temperatures in the Panhandle 20 degrees an hour in a phenomenon locally called "a Norther." We were forced to buy surplus gas at $0.60 and Perryton threatened to hold us to a $0.25 price. I called a meeting in Austin of all of our cities and every mayor showed up except Perryton's. I announced that it was not my obligation to lead High Plains into bankruptcy; the mayors said they did not want their gas service to suffer because of Perryton's intransigence. So, in front of these mayors, I told our president, Paul Wilson, to equalize pressure throughout our system. He protested that the configurations of lines required higher pressure at Perryton than Spearman to the west or Booker to the east. I said, "Paul, you have five minutes to either equalize pressures or resign or be fired." So Wilson instructed our field personnel to adjust valves accordingly.

The pressure within Perryton dropped to the point where gas service was interrupted and the piping in their new schoolhouse froze and ruptured. The Perryton City Council was after my scalp and threatened a criminal complaint. I regretted what had occurred on this very cold day but felt a citizenry in a democracy is responsible for the actions of its officials. Then we learned what really happened. The city's engineer had reacted to the declining pressure by breaking into our locked border station and turning a valve. But instead of increasing the flow to Perryton, he was actually diverting gas away from the city. By the time he reversed his motions every pilot light in town had gone out. The threats of law suits quieted once it was known that an inside source had informed me of what really happened.

The city of Perryton is unusual in many ways. This town of 6,000 was honored when its newspaper editor served as president of a national newspaper association, and a local independent oil producer simultaneously served as president of the Independent Petroleum Associations of America. I learned never to persist in an argument with a local newspaper—the newspaper has the last word. The Perryton editor was a very clear thinking, outspoken, and conservative philosopher who used me as a target during our regulatory difficulties. The fact that we finally defeated Perryton in the Texas Supreme Court never was published in their newspaper.

When we acquired the pipeline, it had a line loss of 12 percent, which meant that 12 percent of the gas entering the line was lost either through leaks or faulty measurements. If you remember Boyle's Law, gas volume is affected by pressure and temperature, so unsophisticated metering is not really exact. In Texas, for rate-making purposes, a utility is allowed a 5 percent line loss in local distribution and a 3 percent loss in main-line transmission. After nearly thirty years of hard work and the expenditure of bushels of money, High Plains' 62-year-old line has a line loss of about 1 percent. So what we lack in earnings we make up with legal victories and proud housekeeping. But that was not always the case. In the seventies our line from Magic City to Canadian was losing 75 percent–4,000 MCF/D was going in at Magic City and 45 miles north at Canadian 1,000 MCF/D was coming out! Leak detectors on the ground or in the air could not pinpoint any leaks. Having heard stories of hard-playing Phillips Petroleum, we dug up the ground where their line crossed ours but could not find any bootleg connection. Ours was a Dresser-connected rather than welded line with 4,000 screw-tightened fittings. The ultimate diagnosis was that when Warren's plant had switched to a modern refrigerator facility, our 8,000 rubber gaskets had dried out and each was leaking a small amount. My friend Neil Mallon, president of Dresser, located the mold from which these gaskets were made back in 1927, but the metal casings had altered and replacement gaskets would not hold tight. So we ended up welding each coupling in place. This did not violate existing safety codes because no one had considered that procedure as an option.

Naturally, this experience meant several years of red figures, but the banks did not panic. In those days there were real bankers. We had the funds to stay afloat, but to strengthen our balance sheet we sold our adjoining towns of Shattuck, Gage, and Fargo in Oklahoma. Well, Oklahoma was something else. At one time two of its state supreme court justices were in prison for fraud, and the last to be incarcerated publicly protested that those remaining on the bench should join. While I was still in Dallas, we filed for a rate increase with the Oklahoma Corporation Commission. I received a call from B.A., the Commission's general counsel. "Sam, who is going to handle your rate case?" "Well, Luke Lupardus from Tulsa will be representing us." "Now, I don't want to take anything away from Luke, but I could represent you." "How in heck can you represent us when you will be representing the Commission?" "Now, Sam, there is nothing to keep me from practicing law after hours and I've done that before." Here was this brazen interstate call proposing a flagrant conflict of interest so I got rid of him in a hurry.

Around 1966 a chauffeur whom I had employed in Haiti wrote that conditions there were becoming ugly and asked if I could get him a job so he and his wife and children could come to the states. The family had left a very fine impression on me. I tried to convince the Texas Department of Labor that they would tutor our children in French, but I never could get the necessary permit. So I told Ivan Conklin, our general manager in Canadian, that this family of digni-fied black Haitians would be coming to join our pipeline crew. "Now, Mr. Ballen, I have the best interest of the company in mind, and I must tell you that no black man has ever spent the night in Hemphill County or north to the Kansas line."

Conklin had worked for the utility since 1928 and knew no life other than our pipeline. The main-line pressure gauge was over his bed, and each winter night he would look up at it in the wee hours. His wife, Addie, with no pay, would operate our short-wave radio system from her kitchen. They were the most solid, honest people, even if he would not come to his company retirement party after more than fifty years of service. But I did not know his innermost thoughts and suspected I had run into a bigoted fanatic, so I dropped the subject. Figuring this Haitian must be Catholic, I got an introduc-tion from the bishop in Dallas to the priest in Canadian and alerted him to the prospect of this Haitian coming to Canadian. The priest told me, "Mr. Ballen, OK, but the only place they can live will be in the apartment in back of the church. OK, then I will lose half of my congregants but, OK, I will do that. Mr. Ballen, why are you doing this to me and them?" Well, there is a pleasant "rest of the story." During the height of the oil boom, and labor shortage, oil contractors brought black roughnecks to Perryton. Its newspaper reported a car caravan of mothers showing Blacks to their children. And in 1991 the daughter of our company president had a black bridesmaid from her college in Austin at her wedding and nary a fuss. Decent people do learn, and progress can occur.

Around Canadian are towns like Darrouzette and Follett and Kelton and Glazier, a former incorporated place wiped out by a tornado, and Twitty and Roll and Miami. Locals used to tell the story of a quiz on a religious radio station when the contestant was finally asked "where our Lord lived." The contestant answered Detroit (wrong), Paris (wrong), Pittsburgh (wrong), and Italy (wrong). When the questioner finally interrupted with the correct answer of Palestine, the contestant said, "Well, I knew it was somewhere in Texas."

While we were struggling to turn High Plains profitable, Bud Mandell wanted to make an acquisition of some town distribution systems around Brownwood, Texas, which were owned by Pioneer Natural Gas. I was less enthusiastic. We agreed upon a price for each other's stock, and Bud attempted for ninety days to buy me and my associated stockholders out but he couldn't swing the deal. Although he was respected as a most decent Aggie and a good practical petroleum engineer, he did not then have sufficient wheeler-dealer motivation. So I bought him out at the same price, and each of his associates elected to stay with me. But before that happened, our very efficient accountant left to become head bookkeeper of Ling & Co. Bud had the responsibility of finding a replacement. Returning from a trip one day, I found seated at Judy Price's desk a bosomy, peroxide blond with an inviting expression. I asked, "Bud who is that outside?" "Sam, she is our new bookkeeper." "Bud, there are many things I don't know, but I surely know that there is no such thing as a big-titted, blond, sexy, bookkeeper." Sad to say, I was correct. It took us seven months to realize that while she had no trouble typing in figures for regulatory reports, her data came out of thin air.

The three commissioners of the Texas Railroad Commission are elected by the citizenry and are among the most powerful officials in Texas. From the mid-eighties on, Jim Nugent emerged as the most domineering, populist commissioner. He rather abused the employee examiners by his insistent interrogations of them. Around 1988 I received, on Railroad Commission stationery, a request from him for a contribution to the Jim Nugent Fund. This seemed like an old-time "Oklahoma solicitation," so I threw it in the trash basket. A month later, again on Railroad Commission letterhead, came a letter saying I probably hadn't received the first request. A friend in Austin said, "You'd better not ignore that; he keeps track of those things." Well, I guess I committed a blunder by sending a check for $100 because a "show cause" order was soon pursued against us claiming improper calculation of severance taxes back to 1984. It was a very complicated matter, but our accountants and lawyers stated our treatment of the taxes was correct. The Examiner of the commission recommended a compromise that we were willing to accept (to avoid years of legal expense), but Nugent bull-headed through a 100 percent refund order against us in early 1991 with 10 percent interest back to 1984! After the case was over, I wrote to Governor Ann Richards that I wanted to come down to Austin to discuss an ethics question, but I was never invited.

With the decline of the domestic oil and gas business, towns like Canadian lost 25 to 50 percent of their populations. But the spirit of the old-timers holds and everyone is awaiting the revival of deep drilling, which undoubtedly will occur in fifteen years or so. Prosperity could not come to a grander town or a more deserving citizenry. Whether or not our customers appreciate that we have saved them from sharply increased rates, I often wonder. Every utility executive is a whipping boy for an element of the community. But while nearly every pipeline in the country panicked and contracted for gas at prices up to $10/MCF (now $1.60/MCF), we held firm and I do not know of another gas utility that did not commit to at least some high-priced gas. In May 1994 we sold the assets in a clean transaction to West Texas Gas after a process whereby prospective interested buyers made a contribution to the Texas Gas Association scholarship fund. Thus the TGA honored me at its twentieth convention. I got by with one off-color story and then introduced Ethel as my wife for close to forty-nine years, which included six of the happiest years of my life. One engineer shouted, "You'll pay for that."

We also supplied domestic water to the city of Miami. Miami is the only incorporated town in Roberts County, with the only school, the only post office, and the only bank. It's a city of less than 1,000 population but has a paved air-strip and an annual hog-calling contest. We donated the water system to Miami and they designated—in perpetuity—June 20 as Sam and Ethel Ballen day. This came about because the editor of the Miami Chief—yes this city of less than 1,000 souls does have a weekly newspaper—made the outrageous suggestion that we would be better off donating the water system rather than accepting the City's purchase proposal. After examining the vagaries of the IRS code, we realized the imaginative editor was correct.

17/ PRELUDE TO AFTERMATH

FRIDAY MORNING NOVEMBER 22, 1963, dawned as one of those gloriously clear and invigorating days in Dallas. Strangely, foreigners from both coasts usually were anguished at Dallas' notorious hot summers and unexpected "norther" freeze-outs in winter. In fact, the year-round temperature in the black land near the Trinity River was invariably pleasant and a haven for both golf and tennis addicts. That, no doubt, contributed to the inordinate number of superior players of both sports who chose Dallas for home.

I could tell when I rose from our makeshift bed in our living room that this was going to be one of the good days. Three months previous we had indulged a touch of opulence and moved into a rambling old mansion on three and a half acres just a stone's throw from Love Field. To the amusement of our belittlers with their vague reference to *nouveau riche,* Ethel and I were camping like gypsies in our downstairs living room while formulating plans for redoing a sensuous master bedroom suite upstairs.

A cardboard moving box served for my wardrobe. I selected one of the better pin-stripe blues as I recalled that this noon I would lunch in the officers' dining room atop the Republic National Bank at Ervay & Pacific. Also early in the afternoon there was scheduled a conference in my office on the next step in our attempt to sell a computer project to the oil industry on digitizing oil well logs.

Ethel and I, like so many other Americans, were constantly conscious of our waistlines, never really making headway despite the Fat Boy Diets and calorie counters. So, as usual, I prepared a breakfast of skim milk, Rice Krispies, and black coffee. As I opened the *Dallas Morning News,* the morning took another pleasant upward turn when I realized this was the day of the President's visit. Although I had voted for JFK in the mistaken belief that a missle gap actually existed which he would energetically and realistically correct, I had early turned into one of his critics when he appointed his brother "chief of police." This just didn't seem cricket and in the traditions of

155

this land of the free.* Having taken a jaundiced view of the President, many found it easy to fall into a pattern of noticing faults and deficiencies. When Kennedy seized the steel mills during a strike, we all quipped after the stock market fell thirty points that "Kennedy destroyed more Jews than Eichmann." But all that aside, his energy, elan, humor, culture, and ability to learn from mistakes and recover from losses made me an admirer of the man. It was, therefore, satisfying to see that the *Dallas Morning News'* coverage was rather decent and respectful, which is what our President deserved in any event.

This pleasant euphoria abruptly sank when I came to the full-page vulgar ad with black border inside the first section. My God, I thought, the John Birchers are at it again with their smear of JFK. What a dirty trick—they've used some Jew to sign that insulting intemperate rot. Of course, I quickly reflected, as a member of the ACLU, the *Dallas Morning News* was right to run the ad but couldn't they have moved it up or back a day? What lousy taste to besmirch Dallas on the day of the President's visit.

A second uncomfortable thought crossed my mind—that I would again have to apologize to Lev Aronson, who at our small dinner party the previous evening had sputtered in his usual emotional staccato that he feared for the President in the presence of those John Birchers. We had resumed our incoherent arguement, now in its seventh year, when I patronizingly told him his concentration camp days had distorted his thinking and he really didn't understand the beat of America despite his citizenship papers.

And, so, down to work to the Southland Center and an easy morning of good tidings and no reminders that ours is not a profit system but a profit-and-loss system. Towards 11:30 it was Ray Pulley, vice-president of the Republic National Bank, on the phone with the suggestion that I drop by his desk around noon and we could then go upstairs and discuss the renewal of my note. When a former partnership had dissolved with some rancor in 1958, I was left with most assets dissipated and a pro rata debt, funded through the Republic, which they had handled courteously.

As I left the Southland Center to walk the two blocks down to the bank, I enjoyed the warm clear day that the morning had portended. It seemed that the people had a touch of briskness to their steps and a trace of sheepishness in their knowledge of our city's reputation for

* Santa Fe's unusual Mayor will of course pay the price for appointing her brother City Manager and her brother-in-law Chief of Police.

extreme conservation. We harbored some highly placed kooks who had acted as truants towards Lady Bird Johnson and Adlai Stevenson and many others not so well publicized. Yet, unmistakenly, there was friendliness in the air and on the faces and in the figures, mostly female it seemed to me, who had started to line up on St. Paul Street.

Ray Pulley and I rode the attended elevator to the bank's private dining room on their thirty-ninth floor. All of the occupants were clothed in pressed, narrow-shouldered handsome Neiman's look—so much more appealing than the formal, vested fabrics of Fenn Feinstein or Brooks or Savile found back east to intuitively remind you theirs is a class society. Someone remarked, "Well, looks like he picked one of our good days," and everyone chuckled an agreeable consent.

The dining room is just the right combination of simplicity and elegance—that is true of both the furnishings and colored human wait staff. None of the phoniness of the Petroleum Club where you instinctively brace your shoulders and wear the wiseguy expression, none of the establishment formality of the City Club where the bored and mean look is *de regueur,* none of the washed out atmosphere of the Athletic Club where the fatigued slump of the guests and the salads reflect that you're now going second class. No the private dining room of the Republic National Bank has the calm dignity of those who've achieved. They know they're in decent company, where shrewd thinking will be merged with an undercurrent that no deal is really a success unless both parties walk away content and better off.

While looking at the day's printed menu—all gratis of course—we gave our order to the handsome thirtyish ochre-turned waitress with the demeanor that showed unquestionably she would be the mahjong and garden club type "if only." I chuckled with the passing thought at how much better off she was in her present circumstances, with her open face and controlled curves and strength of knowing she was making it on her own. Then Ray and I noticed a stirring in the assembled guests, all drifting towards the windows facing south to the Elm Street intersection. "The caravan is passing; he'll be along any minute." Somewhat apologetically, but also enthusiastically, we walked over to an empty window and looked straight down thirty-nine floors to the intersection, now packed with mid-day humanity, including police and dignitaries, and in a flash his car came and passed with a spontaneous ovation from the crowd below and a distinct indelible view of his erect back and outstretched arm. We lingered at the kaleidoscopic view of the balance of the caravan and heard someone exclaim, "That's Lyndon just went by!"

Quietly, as in the pomp of any private downtown club, we edged back across the room to our small table against the wall and sat down. We skirted around and reached agreement about renewal of my note without ever directly addressing that question. Suddenly our handsome waitress burst through the swinging kitchen door and whispered to us, "They've shot the President."

"Oh, no, you're kidding; we just saw him go by."

"No, it came over the radio, they shot him." And she disappeared back into the kitchen.

By now all the small tables had learned the news. There were no loud voices, everywhere a dark cloud sifted down to hush and sober the previously happy crowd. Ray and I pecked at our small steaks without saying a word. Although Ray had been my banker since Jim Grisham had left for Houston six years previous and although we saw each other every month, our relationship had always been at arm's length. We had been assigned to each other without much choice and were both quite nicely making the best of it. I knew his son was Mayor Cabell's son-in-law and took for granted that he was a proper Dallasite, utterly reliable, kind, charitable and an altogether good man who never had been called upon to sharpen his bite or wits, if indeed he possessed them. In the same way I imagine Ray had assumed me to be another transplanted Yankee whose perspective had been improved in the gentile Dallas climate but whose genes probably still carried traces of eastern liberalism. Therefore, politics was never discussed.

"Ray, this is the finish of Dallas. We've all stood silent and let Walker and Hunt and Alger spew their hatred and now we'll pay the price. There's been a sickness growing in Dallas and now the damn thing's erupted and you can just forget about your Republic Bank stock." To myself I wondered what Cleaver would say now, thinking back to that afternoon when that handsome, intelligent, worldly friend had called one afternoon in a spasm of glee, "We wouldn't let the son-of-a-bitch into the Baker. Sam, you should've seen J and M and the other girls surround the bastard and that filthy Lady Bird and let them have it."

"I don't agree with you, Sam," was Ray's quiet and composed reply. "We don't know what this is all about, but it's not the act of Dallas."

I was calmed down more by his dignity than his words and I realized that as a native he was really shook more than he showed.

Tears streaming down her face, our colored waitress reappeared.

"He's dead. Oh God, I liked that man…he was a good man. Why did they do it? What will become of us?…Excuse me, will you have dessert now?"

I walked slowly back to my sober office at the Southland Center to prepare for a meeting with Bob Seale. He was beside himself with grief and couldn't control his tears. I knew how politically conservative he was, but his view of life was based on decency and integrity. This incident in his beloved Dallas was beyond comprehension. "Bob, I am closing the office. Our discussion will have to await another day." And off he went.

I drove up Central Expressway slowly to the Lemmon Avenue exit where I could swing home to Bluff View. Over the car radio I heard, "A suspect has been arrested in Oak Cliff…a Lee Harvey Oswald." Lee, LEE! Oh, gosh, he is the creep George de Mohrenshildt sent to me six months ago. So this was the start of my subsequent appearances before the FBI, the Secret Service, and the Warren Commission.

18/ *MISCHKA*

FOR TWO DECADES George de Mohrenschildt and I were the closest of friends. There were wonderful dimensions to him, certainly surpassing his ill-concealed parlous blemishes of character. But, alas, now he is remembered as Lee Harvey Oswald's closest acquaintance. The Warren Commission Report devotes more pages to him than to any other witness. Those investigators attracted to conspiracy theories try to stain his memory, but that is nonsense. I will try to set the record straight.

It was early in 1952 that Joseph P. Downer came up from Houston to be my assistant at the Wertheim office in Dallas. With his arrival commenced a very satisfying professional and social friendship that has endured up to the present. Downer was not brilliant, but he was very solid and decent and organized, with wide Ivy League bonding. His father was a professional army man, erect and wiry and a World War I hero. Joe somehow always seemed to reflect some sternness from his father overviewing progress in Joe's own life. He went to Harvard, where his roommate was Bud Kelly, of the old-line Santa Fe family. Then he graduated from the Harvard Business School and was assistant to Continental Oil Company's economist, Sergei Jurinov, in Houston. But Joe rather correctly understood that he was not going to learn the real intricacies of the oil business while in the disciplined arena of Continental Oil. It was my good fortune that he decided to leave and join me in Dallas. As much as Ethel and I liked Joe, we were equally attracted to his wife Jeannie, who had also been part of the women's Ivy League back east. She basically had a dramatic and artistic flair, which she kept in check while her husband was moving in more "proper" circles. Ultimately, this conflict of personalities ended up in a divorce, which was probably the best for each of them. Joe remarried a more statuesque country club lady from the north shore of Long Island, and she more closely flattered Joe's aspirations. But I thought Jeannie had perhaps too deep a love for her father, who was the vice-president in charge of South America for the

Schroeder-Rockefeller Bank. Ironically, Wertheim Schroeder has now become Schroeder Wertheim.

Joe and I worked together until I went on my own in 1956 and he went back to New York to be Wertheim's oil expert. Only once did we have any misunderstanding; that was when he resented a letter I sent out announcing the opening of my independent consulting office. Upon reflection, I decided that his objection was well founded and changed a crucial sentence in my letter. Joe went on to become treasurer of Sinclair Oil. At that time he sent me a kind letter stating that everything truly important about the oil industry he had learned from me. Naturally, I treasured that letter. Ultimately, Sinclair became part of the Atlantic Refining family and then Joe became vice-chairman of Arco under R. O. Anderson. I don't mean to be belittling when I say that Joe was the perfect adjutant or number-two type. This included the time when he was adjutant to the commanding general of the Tenth Mountain Division of ski troops who ended up in Italy in World War II. That famous division included Senator Dole and Rabbi Schindler, both wounded the same day.

It must have been the summer of 1952 when Downer introduced me to George de Mohrenschildt, and almost immediately George and I became brothers under the skin. George had one of the most fascinating and complex life journeys that can be imagined. At that moment he was an independent geologist in Abilene, living off the savings and the contacts of his then number-three wife, Dede Sharples. She was a physician and daughter of the socially prominent Philadelphia family of Sharples Tool Company, which had extensive oil operations in the Rocky Mountains. Shortly thereafter, the de Mohrenschildts moved to Dallas into a rather prestigious estate on the north side of town.

George was a handsome man, six feet, 2 inches tall, with arrogant charm emanating from every pore of his body. He had a command of some nine languages. (After moving to Haiti years later he was able to pick up Creole in about six weeks, and that reflects his ease with any foreign language.) It was well known in Dallas that he had a roving eye, which was not just theoretical. At his very first meeting at a dance with the graceful Jo Cleaver, he wanted to know if she and her husband Jim had an understanding so that he could feel free to call Jo occasionally. In those very conservative times in Dallas when the John Birch Society was well entrenched, it was typical for George to escort some young lady, whether white or brown or black, through the lobby of the Baker Hotel to a private room for a lunch, and so forth. The dowagers of Dallas glowered at every step of his way. It was also no secret that shortly after he and Dede moved to Dallas, he selected as a friend a very appealing and exotic young Russian-English emigree who lived with the philosophy that the most friendly thing a man and a woman could do is to make love.

I believe George was born in the Crimea, where his father was overseeing the Baku oil fields owned by the Swedish Nobel interests. His mother was Russian. George's Scandinavian father carried some form of nobility but harbored liberal notions. He and his family had to flee to Poland after the Bolshevik Revolution when the White Russians invaded the Crimea. George's political tendencies were opportunistic and certainly not patriotic. He floated from right to left and vice versa, but there was always within him a liberal residue, tracing his exposure as a youngster to Bolshevik idealism. His brother, Von Mohrenschildt, ended up with a more conventional White Russian philosophy as a professor at Dartmouth. I believe that after the Kennedy assassination complications he migrated to India.

At an early age George had to fend for himself, and he made good use of his handsome looks. He depended on the generosity, with friendship and finances, of better-established women in Western Europe, where he matriculated at a university in Holland. Ultimately, he came to the United States and for a while worked in New York City with a perfume importer. In that arena he gained entree into the upper social set of Long Island and became friendly with Mrs. Bouvier and also with Jacqueline Kennedy when she was a youngster. He was a sensation at some of the classier North Shore country clubs. He also worked for a while in Venezuela under the tutelage of a man named Smith, with Pantepec Petroleum, which was controlled by William Buckley's father.

George was encouraged to enroll in the geology department at the University of Texas, where he made a close friend of the very eccentric Tito Harper, who had many characteristics similar to George's. Tito was the heir to a well-respected ranching family near Eagle Pass, Texas. He had a rebel's streak in him, which took the expression of marrying a beautiful Mexican girl named Conchita. He then moved across the border and lived in Piedras Negras. All of ranching society in West Texas was shocked at this indiscretion. That was more than true of the border patrol, who questioned Tito each day when he took his young daughters across the border to school in Eagle Pass, using his mother's connections. Each day the border patrol would examine Tito's immigration credentials. Tito developed a serious alcohol problem plus some other psychological difficulties. He was a big man and beat up his psychiatrist after one difficult session in Mexico City. Ultimately, he died before his time in some incident with violent undertones.

In the late forties George was petroleum engineer for the unitized* Rangley Oil Field in Western Colorado. He set up housekeeping with a new and beautiful wife, Phyllis, the daughter of an investment man, Bill Wassermann, from Philadelphia. Wassermann was also a promoter of oil exploration syndicates. George summarized Wassermann's investment philosophy, "If the well was dry, you lost your money; if the well came in, you ultimately got your money back." The environment at Rangley was not salutary for this beautiful young socialite from Philadelphia. She must have gotten bored by the lecherous looks of the oil field roughnecks. That marriage broke up, as did all of George's marriages, before and after Ms. Wassermann. But in the late fifties George welcomed this ex and her new husband (a French TV producer who had discovered the diary of Anne Frank) and provided them an elaborate cocktail reception at the Dallas Petroleum Club.

One of George's experiences at Rangley had a lasting effect in his practice of walking away from physical conflict. He explained that one Saturday night everybody left the oil field to go into some bar in Rangley frequented by cowboys who were also searching for weekend enjoyment. It was not unusual for drunken brawls to erupt. That particular night a tiny thin drunken cowboy tried to pick a fight with George, who towered over him. Nothing George did to discourage notice of this tiny twerp was successful. Finally George shrugged his shoulders and put up his dukes to fight. The tiny cowboy whipped George to a pulp. But George was also scornful of my proud wartime service, saying it's silly to get involved in the senile tribal conflagrations of mankind.

When George and Dede got to Dallas, they moved in proper conventional circles. George joined the Dallas Petroleum Club and was initially sponsored by a very wealthy and religious White Russian process engineer and independent oil man, Paul Raigorodsky, whom I never felt comfortable with. I probably wasn't the only one who harbored some suspicion of Raigorodsky's past. It was well known that the Dallas Petroleum Club did not admit Jews, other than Fred Florence, who was head of the Republic National Bank, and Buddy

---

* Such a field is operated collectively rather than with individual ownerships.

Fogelson, husband of Greer Garson, who concealed his ancestry. Another member, Pat Marr, had become a Presbyterian as a young man out of religious convictions but then had to reveal this background to his beautiful daughter, Marilyn, when she became engaged to a Jewish physician. George jokingly complained to me that I had an advantage over him in starting in business on my own since it was not obligatory for me to pay the initiation fee and monthly dues to the Dallas Petroleum Club. For a decade we probably spoke to each other at least once a day. A typical call from George would start with: "Eh, chico Samson, did you see that ugly highrise on Turtle Creek? The C of C is syphilizing Dallas and the hillbillies think it's progress."

George's marriage to Dede was doomed to failure, but I am certain that for a while he made her life very happy. Unfortunately, their two children were afflicted with cystic fibrosis. No cure was known and the two lovely delicate children died. George tried to solicit friends for a C.F. Foundation, but he was not particularly successful since he was so close to the vest in other public charities. Dede was a physician and naturally curious whether the genetic defect stemmed from the father or the mother. The resultant strange episode can then be understood. George noticed that after their night-time romantic activities Dede would disappear for some interval. He quietly followed her one night into her laboratory where she was examining his semen under a microscope.

When George walked into a room, his hauteur and dark good looks brought all discussion to a close. All eyes would concentrate on his arrogant steps. There were many women in Dallas who found him irresistible, and his infidelities became too flagrant for Dede to tolerate. The marriage came to a close. While he had numerous talents, being a businessman was not one of them. Nor was he a competent geologist or petroleum engineer. However, despite the skepticism of so many others, I found him to be professionally honest. Together with an associate, he brokered a large tract of oil leases to John Mecom of Houston, and that nest egg enabled him to open an office in the Republic National Bank. From there on his finances went downhill, ultimately contributing to his suicide.

As a bachelor he set himself up in apartment 707 at the Stoneleigh Maple Terrace Apartments, which in those early years was a magnet for fringe operators who rotated between the gambling tables of Las Vegas and the speculations of oil drilling. The poolside included wildcatters like Blondy Hall who would telephone Las Vegas hotels and see what they bid for him by way of accommodations, limousines, female companionship, etc. All the poolside cronies listened in and shared this frivolity. It was there that George met Jeanne, a person with almost as colorful a history. It turned out she had the stronger backbone of the two. Jeanne was born in China of a Russian father, manager of the Russian-Chinese railroads, and a French mother. After the Communist revolt in China, her father was executed by the Reds. She married a Russian named Bogoyavlensky and supported the two of them as a high-society model and dress designer in Paris, going under the name of Jeanne Legon. She was a most handsome woman, a fine ice skater, a great cook, and quite charming—but as outspoken as anyone could be. She would, literally, give a deserving soul the shirt off her back. She had a beautiful daughter named Chris. Jeanne took up residence at the Stoneleigh Apartments, where she flipped over George. Before Jeanne and Bogoyavlensky were divorced, he made several amateurish attempts to assault George.

Jeanne and George got married and there is no question that he fell completely in love with her and was captivated by her. However, he stated in his Warren Commission testimony that the young lady in Mexico, who was the Mexican President's mistress, was the great love of his life. After the death of his beloved son, Sergei, George was totally disconsolate and felt that he needed to make a personal pilgrimage, a walk from the Mexican border to Panama. Jeanne agreed to go along with him, together with a mule and a tiny Manchester dog of hers named Nero. They started off from Torreon, taking the back trails, and nine months later ended up in Panama. In some of the isolated villages in Mexico, Jeanne said she could understand the tongue of the Indians from the Chinese she remembered as a young-ster. Periodically, George would send me a letter when he reached a community with a post office. Unfortunately, I did not save them. After the Kennedy assassination some of the right-wing critics claimed that the journey had never occurred, asserting George had been in a KGB training camp. As is typical of the coincidences in George's life, they arrived at the beach in Guatemala where the invasion force was being trained to invade Cuba. George and Jeanne witnessed some of the maneuvers. But coincidence for them was not unusual. At the depths of the Cold War, they landed in Mexico City in a private plane just when Mikoyan's Soviet plane taxied up close by. Jeanne ran through the security people and in Russian exclaimed, "Welcome, Comrade Mikoyan!" He almost fainted in expectation of an assassin.

When George and Jeanne returned to Dallas, we welcomed them with a party to show some of their slides. These included some risque sauntering by Jeanne in her bikini, which was somewhat indiscreet in those times. Many notables came to this party—at that time George was still a part of accepted society. But something deep and basic had happened in their Hegira. George was now completely under the domination of Jeanne. I suspect that in some tense moments in the jungle she had proved to be the more manly of the two. George, who had spent a lifetime bowling over women, now was caught in the web of the one he really loved. But money problems were really pressing on him, even though Jeanne had gone back to work with a dress manufacturer in Dallas named Ike Clark. In order to promote money for oil drilling, it is necessary to move in wealthy circles. But, one by one, the doors were being closed in George's face because of the outspoken leftist expressions from Jeanne. She was even praising the Mao Communists who had murdered her father. George went off to Yugoslavia to make a geologic survey. While he was gone, I was visited by the FBI, who inquired of him—supposedly in connection with a pending visa application to Yugoslavia. I told the agent that George was already there.

George's problem with respectable society was accentuated by the extreme and intolerant atheism broadcast by the two of them. One day I told them that an intelligent and courageous rabbi from the Chicago area would be talking at Temple Emmanuel in Dallas, and I invited them to attend as my guests. Temple Emmanuel was a handsome building with gilded dignity in its walls and its membership. That afternoon George showed up in sneakers and wearing a T-shirt and tennis trousers. Jeanne was dressed in a tennis brief and slippers. After drawing my breath, I said, "Okay, you rascals, I can play your game. Come on in with me." So, to the amazed look of the audience, I escorted them down the aisle to one of the benches. Although Jeanne on several occasions chauffeured our daughters to Temple Sunday School, her and George's atheism knew no limits. Natasha and Igor Voshinen were an attractive White Russian couple from Yugoslavia, he an engineer and she a geologist. Both were devout members of the Russian Orthodox Church in Dallas. At one of their dinner parties, Jeanne proceeded in a most uncalled-for way to criticize their upcoming Christian celebration, and George joined in with vulgarity. After the two of them barged off, George then returned with some supplemental base behavior before he left for good.

Around this time George had done some geologic work on some off-shore prospects in Nigeria and then made a legal claim against Phillips Petroleum Company, which had made a large discovery there.

George pretended that it was due to what they had learned from him, but I very much doubt that this was the case. He was able to find an attorney named Patrick Russell, who moved in open gay circles in Dallas, to present this claim to Phillips Petroleum. There may have been a token settlement with Phillips. We knew that George and Jeanne were not conventionally upright, but they treated any underdog with respect. Their entry into a household brought excitement and joy, and our daughters were elated when they showed up.

When I went on my own in 1956, I journeyed to Los Angeles to promote the hotelman Arnold Kirkeby as an investor in my oil syndicate. George arrived and stayed several days at my room in the downtown Hilton. I was also feeding him. But one day we bumped into his acquaintance, Dimitri Diamtoptropf, a Hollywood composer. George said he owed me a dinner, and Dimitri recommended a French spot. As soon as we sat down, I knew he was in trouble because there were no prices on the menu. A French waiter hovered over us, joining in our French discourse. He finally leaned down and drawled, "You boys from Texas? I'm from Waxahachie." Well, George gasped when the check arrived. He counted out his money, and the waiter left. George pulled on my sleeve and walked to the door. When I looked back, I saw that he had left a dollar tip. Several years later Dimitri sent George a telegram from Paris, "Send $500, will explain later." I asked George how he responded. "Oh, Dimitri can take care of himself. I didn't want to cheapen him, so I wired, "No, will explain later."

At this time Jeanne's luscious and well-endowed daughter, Chris, moved into their apartment. Everyone was shocked when at, I guess, the age of fifteen, she painted in a hall closet a beautiful Pompeii-type scene of all of the imaginable forms of sexual intercourse. In her defense the fresco was really lovely and artistic. Chris had her own charm, aside from her physical magnets, and through some of the Marcus family was able to get the interesting puppets she was making offered for sale at "The Store." After she married Rags Kearton and moved to Alaska, she learned that her name was Bogoyavlensky and not Legon, and she asked me for an affidavit so they could change their name. The judge said he could understand changing Bogoyavlensky-Kearton to Kearton, but they said it was the other way around. The judge wanly granted their request in a lackluster decision.

Probably George knew that he was now on a downward treadmill of nihilism, but he still managed to maintain some contacts with the uppercrust of Dallas society. In the Warren Commission testimony, Jake Hamon, former president of the American Petroleum Institute, stated something like "I can take George or I can leave him and I prefer to leave him." But ultimately George's fine associations were limited to John Jacobs, president of Texas Eastern, and Bruce Calder of Horizon Oil.

It was in this setting that Lee Harvey Oswald and his wife Marina and their children showed up in Dallas. Eventually, the White Russians wanted to befriend them in their desperate poverty and provide some children's clothing and the like for Marina. As a result, George became Lee Harvey Oswald's closest friend. George says he learned of Oswald while driving to Ft. Worth with Lawrence Orlov, a colonel in the Army Reserve and a so-so oil broker. But Orlov denied this and said that he learned about Oswald from George. Anyway, in no time at all George became intrigued by Oswald, with whom he could talk Russian. They could discuss what had evolved in Soviet life and how it compared to the socialist dream. In addition, Marina's hungry, sexy looks were not a detriment. George was puzzled by her since her bible was not *Das Kapital*, but the Sears Roebuck catalog. After Oswald physically abused Marina, it fell to George, who was more than twice the size of Lee, to threaten him with bodily harm if he ever again raised a pinkie against Marina. The day after the radio announced that someone had taken a rifle shot at the right-wing General Walker on Turtle Creek Drive, the de Mohrenschildts were at the Oswald's home for dinner. Marina was screeching in Russian how irresponsible Lee was–they didn't have the money to provide adequate food for their children and here he had gone and purchased a rifle. She opened the closet door and showed the rifle to George, who in his typical kidding way, with a Russian accent said, "Ah,...Lee,... den you are de one who shot at Walker!" Lee turned absolutely white and excused himself from the room.

All this time George was keeping me informed of the comings and goings of the Oswalds, and finally he pleaded with me to see Lee and give him a job. Lee Harvey Oswald came down to my office in the Gibraltar Life Building. I did not know then what a facile liar Lee was. When I told him that Electrical Log Services Inc. could use somebody who knew how to operate a large vacuum frame for photography, Lee told me that he had been so trained in Kiev and could operate such equipment. I was intrigued at how a Ft. Worth native could defect from the marines, spend time in the U.S.S.R., then marry a KGB colonel's niece, and then be repatriated back to

Texas. So for the next two hours we proceeded to talk about Russia and socialism and the marines. It immediately became apparent to me that he was intellectually way over his head and was talking about things that he did not understand. It also became apparent that he was fiercely independent, with some enormous chips on his shoulder. He kept saying that I should not worry about him and he could handle himself whether I offered him a job or not. I really intended to offer him a job, but as we talked I just had the overwhelming feeling that he was a stray dog who would be a magnet for trouble. He talked himself out of any prospect of employment with me. The two of us then walked down toward the Republic Bank Building. He kept saying, "Don't you worry about me, I can take care of myself." We said goodbye, and that's the last I ever saw him in the flesh.

Throughout our acquaintanceship, George and I played tennis at least three times a week, sometimes with Jeanne and a fine Chinese lady, Irene Chu, who, by herself, raised six kids and put each one through college. Everyone called George "Mischka," which is Russian for bear. They called me Samson. You can tell a great deal about someone playing tennis. George was honest in calling the line shots, enjoyed the game, controlled his aggressiveness, and was just out for a good time rather than winning being his number-one goal. The industrialist Troy Post was another matter, and I gave up on him when he continued to cheat when calling the balls. George had good control of his huge frame in other pastimes as well. For example, he stood on his head each morning for twenty minutes, reading paperbacks.

When we circled Navajo Mountain for three days on horseback, all of our group had exhausted horses except George, whose mount still had a spry step. George said we knew how to handle neither women nor horses. Jeanne became a passable tennis addict, and our foursome with Irene Chu would play every Sunday near Highland Park Methodist Church.

In his prime, George was the grandest person to be with, spewing out intelligent and spontaneous humor and restoring to each of us the joy of our youth. His serious decline and loss of confidence and spontaneity, leading to his ultimate tragedy, commenced with his failure to secure a publisher for his memoirs of his journeys through Central America. His purpose in writing up this experience was to record for posterity their interesting time on the back trails through isolated villages. Equally important was his hope that his writing would be financially successful and might even end up as a movie. It was a shock to all of us that someone who had such a great command of language and such an easy flow of words produced a dismal, sterile, and boring account of his trip. He never could gain the attention of a publisher, even after he had it professionally rewritten. This hurt him deeply.

From there on to the end of his days he drifted from one aberrant business scheme to another. He was completely out of the main stream of the oil and gas community. Around 1960 he secured a little commission to go to Poland and make a geologic overview, which essentially consisted of translating Polish professional papers. He came back saying that the country was so dismal and depressed that you couldn't even get an erection. He was able to get his Yugoslav geologic report published in the *Oil and Gas Journal,* but it was not of high professional quality. Then came his complex experience in Haiti.

I think it was a contact in New York who put him in touch with a Russian Jew named Breitman who lived in the Russian emigre community of Kenskof, situated at 5,000 feet overlooking Port-au-Prince. Breitman was a good family man despite the disenchantment of his daughter in New York after she learned that he had a Haitian mistress, but that was not any particular rarity. A step-by-step deal was arranged through Clemard Charles, a talented Haitian who had grown up in the bush and then ended up as president of a bank and a financial crony of Papa Doc. Ultimately, Clemard Charles had to flee to Brooklyn, but at that time he was at the top of Haitian intrigue and had considerable power. His cheerful and intelligent receptionist commented to us, "I'm not a Victorian, but I don't want a man to take his anger at society out on me." That's a variation of the words of an English receptionist at the Dallas Petroleum Club, who said, "I'm not a prude but these oilmen dispense with the preambles." Anyway, through some United Nations seed money, Haiti gave a substantial contract to George to conduct a complete geologic survey of the country. Because Haiti didn't have the funds to pay totally for the contract, they also gave George a lease on a sisal plantation, with arrangements for him to sell the sisal on the international market through Clemard Charles' bank. George and Jeanne, with their two Manchester dogs, moved to Lyle Estates, just outside Port-au-Prince and about 800 yards from Papa Doc's residence. That meant there would always be tough security guards nearby.

Although George hired a few well-trained young field geologists from Sweden and Italy, the project ultimately collapsed. Amateurs were involved so it was destined to failure, but in the interim, he and

Jeanne had some of the grandest times of their lives. They had an off-the-road Land Rover and three servants at their house and were soon part of the social scene of the international diplomatic "corps." Although Haiti is one of the poorest nations on earth, it was the first independent black country and the first country to militarily defeat Napoleon. As a consequence, many nations had embassies there.

The most interesting consul I got to know was ostensibly the Polish Commercial Charge d'Affaires, who was named Galitsky. I am sure he was an intelligence agent because of his great shrewdness, and he was always accompanied by a tough-looking Polish security guard who claimed to be a secretary. This was at a time when Washington was lying to America about the goings-on in Vietnam. Time and time again Galitsky would humiliate me when we played tennis or went snorkeling. He would say, "Well, Ballen, the Vietcong knocked down six of your helicopters two days ago." "That's nonsense. The *New York Times* said two helicopters were knocked down." "Ballen, I assumed you were experienced in the world and would not swallow your own government's propaganda." Invariably, with the passage of time, Galitsky's information proved to be correct, in direct opposition to the blatant lies put out by our own government and repeated by our otherwise respected papers.* Galitsky had been everywhere, and that included Vietnam. Very early on he said to me, "The Vietcong are going to defeat you. I have been there. Believe me. If you declared war against Poland, we would surrender in one day. If you declared war against the U.S.S.R, they would surrender in three days, but I have been in Vietnam and the Vietcong are going to defeat you." This is what he said in mid-1964!

Back in those days Haitian society was topped by the one-hundredth of one percent of its population that were handsome, multilingual, wealthy mulattoes. In contrast to the brutality of the Ton Ton Macoutes, who were teenagers with submachine guns, the aroma and visual impact of bougainvillaea pleasantly filled the entire landscape. Tamara Bousson, a Russian Jewish poet, was married to a handsome Haitian architect who owned a hotel in Petianville and also one on a nearby island. She felt that despite Papa Doc's cruelty, he could not destroy the people's spirit and romance was in the air. Unfortunately, I somehow feel that this overview is no longer true

---

* One recalled Montaigne's expression: "This world needs more unreasonable men. A reasonable man says, 'Don't burn too many heretics at the stake.' An unreasonable man says, 'Don't burn any heretics at the stake.'"

today. At that time it was the challenge for these young, handsome, cultured male Haitians to deflower the female tourists from the Mainland. Who knows whether there was any truth in it, but through the countryside ran the rumor that this had included the wife of the U.S. ambassador named Timmons, whom the Haitians subsequently called Timoon, which in Creole meant "little man," (the slang of *petit homme*). On one of George and Jeanne's airplane journeys back to the states, they left one of their Manchesters named Papeya with the ambassador's household. When they returned, the dog had been attacked and was injured and needed medical attention. When Jeanne learned this she barged into the ambassador's office at the U.S. Embassy and chewed him out with the roughest possible language and humiliated him in front of his subordinates. No longer was the U.S. Embassy a refuge for George. One by one the doors were closed to the other embassies, other than that housing the very handsome, tall couple from Ethiopia.

After the Kennedy assassination I was really concerned about George and Jeanne. In January 1964 I went down to see them and noticed irrational extremism had enveloped Jeanne. George was reconciled to the probability that Oswald had pulled off this dastardly deed, but without any information whatsoever, Jeanne was now starting to put together a scenario that this had been a plot of the CIA and of H. L. Hunt and that poor Oswald had been set up by the reactionaries in the United States. I was unable to reason with her. Since she was sounding off in this fashion to the distress of Ambassador Timmons, George's future in Haiti was now dated.

Before they left, they chartered a sailboat and spent about two months going around the island to all the most remote spots, living off their fish catches and enjoying native hospitality. No one related easier to native peoples than George and Jeanne. For my part, I learned that there was a 9,000-foot mountain called Foret de Pine with some semblance of a lumbering operation. Despite its tropical latitude, there was frost at the top of Foret de Pine, as I learned to my regret, when I tried to camp there one night with only a sheet for a cover. A U.S. AID mission had put in a skyline to carry cut lumber from the mountain down to market. At a grand-opening ceremony one of the towers collapsed and killed the U.S. engineer who had directed the construction. My commercial interest there ground quickly to a halt when I learned the number of different Haitian officials I would have to pay off. I was regretful because there was so much charm to the Haitian people who lived outside the big cities. There were no solid walls to the fine homes in Lyle Estates, but open, filigreed concrete tiles. One woke up in the morning to the lovely sound of the singing Haitian women carrying their produce on their heads, walking from their plots on the hillside down to the Port-au-Prince market. At one party I was chastised for asking the little daughter of the maid what her father did. I was then advised that one never asked such an indelicate question of a child.

As Jeanne's coterie of human friends disappeared one by one, she turned her maternal instincts to her Manchesters and to other animals. One day while we were driving through heavy traffic in downtown Port-au-Prince some Ton Ton Macoutes with submachine guns kicked a stray dog. Jeanne, who was at the wheel, ground the Land Rover to an emergency stop. Out she leaped and to the horror of all passers-by, she cursed the Ton Ton Macoutes in the crudest Creole while the other cars were honking behind the Land Rover. On another occasion, we were driving down from Kenskof, past a tiny suburb in the Plaza in which was a five-foot-square cage restraining a completely cowed monkey. It was the favorite sport of all of the Haitians in this village to torment the monkey verbally as well as with poles, pebbles, and rocks. The monkey was afraid of its own shadow with a complete paranoia. Jeanne insisted that we stop, and she played a good samaritan to this monkey with the cage separating the two of them. After two hours the monkey would let her pet him, and the two of them were cooing together. There was deep sadness when we left because we knew as soon as we turned the corner the inhumane tormenting would resume.

One day in 1965, while we were driving to the beach, an episode occurred that at the time, and now in hindsight, seems to be a replay from a Dashiell Hammett mystery. We detoured through some rundown warehouses in Port-au-Prince and came to a halt while George went to meet a shadowy, trench coated European. The two of them talked for about five minutes, and when George returned, he and Jeanne exchanged some words in Russian. When I inquired what that was all about, they passed it off with some platitudes. We then proceeded to Iboleli and went swimming in the reef.

George and Jeanne crawled out of Haiti totally destitute. I offered them our guest house in Dallas to stay in until they restored themselves. Jeanne maneuvered matters to a showdown. With their few possessions they drove in their convertible car from Miami and arrived one night most travel weary. Ethel had stipulated, since we had a magnificent German shepherd, that the Manchester dogs could not come into our house. Ethel made an excellent *coq au vin* dinner for them and we invited some mutual friends over who had not seen them for many years. To Ethel's absolute irritation, Jeanne fabricated some excuse to bring in the two Manchester dogs and she sat at the table feeding the *coq au vin* to the Manchesters. Ethel was quite disillusioned with me when I did not turn this incident into a confrontation with Jeanne. My father enjoyed breakfasting with George and Jeanne in our guest house, and our girls were thrilled to visit with them there.

George McMillan had come down to Dallas to produce an NBC television show on the November 22, 1964, anniversary of the assassination. I put McMillan in touch with the de Mohrenschildts in Haiti, and a deal was worked out whereby NBC paid their expenses to come to a lavish suite in New York and then must have given them over $15,000 to make an appearance on the anniversary TV show. On their first public appearance they did not display anything but the distress within them. McMillan offered me $5,000 to go on the show, but I told him that would be fraudulent because I was only a two-hour expert on Oswald, but McMillan said I was the only clean-looking businessman among the cast of characters. He did not convince me.

The great bonus of all this was that McMillan met Priscilla Johnson, and they ultimately married. But McMillan left the lovely Priscilla for a younger woman in North Carolina and then was diagnosed with Lou Gehrig's disease. Since generous Priscilla had maintained her love for McMillan, she attempted his rescue during the final stages of the illness. A warm friendship between Priscilla and McMillan's second wife led, shades of Dostoyevsky, to the widow and son becoming permanent guests at Priscilla's home in Cambridge! A week after the NBC anniversary show, an FBI man called and said a scrap of refuse in Room 560 in the Statler Hilton had my phone number and LHO* scribbled on it. Then I recalled this was George McMillan's guest room. This gives some idea of the depth to which our security people were searching.

During the period when George and Jeanne were in our guest house, she began drinking excessively and hiding bottles under her mattress. The two of them started grinding on each other's nerves with daily scenes from a Virginia Woolf script. One day I came in when they were verbally at each other's throats and George said, "Well, now I have had it for good and I am leaving," and he headed

---

* Lee Harvey Oswald.

for the door. Jeanne said, "You'd better not, or I will spill the beans," and George stopped in his tracks. I have no idea what this means, but I doubt if it has anything to do with Lee Harvey Oswald.

There was no fun with these uncivil guests, and I was worried about our five daughters. It was quite possible that I might come home one day and find the de Mohrenschildts in physical disarray. And so, when I left for a trip to West Texas, I wrote them a note saying it probably would be best for all of us if they moved out of our guest house. They managed to find another tiny apartment, but Jeanne was furious and started spreading lies about me and falsely claimed that I had cheated a former business partner and lord knows what else. As for me, I preferred to think of the times when George and I were drilling a well down near one of the German communities in Yoakum, Texas. We would buy a steak and a loaf of bread and a tin of frozen strawberries and stop by the road and cook our absolutely delicious dinner. Then George would, from the highway bridge, dive into the solid green of a limestone-tinted river while I tiptoed into the darkness. How we laughed when the drilling crew could not keep their minds on their job when the teen-age daughter of the land-owner where we were drilling the well would come out and practice her cheerleader routine. I also prefer to remember when we went out on a journey towards Jacmel on the south coast of Haiti. George and Jeanne huddled together in the cab of the Land Rover while I spread out some pine cones and then knew that around 3 a.m. she came out and covered me with some of her clothing to keep off the night chill.

I did not hear from them for several years, and then one day here in Santa Fe came a long letter from George. Unfortunately my secretary opened it, and it started out, "I still think you're a rotten, fuckin bastard, but...." During those times George reached the low point of trying to borrow money from some of his former friends, but he was not too successful. He asked Henry Rogatz, former president of the Dallas Geologic Society, for a loan. The two of them had spent many intimate times together in Mexico and at Navajo Mountain. But Henry turned him down, and George almost stumbled in his fury. He never did ask me for financial assistance, but his petitions included requests for money from a former ideological enemy, Ilya Mamontov. A refugee from Latvia, Ilya was a virulent anti-Communist besides being a good geologist at Sun Oil.

Mamontov had become a 110 percent American and had aligned himself with the Republican Party in Dallas. He assisted the campaign of Jack Creighton, who was running against an Abilene drilling contractor named Cox for the Republican nomination for governor. Mamontov tripped on his confused command of English. He was trying to enthuse a gathering of supporters for Jack Creighton. Mamontov highlighted his speech by saying, "This Cox has his testicles spread out." Naturally, the audience roared at Mamontov's confusion with the word tentacles, but Mamontov looked up surprised at the joy of his audience and repeated the expression. Well, the irony is that Mamontov did loan George some money even though the two of them had been opposites on the political spectrum. George's philosophy was "live and let live." Consequently, George was more pro-Soviet status quo and did not align himself with White Russians. His appreciation of the harsh practicalities of life was typically expressed when a statuesque redheaded receptionist at one of the downtown banks, whom we all ogled and knew, asked him for advice regarding an overture from a more-than-middle-aged oil man in the building who wanted her to marry him. George's advice was that she was just a product of the countryside. If she married this oil man, she would only be burdened by him for a decade and a half and in that interval she could improve her education, travel widely, become cultured, and then end up as a wealthy widow—and that is precisely what transpired with this young lady.

The financial pressures drove him to some near-unethical conduct, encouraged by Jeanne, but George swallowed his pride and went along. When George learned that his son was an heir to P. T. Sharples' will, he undertook, through the attorney Patrick, to pressure the noble Sharples for a portion of what would have been his deceased son's estate. There were some threats regarding Dede's lifestyle which would have been a discomfort to her new husband, a respected physician doing commendable research on cystic fibrosis. This friction undoubtedly tore at what was left of George's ethical sensibilities.

While teaching French in the early seventies at the black Bishops College in Arlington, George suffered a nervous breakdown and was hospitalized and given electroshock therapy. Then he and Jeanne were divorced, with George saying he loved her too much and had to regain his independence and sanity. The last I saw him was at the Stoneleigh Hotel in Dallas. I shared a room with my long-time partner Jim Fouts, a very conservative Texas Aggie who was bored silly by George's ramblings and went to sleep while George and I still reminisced about old times. The experience was most disquieting. Most of the time he was his usual lucidly analytical self, but then he would come forth with absurdities and errant guilt feelings. He recalled that he had cheated Morris Jaffe in an oil deal and then claimed the Israeli secret police were trailing him and had him as a target. Jaffe was the senior partner of Angus Wynne's law firm and well knew how to handle an oil deal.

George said a Dutch communist journalist named Oltmans had paid his way to the Netherlands and was prepared to pay George $25,000 if he would sign an affidavit connecting the CIA to Oswald. George sized this up as a homosexual trap that he might not survive if he refused to sign. He managed to escape the hotel suite without his passport or money and then, using all his contacts, worked his way through three weeks to the United States. How much of this was fantasy I do not know, but after George's death a U.S. congressman provided a pulpit for Oltmans. George told me he was tired of being hounded by the press on the Kennedy matter and was thinking of suicide. We spoke about depression as a defined illness. I convinced him to come to Santa Fe where we would hike the Sangres, and a date was set. When he did not show up, I was prepared for the worst. The similarity to Hemingway's final days was inescapable. George called and emphasized his financial distress. Consequently, I put him in touch with Edward Jay Epstein, a reporter for *Readers Digest* and the *Wall Street Journal* and an author who massaged his connection to the CIA counter-intelligence chief Angleton into several books. George was promised a good sum of money, and he went to the Palm Beach estate of the aunt of an ex-wife. Epstein arrived for the interview. I was in Austin at a Railroad Commission Utility rate hearing when a call came from Epstein in Palm Beach, and I knew that the message would be "George excused himself from one of the sessions and shot his brains out with a shotgun."

Congress tried to connect it to the Kennedy affair and so will those attracted to conspiracy, but they are off the target. George was in the mold of Hemingway but much more intelligent, more handsome, less alcoholic, loving to children, and not a brute. Bruce Calder summed it up, "George was bound to end up as he did. He remained a rebellious child who would not submit to the conformity of society. There should be a national fund to take care of the material needs of such people since they add so to the joy of others."

Sometime afterwards Jeanne called, and I visited her humble apartment off of Lovers Lane in Dallas. She was in bad health and was using her few dollars on heart medicines for the sick Manchester, Nero. Besides social security, she was receiving assistance from the attorney Patrick. Jeanne was making glass jewelry, and I bought some rather than offering money. She started to call periodically and then fell into good fortune. A long-time Neiman executive, Gretchen Hartzel, was nursed by Jeanne in her convalescent years and remembered Jeanne in the will. Jeanne then retired to southern California. She recovered her health after a stroke and regained her exciting spirit of old. But I feared that she would fall into the hands of some irresponsible conspiratorial journalist who would play on her passions.

I sent her a draft of this chapter and then called her on the phone during a visit to Los Angeles. Jeanne was inconsolable. She said, "I thought you were the last one to stand by George and now you've surrendered like all the others. How dare you call George a poor geologist. Have you forgotten how we gave you and Ethel our master bedroom in Haiti?" I replied, "Now, Jeanne, unless I report accurately, there will be no credibility to the recitation." She then said, "I never did admire you like George and always suspected you and now you've shown your true colors of deception." Her words shattered me. I did not write another word for a year. She died of a sudden illness in January 1994, without any reconciliation between us. Meanwhile, a journalist in California is assembling illogical pieces of coincidences in an attempt to smear George. He is getting all excited over such trivia as the fact that Jeanne and amateur photographer Zapruder worked together at Nardis in Dallas. And Norman Mailer's recent book on Oswald plays around with unjustified speculations about dear George.

19/ WEST TOWARDS HOME

WILLIE MORRIS, NATIVE OF MISSISSIPPI but campus leader at University of Texas, married one of Austin's beauty queens and then was editor of the ultra-liberal *Texas Observer*. He published *North Toward Home* to explain how he accepted the editorship of *Harpers* and became a Yankee. How times change–he was fired as *Harpers'* editor after he published the "f" word. Over a three-year period it gradually dawned on me that to be true to myself I would have to find my way "West Toward Home." This discomfort with Dallas was gnawing at me even though we were living in absolute luxury in Bluff View on three and a half wooded acres with a guest house, tennis court, and nine tons of air conditioning. It was a distinctive frontier-style home cum heated swimming pool. Most important of all, we had a dozen close friends. There were other places to scuba dive, or rock climb, or ski, but Dallas specialized in warm, genuine friends.

I had hit another home run in the gas business in Fri-Tex Oil & Gas and was afforded the appropriate respect. But my contribution was less than passive. Curtis Fisher was a former vice-president of Houston Natural Gas, now operating as an independent in Corpus Christi. His was the broadest talent in the gas business; he knew every aspect of it. His wife Sammie, named by her father, who had anticipated a son, was a social asset to him. Curtis and I hit it off, and we worked together on several deals with mediocre success. Then we had a chance to buy a gas field southwest of San Antonio. The lion's share was taken by the partners of Fulbright & Jaworski. Our attorney was John Jamison, as shrewd a corporate attorney as I have ever known. Things were going relatively well when Fisher said he would try to get a farmout from Phillips on adjoining acreage. I asked, "How will you ever succeed in that–it's semi-proven acreage?" "Don't worry about me, Sam. I'm going to move up to Bartlesville for a couple of months at our company's expense." Incredibly, he returned with an enticing farmout of the Phillips acreage. I was called down to a special board meeting in Houston. Present were two strangers. When I asked, "Who are they?" I was told, "She is the wife of the manager of the gas

181

department of Phillips, and he is her accountant and we are going to sell him a block of cheap treasury stock." I was dumbfounded. Here were these top-flight respected attorneys while I was young at this game. I announced I had to go to the men's room and would return after this resolution was voted on. Jamison worked out a plan to borrow all the development drilling capital plus some, so we donated the excess money to Rice University. Naturally the deal was a huge success. Frio-Tex Oil & Gas was then sold to Suburban Propane Gas.

The effects of male menopause probably made me receptive to the intrusion of four influences arguing for change of scenery. For the first, Ethel never really became a Dallas girl. Her hands were full with our five daughters so she never engaged in the routine of beauty parlor, luncheon club, tennis at the Dallas Athletic Club, and then bridge or Temple Emmanuel Sisterhood. She had a handful of good girlfriends who were not the type to grace the pages of *D* magazine. She did not champion enrollment at Hockaday for our daughters, rather Greenhill was her selection as our girls came of age. Ethel was ready to consider relocation to a less-elegant community.

For the second, we were accumulating quite a library of maps and papers on the Navajo Country and were scooting out there with regularity as if it were around the corner. The *Dallas Morning News* ran several articles on our "exotic" trips to Navajo Country. To my shame, I sneaked around a corner when some primitive Navajos came looking for me at my Southland Center office. I really was not the sort to just accumulate wealth or let comfort be the centerpiece of our life. Instead, I was attracted to some stark change of lifestyle, which my modest capital would now make possible.

For the third, co-investor Gary Morrison felt it was simply a case of slowing down. His interpretation was that I had started that process in the move from New York to Dallas and now that the pace was quickening in Dallas, I was looking for a quieter landscape. Whether he was right or not, incipient traffic jams on Central Expressway and Loop 12 did portend that Dallas had adopted growth as its god and I wanted to be free of that rat race.

For the fourth, I started to feel troubled that the Dallas Petroleum Club would not admit Jews. This must embody a foulness of deeper significance in the city's climate. I was a member of the Ft. Worth Petroleum Club, courtesy of the outspoken Park Weaver. He was the rare investor to openly disagree with Amon Carter. It was known that when the Houston Petroleum Club expanded to the Exxon Building with a gentleman's agreement not to admit Jews, Bob Smith told them to include him out and the bigots backed down. That voice of decency was not heard in Dallas.

It so happened that there was an admirable group of Jewish oil attorneys in Dallas as well as Jewish geologists and Jewish petroleum engineers and Jewish promoters and only two or three for whom we had to apologize. So I scheduled a luncheon at the Chaparral Club of about fifteen of these esteemed fellows. I said, "Now, like you, I don't really care to enter the Petroleum Club, but we have a responsibility to our children not to tolerate such archaic prejudice. The Insurance Club has no such barriers, nor does the Bar Association. We should in a dignified way bring this to the attention of Herb Hunt, who is president of the Petroleum Club, and Bobby Stewart, president of the First National Bank, who is their landlord." Well, I got only lukewarm support from one attendee. All the others said life was fine for them and this exclusion policy did not spoil their days. I was troubled deeply by this acquiescence to a golden ghetto. I wrote to Herb Hunt, who replied, "Sam, a reactionary is head of the Admission Committee. I cannot do anything, although I agree with you." I also wrote to Bob Stewart, who said a tenant's policies did not concern him, although he agreed with me. These two men were at the very apex of Dallas commercial and social establishments. What irony that both fell so precipitously on hard times and were knocked from their perches during the eighties.

In 1967 we rented a truck home and the entire family took a leisurely six-week swing through the Midwest and into Canada to Expo at Montreal, then through New England and down to Washington and back to Dallas. It was good that I carried my .22 rifle—we had to spend the night in a District of Columbia ghetto park and another night on 8th Avenue in Manhattan. We visited over twenty friends in different cities and had a grand time. But by the time we returned, we knew Dallas was not our home even though our final resting place would be there, alongside Nina. For Easter 1968 we went to Santa Fe on a spring skiing trip, stayed at La Posada, and then stopped at Fort Sumner for breakfast on the drive home. I explained to everyone that there would be a closed vote on whether or not to move to Santa Fe—and the voters would include six year-old Marta. Seven pieces of paper were passed out with a yes-or-no ballot space. When they were unfolded, there were seven yes votes to move to Santa Fe. Its physical beauty and small-town serenity had conquered us all. It would not be easy to leave Dallas. We appreciated what Charles Mayer, the father of the proprietor of St. Bernard at Taos Ski Valley, after arriving from France and opening a restaurant in Red River said, "It didn't take but 45 days and I realized there were two kinds of people here. There were Americans and there were Texans."

In 1968 the only franchise food outlet in Santa Fe was KIPS. There was no Hilton, no Inn at Loretto, no Eldorado, no Picacho Plaza, no Quail Run, and of course, no bed and breakfasts. The renovated and reconstituted Rancho Encantado opened that year. A good eatery on Cerrillos and St. Francis was El Comedor, whose welcoming sign read "We don't care how they do it in Texas." Walt Keesing and Mark McAuliffe were the dominant realtors, but fewer than six homes were advertised in the classifieds. The only modern apartments were in the recently completed Casa Loma complex. An ingenious Texan from the Panhandle, Hubert Hatch, had conceived of this project and promoted it 98 percent to the finish line through the FHA. He then could not reach home plate so it passed to the Greers after foreclosure.

The prime restaurant was the Compound on Canyon Road but Victor Sagheer was the maitre d' then rather than the owner as he is now. The Nirvana, also on Canyon, was the admired international cuisinery with chilled salad forks. It closed after the proprietor's wife was killed in an auto crash. The Gates of Spain formal restaurant at La Fonda, where now sits the Carriage House, scheduled every Wednesday a popular style show by Suzette. After the quality of food and service declined under my inexperienced, amateurish leadership the style shows were abandoned. There were no shopping malls in Santa Fe, no copies of the *New York Times*, no taxis, no buses. The postal cars drove into the driveway rather than up to the street-side mailbox. The Sangre de Cristo Tennis Club was just getting started. The Downs did not exist nor the big poma and certainly not the triple chair to the 12,000-foot level at the ski basin. The primitive, unpaved ski road without drop-off barriers had its quota of car and bus turnovers but miraculously without injuries. Ruth Leakey's *La Tourista* was the only subscription-free weekly; the avalanche of imitators did not come until later. The artist community included Giuseppe Olmi, whose latest wife, Winnie Beasley, rode a side-car motorcycle. Bull snakes had the run of her large house on Bishops Lodge Road. This was before Olmi wintered each year at Guymas, where his first order of business was to locate a "donna tutta fare." Jean Seth had a going gallery on Canyon Road, but Margaret Jamison in her gentle way quietly promoted Western art across from La Fonda. The heavy merchandising of Forrest Fenn or Elaine Horowitz were not yet part of the scene. Instead, Pansy Stockton, with her scenes of natural materials, was held in high esteem despite rumors that her husband had fried to his death while taking a roof-top nap after too much libation.

In those days before East and West Coast waves of newcomers, Texans were the locals' whipping boys. Three months after our change of domicile, our five native Dallasites in unison said "damn Texas" when a Cadillac bearing a tag from the Lone Star State was tardy in moving after getting a green light on the Old Santa Fe Trail. They had forgotten that Ian Fleming said, "During World War II I met many fine Yanks and most of them turned out to be Texans."

Our family settled into two apartments at opposite ends of the second floor at the Casa Loma complex while Mark McAuliffe tried to find us a home. Former Governor Dempsey's widow in Idaho offered her home on Circle Drive for $80,000, but it needed lots of repair and we knew we had to construct another two bedrooms. When I asked her Indian caretaker if a path through the junipers marked the city water line Governor Dempsey had engineered up to his acreage, he said, "No, dat's where we Indians sneak into Santa Fe and scalp dem Spanish priests and run dem out of town." As Mark and I retreated, we didn't know whether he was having a good laugh at our expense or this was oral history about the 1680 pueblo revolt. In any case, the widow was insulted when I counter bid $75,000 and she took the house and its five acres off the market.

One evening at 9 p.m. we walked down to the other apartment to say goodnight to our girls only to find that all five were out on the street. We redoubled our efforts to find a home. That weekend the *New Mexican* front-paged the death of Mrs. Peabody, a unique local eccentric. She had worked alongside her highway contractor husband from El Paso, and when they retired, they built their dream house in 1935 with John Gaw Meem as architect on six piniomed acres only two miles from the plaza. Within a year Mr. Peabody had died, and Mrs. Peabody spent the next thirty-three years as a widow, shooting a BB gun at "trespassers" across her cattle guard. Her gardener-chauffeur, Jimmie Gonzales, drove her to shopping and kept clear of the ruts of the real old Santa Fe wagon trail running through the front yard. Since the living room fireplace smoked against the second-story bedroom suite, she had some workmen extend the chimney ten feet higher. Meem protested the inappropriate contour so she discharged this most famous of New Mexico architects.

I immediately called Ruth Leakey and said we would buy the

Peabody place. Ruth replied, "Stan Brumlap is the executor, and they have not yet set the price." "Well, get a price because we will buy it." So a week later we met with A.K. Montgomery and Brumlap, who represented the estate, and finally Brumlap got up enough courage and said $95,000. I said, "OK, we'll buy it." Then Brumlap felt bad because he suspected he could have said more. On January 1, 1970, we had a party with 100 guests plus the *de rigueur* mariachi band. Mrs. Garland of Swan Lake Ranch told us she was available if we needed a decorator, and when we were introduced to Mrs. Moses, that well-groomed lady extended her hand and announced "Kennecott Copper Moses."

But Marc McAuliffe was not left to hang out and dry. In June 1968 he mentioned that Walt Keesing had been referred the sale of La Fonda by the Santa Fe Railroad through a broker who had an oral offering. It was soon apparent that Van Scoggins in Las Cruces was a true-blue, honest motel broker who would not be manhandled by the Santa Fe Railroad. Elemental research showed that this world-famous Western hostelry where presidents and movie stars had registered was in a state of sad neglect. It had been offered to numerous hotel chains all across the country. They had backed off because it was an old property and in the core of a city. It also had another year to run on a lease to Fred Harvey. ELSI was then coining money, and I convinced our directors that the purchase of La Fonda would be a contribution to society and that buying it was a good gamble even though we were amateurs. I suspected that the lore of the West and the Indians would become ever more popular and La Fonda could not be separated from the two. For four months we poured over historical data on the hotel but could not make up our minds until mid-November 1968. The president of the Santa Fe Land Improvement Company called and said they had another interested party but would give me one week to firm up a proposal. We signed a contract to buy the hotel for $150,000 cash with the seller keeping a one year $1,250,000 first mortgage. Our obligation was to spend $250,000 the first year on improvements. As commission we gave Scoggins, Keesing, and McAuliffe 5 percent of our common stock. So in the same fortnight of December 1968 we bought our home at 1020 Old Santa Fe Trail and La Fonda at 100 East San Francisco Street, not knowing that our immediate neighbors to the north were Stewart and Laura Harvey of the Fred Harvey family, with their two tennis courts.

But on December 8, 1968, when we closed the La Fonda deal in the office of Bill Federici, I pulled a smart-ass stunt that still has me blushing. The very decent railroad executive Jim Scott signed the deed, and I direct-dialed the Republic National Bank in Dallas to release our $150,000 cashier's check to the Santa Fe's messenger. Federici then sent his runner to the courthouse to record the deed. Much relieved, Scott put on his winter overcoat and headed for the door. Before he reached it, I asked, "How do you know I was actually speaking to the Republic Bank?" With a frightened start, Scott pulled off his coat, prepared to stay, but satisfied himself after a telephone call to Dallas. Well, I guess I was still growing up and had a ways to go.

20/ EARLIEST MANAGERS

Since everyone in Santa Fe back in the '60s felt that by birthright they owned a piece of La Fonda, I wanted to make the board of directors exclusively Santa Feans, but I included my long time associate from Monroe, Louisiana. Each initial director purchased 100 shares of stock at $5 per share, and the group included Bud Kelly, Jimmy Russell, Ralph Lopez, Peter Price, Bill Vance, Leonard Valdes, Joan Greer, Tim Skinner, Gene Petchesky, and Eugene Zacher. Over twenty-seven years, each dropped by the wayside with the exception of the Louisianan Jim Fouts and Russell. Richard Weigle, the president of St. Johns College in Santa Fe, was puzzled and maybe a bit put out that we had selected his administrative aide, Peter Price, but I wanted a young person to be on the board. John Gaw Meem was made honorary chairman of the board. However, he visited me one day and said his attorneys advised against his membership. When he handed me his letter of resignation I said, "Well, we will respect that, but this causes me a problem." He asked, "What is that?" I replied, "Our prospectus for our convertible debentures has just arrived from the printers, and you are listed with your title." On hearing that, Mr. Meem pulled back his letter of resignation and tore it up.

Bill Harvey, the grandson of Fred Harvey, was then acting as general manager of La Fonda. He was an affable young man, married to a beautiful socialite, Linda, from Chicago. Together with their two children and their maid, they were living in the second-floor manager's suite, now occupied by our executive office and our accounting office. Bill Harvey was an endearing host and pretty much liked by everyone. The board suggested that we offer the General Managership of the hotel to Bill Harvey, so I invited him over to my offices at Sena Plaza, little anticipating what erupted.

Bill came in rather fidgety. When I told him it was my keen pleasure to report that our board of directors wanted him to continue as general manager, he could not control his rage and screamed that we were a bunch of idiots to think that he would work for us and that there were several members of our board of directors for whom he

189

would never lift his little finger. He was almost foaming at the mouth; the noise level was so high that my colleagues in the two adjoining offices rushed in to see what the trouble was. I was fully expecting him to lose control and call Valdes a spic and me a dirty Jew, but such vituperation never surfaced. After he barged out, I was stunned and fearful. We were newcomers to the city and obviously had an enemy in one of the most important families in town. I then decided on a course of action that proved effective. A strictly confidential letter was sent to each of our directors reporting almost verbatim what Bill Harvey had said. Within thirty hours all of Santa Fe's establishment knew of this conversation, which registered with a reverse twist in the recitation. Each one of the local directors felt he himself was the target of Bill's abuse. The esteem in which the community held Bill dropped like a lead bullet.

Many years later I found out what this was all about. At the time that we were negotiating with the Santa Fe Railroad to buy La Fonda, Bill Harvey, backed by George Dapples, was making his own unsuccessful bid to the Santa Fe Railroad. About a year before George Dapples died of cancer, he told me that he was nonplussed when he read our prospectus on convertible debentures, since he was offering the Santa Fe Railroad six high figures more than our proposition. Eugene Zacher said Dapples, who was related to the Nestle people in Switzerland, was the finest courtroom attorney in Chicago and someone who had to be believed. Assuming that Dapples' story about his bid was accurate, then the only explanation of the rejection of his bid is that the Santa Fe Railroad brass, who officed two floors below the Fred Harvey executives in Chicago, had had their fill of family interference and did not want any further dealings with the Harveys. This is pure speculation on my part, and there may be other explanations to which I'm not privy. Dapples and I both belonged to a men's club, Quien Sabe. With his doctor, he attended his last meeting before he succumbed to cancer and joked to all of us that this probably was the last time we would have to put up with him. This turned out to be true.

Dapples once appeared before a Chicago judge to argue a simple motion. After the judge had unexpectedly ruled for opposing counsel, Dapples walked dejectedly to the rear of a large elevator. When the judge and the opposing attorney entered the front of the elevator, Dapples saw the attorney reach into his coat pocket and hand an envelope to the judge. When Dapples exited, he just said to the judge, "You filthy son of a bitch." Dapples had a wonderfully humorous attitude towards life and respected most people, although he was as deep an anti-black bigot as I've ever run across. As a submarine commander, he took Mrs. Douglas MacArthur and her son from Corregidor to Australia together with a footlocker holding $1,000,000 in U.S. dollars as a present to the general from the Philippines.

After we bought the hotel, the Fred Harvey organization replaced Bill Harvey with a temporary resident manager. (Incidentally, the corporate name was Fred Harvey, not Fred Harvey Inc. or Fred Harvey Ltd.) Bill Harvey and his wife opened a catering service out on St. Francis Drive. During their first year of operation they took the Cattlemen's Convention from us, and then Bill expanded to a public restaurant where he and Linda worked like dogs. Alas, Bill took to drink, and his wife's eyes roved elsewhere. I played tennis with Bill one afternoon on their homestead adjacent to our residence, and the flaw within Bill Harvey was immediately apparent. Even though as a youngster he had been tutored by Bill Tilden, he had *no* inner confidence in himself and offered no rough-and-tumble competition. To everyone's sorrow, he fatally shot himself. I felt particularly bad because two days beforehand he came up to my office with some weight obviously on his shoulders, but it remained hidden and I couldn't offer him what was needed. His father, Stewart, fifteen years later, after an extravagant eightieth outdoor birthday party, also ended his life with the same revolver.

Everyone was telling me that Amy Meadows, executive secretary at La Fonda, was the person who really ran the hotel and had covered for many specious Fred Harvey general managers. We invited Amy to lunch at the Palace and sought to recruit her as executive secretary. In those days no one would think of offering a general managership to a woman. Meadows politely declined, saying she would continue with Fred Harvey at the Grand Canyon to secure her retirement. That is what she did and then retired to Moriarty, south of I-40, where she died. Incidentally, as far as I know, Amy Meadows is the only person at La Fonda that Fred Harvey protected with any form whatsoever of retirement benefits even though many hotel employees had more than thirty years of service.

La Fonda also had a competent stores manager named Art Cantu. When we tried to hire him, he also declined and went with the Fred Harvey organization down to the Alvarado in Albuquerque. He ended up as a stores manager at the Amfax Hotel. To the chagrin of most New Mexicans, the Alvarado was torn down to make room for a parking lot next to the railroad tracks in Albuquerque. Unlike the superb construction elements of La Fonda, the Alvarado's basic structure was wood, and physical deterioration had occurred. Ralph Lopez mentioned that George Beach, then the general manager at the Alvarado, wanted to apply for the job. Lopez had heard good things about Beach, so youthful Beach came on board as general manager. He moved into the suite vacated by Bill Harvey and his family. The property was still under lease to Fred Harvey, but we gave them notice of termination effective after Labor Day 1969. I was not then sufficiently alert to the fact that the profitable season at the hotel ran from June through September and that all the other months had varying degrees of red figures. The lease required that Fred Harvey properly maintain the premises, which they unashamedly failed to do. They even bypassed some deficient electric junction boxes and in one case used a copper penny instead of a fuse. In the kitchen, removal of the plywood covering of one of the leaking sinks revealed that the sink was not connected to any drain at all! I wanted to take legal action against them because we had put them on notice of their failure to live up to their maintenance responsibilities. But attorney Bill Federici argued against it and told me I was too new in town to lock horns with such a respected family, long resident to Santa Fe. I followed Federici's advice. He was probably right—our energies were needed elsewhere. But it was a hard pill to swallow.

George Beach brought up from the Alvarado a good detail man, Arthur Terry, as his assistant manager at La Fonda. Terry's girlfriend was another Fred Harvey lady, and almost senior enough to be Terry's mother. The transfer from Fred Harvey was an unpleasant combat between Beach, Terry, and the Fred Harvey people. Fred Harvey inventoried half-bottles of opened coke and potatoes on the grill. I had to keep fists from flying. We were chumps to buy their old food inventory and never received a note of thanks from them. Beach did a good job of the transition and had a fine feel for the restaurant and lounge. My associate, Tom Ashton, got involved in a potential *menage a trois* with George Beach and influenced me to terminate his employment. Ashton was a very bright young man with a bachelor's degree in geological engineering and an MBA degree. He possessed a youthful devotion to intellectual honesty, which had to be admired. He made many recommendations that I, unfortunately, failed to adopt. I think it fair to say that on two such recommendations we would have been millions of dollars ahead and I would now have fewer lines on my face. But this recommendation on George Beach, which I did follow, did not prove to be a good one. Eugene Zacher tried to discourage me from releasing Beach. He said something like "boys will be boys" and "don't I remember when I was younger," but I was bull-headed and the tension of this new challenge was getting to me so I acquiesced to Ashton's wishes and thereby lost the valuable services of Beach.

Harold Bibo, who was then leaving as state personnel director under Governor Jack Campbell, moved into the general managership. Harold was like a lovable puppy dog and a native New Mexican. His grandfather produced 18 children with an hispanic wife from Hatch. He was one of five Bavarian Jewish-New Mexican peddlers, one of whom married the daughter of the Indian Cacique at Acoma and became governor of the Pueblo. Harold had been deputy to General Patton during World War II and was a good and reliable boy scout in every wholesome sense of the word. He had several marriages, the last one being to a winsome lady from central Texas. She was extremely well endowed, and short Harold just about reached up to her prominence. Before Harold died of cancer he told me that he understood that he was Jewish but didn't know what that meant. I lamely said to him, "Jews are like other people only more so." One June a dowager from Boston called Harold to reserve a suite in July. She was going to introduce her grandson to the Southwest and wanted a fire in the fireplace and an Indian sitting in the parlor when she entered the suite. That is exactly what Harold arranged. But one day Harold came to me and said that this job of trying to rebuild La Fonda was too much for him and he wasn't able to sleep at night. He told me I had better look for a more experienced manager. In the seventies, Jim, Harold's son from an early marriage, showed up and opened the gourmet SantaCafe. Jim never knew Harold; he was raised by his mother in Houston after an ugly divorce. It was my pleasure to tell Jim what a great guy his father was. "Gee, mother never said that." But before he left, Bibo saved us from a mishap.

New Mexico had a unique Republican governor, an attorney from Michigan who was married to an appealing Spanish lady from Villanueva. Dave Olmsted told me that after a first-year review of Cargo's performance at a top-line Albuquerque law firm, the senior partner groaned that Dave Cargo really hadn't accomplished anything. In response, Cargo commented that he came to New Mexico to become governor, not to practice law. The senior partner just laughed and laughed, but lonesome Dave had the last laugh.

He had attended a meeting of the Republican Governors' Conference, a structured organization that met quarterly in different states. Governor Cargo had volunteered Santa Fe for the next meeting, and no place was even remotely available but La Fonda. Bibo worked day and night to try to make the rooms presentable, but even our newly installed air conditioning was not operable, and the mattresses were lacking structure. Bibo told me we needed financial guarantees. When I disputed, saying the governor was signing for everything, Bibo said, "I wouldn't rely on his guarantee for a moist enchilada." When Bibo convinced me he was serious, I made a couple of phone calls and learned our flanks were exposed. We demanded a responsible guarantee other than that of the governor. Tim Skinner, a member of our board and president of the First National Bank, protested, "You're not seeing the forest for the trees–this will put Santa Fe on the map." I said, "Let the First National Bank be an underwriter and we'll see both the forest and the trees." Skinner resigned from our board. Four days before the conference was to open I issued an ultimatum–no guarantee, no conference. The governor's secretary called me to object with a marine's vocabulary. But she learned I was serious. So the governor's office approached R.O. Anderson, the lone Republican on the National Committee from New Mexico. "What? You haven't arranged for the conference financing?...[expletives deleted]." Anderson really had no choice; he sent us a telegram committing as underwriter.

It now became a Mack Sennett comedy. The executive director of the Republican Governors' Conference moved into the hotel and announced that he and his staff would take over reservations. He was obnoxious to everyone. When a chap appeared at the front desk and said he was President Nixon's advance man in case the president showed up, the desk sent him to a guest room and immediately called the executive director, who fumed that no one could come into the hotel without his clearance and we should evict this guest. After he refused to leave, the police were called. He pleaded with them to use his secret phone number to call the White House. Yes, the next day it was confirmed that he was Nixon's man!

The opening day of the conference coincided with the Kent State massacre. At 2 p.m. Governor Scranton of Pennsylvania cancelled the conference so the governors could return to their states, where protesting college campuses were rioting. R.O. Anderson's man asked how much money we were out. I replied, "Forty thousand dollars of labor plus lost revenues of perhaps thirty thousand." He said, "Well, this is an emergency. Will you accept ten thousand dollars?" Since it was such a unique disaster for the entire country, we consented and pocketed a check from Arco's governmental affairs division.

These events, together with what subsequently happened at the governor's prayer breakfast, brought about the collapse of Cargo's career with the Republicans. Each year before the New Mexico state legislature met, it was *de rigueur* for the governor to host a prayer breakfast at La Fonda. That year it coincided with some dispute La Fonda was having with the powerful Carpenters Union, which insisted that we had to use union carpenters to rebuild the hotel. We had no financial alternative but to "poor boy" the operation by using our maintenance men, then part of the Hotel & Restaurant Workers Union, to do this work. The morning of the prayer breakfast the Carpenters Union planted some women pickets outside the entryway, making it appear they were La Fonda employees. I called Jack Byer, the union representative, at 6 a.m. and said we expected our staff to appear for work. Every one of our employees crossed the picket line and came to work! The legislators gulped and then crossed the picket line and went into the New Mexico Room for breakfast. With newspaper photographers crowding the sidewalk, along came Governor Cargo who stopped, said he would not disrespect organized labor, and did not attend his own breakfast. You can imagine how his invitees felt.

One of my associates, Bill Hudson, from Dallas told me about a highly skilled man he had met in Acapulco, a Swiss named Edward Walther, who had all forms of appropriate Swiss training in the hotel industry. Walther was tall and macho, with a distinctive profile. On the day he came for an interview, Ethel and I went out horseback riding with him in the Pojoaque hillsides. He was manifestly in control of every step taken by that horse. The fruit on one of our apple trees was then ready to be harvested so Ethel asked Walther if he could help us, considering how tall Walther was. He stood on that ladder for two hours and when he was finished there was not the tiniest apple still connected. And so Walther came on board at La Fonda. It was almost immediately apparent that there were strong pluses and strong minuses. He told our staff, "With Swiss know-how and Mexican labor we will get this job done." A month before the Christmas season he dismantled our fifth floor rooms and, together with American Furniture's decorator, Dick Werthen, pushed our housekeepers and maintenance people to get the rooms reassembled in time for the holiday rush. He hired some carpenters from the state penitentiary's work release program to redo our front desk, which they did most elegantly. He found Antonio Mendoza, the guitarist who appeared in the opening scenes of *Easy Rider*, and put together a tremendous group of musicians in our La Fiesta Bar. Mendoza was then in his prime, and the jam sessions in our bar were memorable.

But I gradually became very concerned. Walther was about to sign an open-ended contract with IBM to develop a hotel computer program with no time or dollar limits. This would have paralyzed us, but I was able to veto it in time. Walther's resume showed he had worked for a Dallas hotel group that owned the Westward Ho in Phoenix and a resort in Nassau. The group's president, John Mills, confided, "Walther is a bundle of creative energy. He is not immoral, he is amoral." About this same time small packages were coming to my post office box addressed to Walther from Tangiers, Hong King, Lima, and Beirut. I wondered what the contents were. I wanted to open one of them, but Federici said I couldn't. After a dinner party at our house, Olmsted's Swiss wife said to me, "I don't know the background of this Walther, but I assure you he is no Swiss."

Walther had hired a lady from the state government as head bookkeeper. One day I noticed that a checks-issued list omitted one numbered check. When I inquired of the bookkeeper as to the reason for the omission, she turned white and said she was following instructions from Walther. The check was to a local CPA, C.R. Sebastian, who had made a secret audit whose results highlighted substantial loss of revenues and who had questioned management's honesty. Neither Sebastian nor Walther realized that there was a reverse entry on the cancellation of the Republican Governors' Conference. At the same time, Walther missed a payment on our first mortgage and Bill Hudson volunteered to supply the funds! When we discovered that Walther and Hudson had planned a Palace insurrection to gain control of the hotel, we fired Walther and bought out Hudson's stock. The next month a bill came in from the Pinkerton Agency in Denver. Pinkerton had been hired to run an investigation and get the goods on someone named Sam Ballen!

But like every other manager, save a Fred Harvey lady from Albuquerque, Walther did leave many positive accomplishments. Our front desk and lobby chairs were originally carved by Ben R. Lujan but looked seedy. Walther arranged for some work-release carpenters from the State Penitentiary to restore them by removing layers of shellac, and they did a superb job. When I tried to advise Walther on some strategy, he replied, "What do you know about it?" He was correct.

21/ CHAPTER 11?

UNDER WALTHER'S STEWARDSHIP, we were receiving daily reports about four days late from La Fonda's bookkeeper and were still several months behind in monthly financial statements. Fearing the worst, I called in an accountant friend from Dallas. He stayed here two weeks and told me the books were in such atrocious shape that it was impossible to tell whether there was just unskilled accounting or embezzlement. In any event our accounts payable to tradesmen exceeded $400,000. I learned that the most skilled hotel accountant in the state resided in Albuquerque. His wife was a senior executive in the Albuquerque Public School System. We paid him a premium salary to leave his family and move up to the hotel to get the accounts in passable condition. I told Ethel early in 1970 that this was going to be the toughest business battle we had ever faced and that we would have to tighten our belts at a time when the girls would start to go off to college. However, I felt we would be able to succeed provided we retained our physical health. Without hesitation, Ethel said she would stick with me and to go ahead. In a dark moment, Laura Harvey, Stewart's wife, also told me to stick with it—"It will work out."

I reported the situation to our directors and to a special meeting of shareholders. Bill Vance, who was the president of Eberline Instruments here in Santa Fe, felt that my supervision had not been businesslike, and undoubtedly he was correct. He tendered his resignation from the board and we purchased his stock. A letter sent to all our suppliers stated that they would have to be patient for 75 days and gave our guarantee to them that they would be paid. The only ones who gave us trouble were the liquor companies, who stated that state regulations required they be paid promptly, and Big Jo Lumber, whose management read us the riot act. Naturally, we never forgot that. The largest creditor was American Furniture. Mr. Blaugrund from Albuquerque called and said he would work with us but that we shouldn't abuse him excessively.

A copy of this letter went to the First National Bank of Santa Fe which held a note for about $150,000. Ed Tatum, the president, called me for lunch. He was a scholarly, dignified, pipe-smoking gentleman who had been a professorial historian. In any event, he was not among the contemporary breed of hard-nosed commercial bankers. Toward the end of the lunch he said, "We will require your personal guarantee on this corporate note." I said, "Well, Ed, the note is not yet due for maturity. Why this fuss?" "Sam, you know that the note form has a discomfort clause, and we now do feel discomfort and are going to call the note unless you give it your personal guarantee." I then said, "I don't appreciate your attitude. I have done more than anybody to save downtown Santa Fe from becoming a ghost town like so many other cities. I have saved La Fonda from becoming a parking lot, and the cooperation that I have gotten from your bank is really minimal. I am not going to give you a personal guarantee. Your note is not in jeopardy. Let's stop this kindergarten stuff."

Well, we finished the lunch, but as we got up to leave, Tatum said, "I will be calling my attorneys to accelerate this note as soon as I get back to the office." I replied, "Well, Ed, you might as well also notify your attorneys to defend you." "What has the bank done which is improper?" "Oh, I will think of something." They never did call the note or file anything against us.

I could not blame Bud Kelly, who was a director of both institutions, for resigning from La Fonda's board, and I hope that he did not blame me for moving all of our insurance from his firm to James Russell, who stood by us stoutly all through those times. Shortly thereafter, I had a call from Nathan Greer, who was on the board of the First National Bank. The Greers were very prominent citizens in Santa Fe, their antecedents being immigrants from Lebanon, like so many other successful New Mexican families. They owned much downtown property. Nathan had made a splash when he arrived at Harvard with several polo ponies. Joe Downer, who had worked for me in Dallas and had been a classmate of Nathan's, told me that the Greers were okay people but that I should never ever borrow money from them. Nathan expressed his interest in buying the hotel, but I knew it would be for pennies on the dollar and politely terminated the discussion. Previously, I had seen how they had acquired control of the Casa Loma Apartments, when a poorly financed promoter from Amarillo carried that project 98 percent of the way to completion and then was unable to meet some final minuscule requirements of the FHA. It was a bargain for the Greers, who still own the property today.

Naturally, word got out of the great difficulties we were in. One financier from Houston came up and said that I should contact him just before I was ready to go under. There were days at that time when the entire La Fonda–food and beverage and rooms–did not gross $800 per day. I described the situation to our attorney, Bill Federici. I told him that I thought we would win this battle but that I had to know the alternatives and was not familiar with New Mexico law. He took me down to Albuquerque where we counseled with a bankruptcy attorney. I then learned, to my dismay, that there were no strong homestead provisions as there were in Texas. But our liquor-dispensing Bell Tower, designed by Erwin Parson, became more and more popular.

In fact, every downtown hotel in Santa Fe has gone through some form of bankruptcy except La Fonda. The powerful Schifanis of Albuquerque could not make a go of the Hilton and had to sell it to some oil people from East Texas. The Lubbock investors who had promoted and built the Sheraton went through practical bankruptcy and disposed of it to some people from Arkansas. Even the excellent Kirkpatrick family from Tulsa had difficulties with the Inn at Loretto and had to undergo a reorganization with their first-mortgage lender. The same was true of La Posada, whose management had to call in additional private capital from California.

So during the next several years I acted as general manager. I was ably supported by Ruffenacht, an Italian Swiss who was in charge of Food & Beverage and by a shrewd buxom blond who had moved into the property with her son and was in charge of the front desk.

We drove our maintenance people very hard. We used them as plasterers, carpenters, and electricians as we went about rebuilding the hotel. In order to discourage the hiring of additional staff, I instituted a procedure in which three different forms had to be filled out every time an employee was hired. This had the desired effect of keeping labor costs down. We also went on a search throughout the storeroom and found two removable grills from which goods secreted in basement crawl spaces could be brought out to Water Street.

Ruffenacht was a professional and had seen service in most of the world. When I complained to him about inventory shrinkage, he laughed and said, "You have dumb crooks here. In Miami, they have smart crooks." Ruffenacht was a loyal employee, and an excellent chef, but his sentimental temperament got the better of him. One Saturday I walked into the hotel and instantly knew that something was wrong when I saw Ruffenacht sitting on a barstool. He obviously had consumed more than a couple of drinks. Bud Kelly came over and pleaded for assistance. I asked, "What's the trouble?" He sputtered, "Well, as you know, old Tom Olds' son is marrying that socialite ranching girl from Chama in the Santa Fe Room. Ruffenacht refuses to put a piano on the second floor of the balcony, and the minister is ready to start the wedding." I went over to Ruffenacht, who exploded like a pressure cooker, "Who do these yokels think they are? They didn't ask for a piano when we made arrangements for this function, so what makes them think they can ask for it at the last minute? I absolutely refuse to put a piano on the second floor. It is they who are the peasants, not me."

I finally worked out a compromise in which the best man and the ushers would carry the piano to the balcony. Ruffenacht agreed to this arrangement. Alas, the marriage did not last, and subsequently the groom was killed on a motorcycle. Old Tom Olds went down into the Arctic Ocean off of Alaska and was never found. On another occasion, for a bridge tournament in the New Mexico Room, Ruffenacht had made arrangements for late sandwiches to be available for $2 each. When the widow of Judge Watson came up to protest the poor condition of the sandwiches, I grabbed hold of Ruffenacht to hear her complaint. He was in no mood for that and screamed at her, "People like you do not deserve the fine treatment of La Fonda. You should go down to Denny's. They are accustomed to handle guests like you." Well, of course Ruffenacht did not survive at La Fonda. The final blow was when I sent him a note after seeing a high food cost on the daily report. I wrote, "You can't win for losing." He screamed to his wife over the phone to pack up that they were leaving within the hour.

Pat Goulden, our front desk manager, knew her business completely. She would come down in a robe each night about 10 and assess the vacancies of the house and make appropriate arrangements for selling additional rooms at the prices that she had in mind. She ran her department like a watchmaker. But she also had a sixth sense about guests, and this was before the advent of credit cards, which now enable the merchant to determine a customer's worthiness on the spot. Pat would look at a guest, and look at his check, and determine instantly what to do. Sometimes she would say that was not going to be any good. A call to his bank would invariably reveal she was right. She also would look at a guest and then tell our bellmen, "Go out to the parking lot (then open air) and get his license plate. He is going to skip." Invariably she would be correct. Once, however, a lady checked into the hotel and skipped. When Pat traced her to Española and called on the telephone, a man answered, "What? My wife has spent the night at La Fonda?"

The Albuquerque accountant stayed with us for a year, during which he got our books into excellent shape, but then he wanted to return to his family. About a month after he left, our replacement hotel accountant, Patricia Gallegos Davis, a long-time Fred Harvey front desk clerk, came to me and said that she could not find where a $300 insurance refund had been posted to the accounts. When I called W.S. he said he would be up to see me the next day. He sat down and said, "Well, I just pocketed that claims check. It was stupid of me, but we were leaving for a family holiday in Hawaii and I needed some extra pocket money, and that's what I did." He had been the highest paid hotel accountant in the state, and I was dumbfounded. "What else did you take?" "Nothing else, Mr. Ballen. That was my only inexplicable failure of judgement." "Will you take a lie detector test?" When he agreed to do so, I went to the chief of police, who referred me to a polygraph organization in Albuquerque, and arranged to have the accountant tested. After a week the polygraph outfit called and said he tested just fine and they would be sending me a report together with a statement of services. After three weeks, when I had received neither, I called again. They apologized for some administrative delay, which they said would be corrected immediately. A month later I called them again and said we had received neither the polygraph report nor a statement of services. Again, they apologized and said both would be forthcoming, but I never received them. We had other areas of concern so the matter was not pursued. Somehow, the accountant apparently had gotten to that agency.

It was about this time that our union contract came up for renewal. It had been inherited from Fred Harvey, and La Fonda was the only establishment in Santa Fe that had a union contract with the Hotel & Restaurant Workers Union. I requested twenty-six changes in our favor. The union agent said that the employees would accept five but wanted another two changes in their favor. I stood by our position, saying that La Fonda was operating in the red and the only chance it had of success was to give not an inch of concessions, but to insist upon these twenty-six changes. One of the requested changes was to eliminate overtime pay for work on holidays. Our position was that holidays were when we did our business and there could be no overtime for such times. The new contract needed to specify that failure to show up for two holidays would mean automatic dismissal. The business agent from the union said that it was unheard of to grant twenty-six changes with no concessions and that a federal arbitrator would be needed. That was when I learned of this wonderful assistance provided entirely at the federal government's expense. A sophisticated professional came up from Albuquerque to serve as arbitrator between La Fonda and the union. At first he said we were making his job impossible by insisting on all of these changes without providing any other concessions. In the end, however, the employees respected him and had confidence in him, so the new contract included each of our twenty-six changes. It was my impression anyway that the reason La Fonda had originally become a union shop was not because of economic demands but because of an anti-Hispanic, bigoted attitude harbored by some previous Fred Harvey managers. In addition, the employees really valued the health insurance provided by La Fonda. Whatever criticism the employees felt of my leadership, they also sooner or later learned that an imperious discriminatory attitude was not part of my makeup. For the first time in the history of La Fonda, there were Hispanic department heads.

All of the long-time La Fonda employees had pride in this unique establishment. They wanted to make it work and were willing to sacrifice to turn it into a success. They felt almost as much pride as we did when various constructive changes cumulatively started to show up. I knew we had to make some sacrifices in order to bring in sustained revenues, so we dug out onto Old Santa Fe Trail, formerly College Street. Thus, commercial shops were created from the basement. One by one, we put in these stores which provided some continuity of rent. Some purists objected to disfiguring the original hotel, and I know we could not do the same today because of licensing requirements from the Historic Styles Committee and OSHA regulations. One of the first lessons we learned was that to use a jackhammer on the concrete poured by the Santa Fe Railroad over fifty years ago was no bed of roses. In two of the excavations we found substantial ancient pottery shards, which were delivered to the Museum of New Mexico. The state people were not particularly excited because ancient pottery would show up everywhere around the plaza, which perhaps had been adjacent to an ancient pueblo.

At that time we also called in some carpenters and put in the display cases in the lobby next to the front desk and the newsstand. These were immediately in demand by local artists. We followed up this defensive financial strategy by leasing out our Indian Shop to the ingenious and successful Ortega family from Sanders, Arizona. The only way an Indian Shop can operate successfully is to have adequate inventory, and we needed that capital for rebuilding the hotel. It was at this time that Bernard and Jo Glicksberg showed up and said they wanted to move to Santa Fe and needed to get hold of something to provide a livelihood. I was impressed by their sincerity and acumen, but I did not learn until later that there was an impetuousness within them. (They had met in Mexico and married only three days later.) We leased them the Newsstand, which they have developed admirably so that it has become a distinct asset to them, to La Fonda, and to the town.

John Sexton, the first general manager of the Inn at Loretto, is largely responsible for restoring solvency to Santa Fe's hotel industry when he courageously began pricing his rooms at the unheard-of daily rate of thirty-five dollars. But it was equally important that the Inn was located downtown and not at the emerging intersection south of town off of Cerrillos Road.

We were not the only ones facing tight-cash crises. When Ralph Petty was president of the Bank of Santa Fe, he asked officer Sergio Viscoli if the burglar alarm had gone off. Viscoli replied, "No, why?" "Well, I just saw developer K. walk through the front doors."

My close calls were not just financial. At one lunch hour, service was at a standstill. When I walked into the kitchen, manager Robert Foree was retreating from a chef holding a cleaver in the air. Said Foree "he refuses to let any of the cooks at the ranges." Without thinking, I walked up to the chef and said "throw the son-of-a-bitch out" and the chef turned and put down his cleaver.

22/ TILL DEATH DO US PART

UNTIL NOW, THERE HAS ALWAYS BEEN at least one permanent guest at La Fonda. One of the earliest was Judge Hudspeth from Texas, who came before World War II. On his arrival, he asked to see the general manager, Dave Cole, from whom he requested a discount rate because he was going to remain a while. "You mean a couple of weeks?" asked Cole. "No, forever," replied the judge. That "forever" turned out to be over fifteen years. Another resident was Lucy McGloflin, one of the owners of the Menninger Clinic, who created her fourth-floor suite facing College Street. She was soon widely heralded for her generosity. Monte Chavez, who was room-service waiter while she was at La Fonda, claimed he could survive just on Lucy's healthy tipping. Monte retired after sixty years of food service, mostly as maitre d'. When Lucy left, Mary Naylor took over and expanded the fourth-floor suite. The suite ultimately became the general manager's apartment after Ms. Naylor became terminally invalided. It is now our grand Suite 410.

I believe Mary's husband was a successful attorney for the Chesapeake and Ohio Railroad, so money was not one of her concerns during her widowhood. She had a classic grand piano in her apartment and would practice each morning, to the pleasure or distress of adjoining guests on the fourth floor. Once a year Mary would dress up as Beethoven and invite her many friends up to her suite for lunch and a Beethoven concert. Her costuming was very impressive and always a hit with the fourth-floor chambermaids, who were more under Mary's sway than that of our head housekeeper.

Many of our maids were long-term employees, and invariably their friendliness brought forth wondrous praise from guests. About twenty years ago, when there were insufficient restrooms on the Plaza during Fiesta, we charged ladies ten cents to enter our ladies room (yes, they are more in need than men). A really long line stretched down the portal from the Coronado Room. I asked the head housekeeper, Cleo, what control there was on the coin collections. She replied, "None, why do you ask?" "Well, to combat theft." "Oh, Mr.

Ballen, none of my girls would do that." And she was essentially right. Once a guest called from Flagstaff to say that he had left a paper sack containing $5,000 cash under his bed. When the maid who cleaned his room was questioned, she brought in the sack now containing only $4,500, and then broke down in tears as she said that her son told her she was entitled to withhold a portion.

Horace Akin's stay at La Fonda preceded and extended beyond that of Mary Naylor. Horace and Mary were respectfully cordial to each other all those decades that they dwelled at La Fonda. Some people considered Horace to be a kind simpleton, but there was much more to him. He came from a respected family of attorneys and politicians in Austin, Texas. One of his cousins once served as mayor of Austin. The firm of Akin and Akin paid Horace's expenses at La Fonda all the time he was with us. Everyone affectionately admired Horace, and not just because of his three paintings hanging in La Fonda's lobby—the Navajo Night Chant, the famous and much reproduced Bell of San Miguel, and the imposing portrait of Brian Boru Dunne.

In his formal bowler hat, Horace would take a two-mile stroll around Santa Fe's downtown everyday with an occasional stop-off at the state library. As a result, Horace, though an amateur, was as much an expert on the history of New Mexico as the professionals. He used his knowledge to compose events going as far back as the 16th century into a play that was included in the U.S. Bicentennial activities. I cannot recall a foul syllable ever coming out of Horace, but his room was a mess of randomly scattered files and memorabilia. We really wondered how he was able to navigate to his bed. As old age caught up with Horace, he would fall asleep in our dining room to the open discomfort of our guests since he could not always hold down his food. I feared discussing this with him, even though he was a good friend. But then he had a fall, and his family knew he had to be moved to Four Seasons Nursing Home. One Christmas Eve when Ethel and I went out to see him, he became agitated and exclaimed that he was going back to La Fonda and started to pack before he was restrained by the attendants. On his death, we advertised a memorial service for him in the Santa Fe Room, but only a handful of locals showed up. We were relieved that his Austin relatives had sent bountiful flowers with apologies for not attending. When Horace was terminally ill, many fringe characters laid claim to his paintings, some with bills of sale hand-printed on napkins. But no one pursued these claims after his death, and the paintings remain on display in our lobby.

Our most intelligent and spicy tenant was Rita Bibo, who had a fabulous history of experiences and a computer-style memory. She had a short-lived marriage to one of the Bibo brothers, who operated a trading post at Bibo, northeast of Acoma Pueblo. She then became legal secretary to Tom Catron's father before joining the Santa Fe school system. She was the first person in the lobby each morning and would enter a spirited conversation with our transient guests. I got along with her just fine, but she seemed to strike up an antagonism with women managers. Once, when Russian scientists arrived at La Fonda, I introduced Dr. Kirill Kondrateyev to her as he left the front desk. Three days later at 5:30 a.m. Rita was sitting in the lobby as the Russians left. She said, "Goodbye Dr. Kondrateyev." She was then 89 years old. She wrote her own memorial service, which said not one word of God but mentioned entering a new adventure. It was September 1995.

While we were constructing our Carriage House, the exit door to Water Street was slammed open one day at 4 p.m. as Rita tried to enter. She was smashed to the street by an exiting maid who then ran away. At the hospital it was discovered that Rita had suffered multiple fractures, from which she would never fully recover. Our insurance company offered a settlement that Rita felt was an insult. She hired the Catron firm and sued us, but my relations with her continued cordial. Of course, all the maid witnesses became fearful and we had five different stories from the five maids. Since it appeared that the maid involved had taken an unauthorized drink from the storeroom upon completing her tour of duty, the court ruled that La Fonda's responsibility was consequentially limited. After years of delay and gobs of legal hours, Rita accepted a settlement less than what was first offered. This was truly a tragedy, but our insurance company played hardball. Rita and I both recognized her increasing physical deterioration after she passed the age of 90, even though her mind was alert as ever. On her own, she precipitously moved out of La Fonda and back to her family north of Dallas.

In the forties Austin Clapp, Sr., became a permanent guest, but one plaza merchant said he feared he would one day address him as Mr. Syphilis through the pitfalls of word association. Then, in the late seventies, a retired railroad man from Amarillo moved into the hotel. As time went by, he became more and more demanding and ended up accosting guests with horror tales of how he was being mistreated by La Fonda. His relatives were incensed when we tried to explain the situation and moved him back to Texas in a huff. But at least we were spared a suit.

These permanent guests adjusted readily to visiting Hollywood stars such as Paul Newman, Robert Redford, Greer Garson, and Martha Hyer, to name just a few. The bellman claimed that John Wayne exited from our notorious downstairs mens' room with wet trousers. At the urinal, a guest at the adjoining fixture turned to him in excitement "Gosh you're John Wayne."

As a general rule, it seems that the best place to spend your final years is in a hotel if you can afford the expense. The younger staff members will collectively adopt you if given a chance to reciprocate cheerfulness. It was touching to see our youthful employees arrange birthday parties for these senior guests when they were ignored by their own relatives.

23/ *LA FONDA'S ROUND TABLE*

DURING THE SEVENTIES I would trip every other month or so to Dallas for a memorial service. Now, in the nineties, it seems I'm off to a church in Santa Fe every fortnight for a funeral. The mass at impressive, cavernous St. Francis Cathedral is something I've never fully gotten accustomed to. The rote stanza, the communion, the specifics of an afterlife all remain foreign to me. I much prefer former Roman Catholic nun, Karen Armstrong, who appreciates man's universal quest for spirituality but feels that "a vibrant new faith for the twenty-first century" need not include God. But, at the Cathedral, it is uplifting to see a melange of citizens, from the most humble gardeners to the lofty politicians, all treated equally at these somber events. Of course, it was an honor, when Judge Torres requested I deliver his eulogy from St. Francis' pulpit. Since I attend Temple Beth Shalom only on Yom Kippur eve, I do not discriminate in my difficulty with formal religion. But Colonel Chipp Woodruff did not get angry when he asked Mac Kriendler of Manhattan "21" what the Hebrew lettering on St. Francis Cathedral meant and Kriendler replied, "For Sale."

A service at the Catholic Church at Santa Clara Pueblo remains perhaps the most indelible in my memory. I was invited to attend because I was then president of the Southwestern Association of Indian Affairs. A famous potter, Art Hangouha (whose first wife was a fatality in a lightning storm at Puye Ruins when she held her aluminum chair over her head as an umbrella), and his wife and three children pulled slowly out from Highway 30 onto State Road 502 between Los Alamos and Pojoaque. A scientist driving back to Los Alamos in his four wheeler collided with their vehicle, fatally crushing two of the three children. In the aisle of the church the wife and mother lay on a bench. She was covered with a blanket, except for her face, and a child was tucked between her legs. On another bench was the father, similarly laid out. After the priest's service, each mourner touched the bodies on the way out to the church's sideyard, where two graves had been dug. The mother's father said some prayers in Tewa and then repeated them in English while a stone pillow and some food were placed in each grave before the bodies were lowered. The simple dignity was overwhelming; there was no brass-filled carved mahogany coffin. I knew I had been right to insist on the most primitive pine box for my father although I had to overcome my sister's guilty embarrassment. Hardly ever is the word God used in the prayers of Pueblo Indians; theirs is a faith of reconciliation to life as it is.

All this comes to mind as I leave the Methodist funeral for 91-year-old Burton Dwyer, who until three weeks previous would daily come down to La Fonda dressed grandly. It was either coffee at C.B. Ogas' morning table, or Jerry Dorbin's 9 a.m. table, or Judge Seth's 10 a.m. table. Burton would annually vacation in Alaska for salmon fishing. His mind remained razor sharp until the very end. As a life-long Democrat he still enjoyed taking potshots at the Ivy Leaguer, George Bush. During World War II Burton, as state highway engineer, was notified on 12/8/41 to post a guard at every major highway bridge. He promptly arranged this by contacting the most reliable person he knew at Las Cruces, a New Mexico State University graduate named Yamamoto. Washington was livid when the list of guards was telegraphed and immediately ordered Burton to select a replacement. He hired a drifter named Rodriguez who two days later built a fire underneath an overpass to keep warm and burned down the structure. As state engineer, Burton loved to remind us, "It takes a ton of paper to move a pound of dirt."

There has been a floating La Fonda round table since before World War II. In what used to be the Cantinita, now the French Pastry Shop, was the lawyers' table of Dave Olmsted, Donnan Stephenson, Harry Bigbee, Fred Stanley—our state attorney general whose only philosophical goal, it seemed to me, was to win—and Ed Felter. Perhaps Olmsted started that greedy gang of executives of Public Service Company of New Mexico down the path of ruin when he won a landmark ruling allowing them to "index" rates of return. They then stupidly bought a Lear jet rather than leasing it, which would have averted public notice. We used to say that it took five years to understand the philosophy of public utility rate-making, but Olmsted became an expert in ninety days. He knew nothing about utilities when he received this PNM assignment in the early seventies. I loaned him some basic textbooks, and in no time at all he mastered the principles. He then broke new ground by convincing the Public Utility Commission to agree on a continuous rate of return. Each quarter, revenue requirements would be adjusted to allow for changes in operating expenses, which, of course, never went down.

Fred Stanley's partner in Oklahoma was one of those who argued the famous NRA poultry case before the U.S. Supreme Court. Before heading to D.C. he purchased a formal suit. During the hearing, he was told he had twenty minutes to argue, but he was interrupted by Judge Frankfurter with a question and then again interrupted by a query from Justice Frankfurter and then a third time by the same judge. The chief justice said to him, "Counsel, you have only five minutes left and you haven't gotten to the core of your argument." Fred's partner sputtered, "Well, if that little guy at the end would let me, I will address that."

When United Nuclear got into a dispute with Gulf's subsidiary, General Atomics, and Harry Bigbee was United's attorney, Stephenson resigned from the New Mexico Supreme Court to assist Bigbee. Judge Felter issued a four-hundred-million-dollar default judgement against Gulf after it stonewalled an order to produce documents from Canada by claiming that national security protected the uranium secrets the documents contained. The real reason was that Gulf executives wanted to protect their hides from a jail sentence. Verily, the last refuge of a scoundrel is patriotism. Gulf's arrogant Pittsburgh attorney would not listen to local counsel and never appreciated, until too late, that they were up against the shrewdest pros rather than yokels. Julian Levy, the brother of the U.S. attorney general, sat in on the hearings and said Bigbee became a brilliant nuclear engineer and had a field day against Gulf's stuffed-shirt innocents. Ann Bingaman, the U.S. senator's wife, there demonstrated her mastery of antitrust law.

In the Gates of Spain room was the luncheon round table of Paul Rutledge, who created the Santa Fe Rodeo, and Chester Spain, who came from Amarillo flat broke with only a billiard table in his pickup. He opened a pool hall and ended up chairman at the State Securities Building on Washington Street. That structure is now the elegant Inn of the Anasazi. He enabled his widow to leave a nest egg to St. Vincent Hospital. Also attending that round table was Ralph "Sabu" Gallegos, who was born on the banks of the Chama River, from which his mother moved the family when the Catrons mentioned trespass. Sabu ended up as a champion Golden Gloves Boxer who was flattened by a Black in Chicago, an impressive New Mexico state legislator, a severe critic of Senator Joseph Montoya, and a successful insurance agent never to be vanquished. In the early sixties when a Texan said to Alfonso, who was the reigning La Fonda bartender behind the circular bar, "Nigger, give me another bourbon and water," Sabu nudged him and said, "We're all niggers here." Every year in July, Sabu's favorite reminder of our state liquor laws was, "Be sure to get a fifth on the third for the fourth." Also at the Gates of Spain table were Toad Leon from Abilene, the developer of the Pendaries Country Club on the east flank of the Sangre de Cristos, and Dr. Ralph Lopez from Gallup, who had become a respected dentist and was vice president of the American Dental Association but, more importantly, on La Fonda's board of directors since 1969.

Lopez was a dedicated Dallas Cowboys fan and close to Clint Murchison, Jr., through his friendship with native Santa Fean Bob Thompson, who ended up one of the important Cowboy executives. Thompson's father was the manager of JC Penney when it was on San Francisco and Galisteo. Bob married a Murchison daughter and moved to Dallas. His Great Dane would gingerly back away from Santa Fe's snow when exiting La Fonda during the winter. Through Lopez's intercession Clint came out one weekend together with the Cowboy team and a bevy of cuties. They sealed off La Fonda's fifth floor for a thirty-hour orgy. Lopez had to come down and give each of the gladiators a vitamin B-12 shot to prolong the festivities. On Sunday Clint demanded the best chile and huevos rancheros so, with the assistance of a state police escort, the Rio Grande Cafe in Española made delivery to the fifth floor.

For a decade the most famous of the round tables revolved around Louis Sutin, a judge on the state court of appeals and a famous Shakespearean courtroom practitioner who claimed he never lost a case before a jury. In the sixties, after becoming a widower and surviving a nonmalignant brain tumor, he threw caution to the wind. He grew an anarchist's beard, let his tongue hang loose, and became a beloved, courageous eccentric who championed humane rather than special-interest causes after Governor Bruce King appointed him to the state court of appeals. In the seventies a 35-year-old woman in Hobbs was convicted of sexually abusing adolescent boys visiting her home. Judge Sutin reversed the conviction with a written opinion that the nation was suffering from a runaway divorce rate, that sexual knowledge was an important ingredient to strengthening the marital institution, and what better way for a young man to learn than from a compliant experienced woman. The next day, on its own volition, the state's Catholic supreme court convened and overturned Sutin's decision. But that was not the end. After the national weeklies reported the episode, Sutin was the recipient of the most vicious hate letters from across the country and, as a result, he fell into a depression.

The Sutin luncheon round table at La Plazuela included Judge Donnelly, Judge Bivens, Judge Neal, Judge Kaufman, Tom and Bud and Fletcher Catron, Pat Casey, Saul Cohen, Bill and Tony Sawtell, Dave Sierra, and a number of drop-ins. Casey came from backwater Mora County and had an Irish father and a Spanish mother. After looking over a jury, he would decide what role he would play; with his sharp wit he was an Academy Award winner either way. Dave Sierra was an unusual Hispanic. He hailed from Vermont, where his Spanish grandparents were granite quarriers, and could not speak Spanish. He served as state liquor director in a Republican administration and then successfully sued Governor Carruthers after he was discharged without dignity. In lieu of an immediate sensible settlement to Sierra, the state paid $140,000 to the Sutin firm to defend Carruthers. We all knew that Dave's temper had a short fuse—even before he beat up an opposing attorney late at night in the supreme court law library. His cutting, Lindy-type repartee caused Rabbi Helman to lose his cool and curse Dave out in front of our bewildered luncheon guests at La Plazuela.

Incredibly, Judge Donnelly was born in the Bronx where his father, president of New Mexico Highlands, was attending Columbia for some advanced courses. In the eighties Donnelly found himself in New York and felt he would like to see his birthplace. But when Donnelly showed his cab driver the address, the driver demurred, saying, "I wouldn't go up there with air cover."

Unfortunately, after the Catron firm abandoned the Plaza for the St. Vincent Hospital area and Judge Sutin retired to Albuquerque, it didn't take long for this intense, lively round table to disappear. This left Judge Oliver Seth's decorous coffee table to take the spotlight with a heterogeneous attendance of a couple of law clerks plus Harold Gans, Tom Moore, George Hocker, and their friends. This is the second-generation Seth table. Before the big war, attendance was restricted to the very formal table of E.B. Healey, E.P. Moore, E.R. Wright, and (to break the monotony) J.O. Seth, and their followers. Some indiscreet excitement was added to the current table when Gans contributed to a discussion of diets and weight loss by his pronouncing, "Heck, I know a fellow who got rid of 130 pounds—he got divorced." And then Tom Moore, who was president of the National Association of Men's Clothiers, told the story of the Irish and Jewish partners who closed for a month to take a holiday—the Irish partner went to Israel and the Jewish partner went to Rome, where he had an audience with the Pope. When the month was up the Irish partner mentioned his great time at the Wailing Wall and Masada. When the Jewish partner was ecstatic about Rome and his audience, the Irish partner became very excited and asked his Jewish partner, "What was the Pope like?" The reply was "Oh, 36 short."

This leaves the Quinn & Co. 9 a.m. coffee table, which was usually joined by Alcalde Sam Pick or former Alcalde Joe Valdes. Each day Kip Smith and Greer Garson's nephew, Jerry Dorbin, raced to finish a crossword puzzle and the very conservative Dave Lunt read the liberal *New York Times*. What distinguished this round table was the generosity of the attendees, who threw dollar bills into a pile, none of which got past the waiters and into La Fonda's till. But George Winneberger refused to give up his cigarettes when La Plazuela was the first restaurant in the state to go no-smoking, and this group loyally moved down the street with George, the top securities broker in all New Mexico.

If you travel west from Socorro, past Pie Town, you eventually get to Quemado, where the Misfits Club meets each morning at 6:30 at the Chuck Wagon Diner. C.B. Ogas' 7 a.m. La Fonda table would properly protest that the distinguished individualists composing this "League of Nations" should not be mentioned in the same breath with Quemado. But, unfortunately, C.B. Ogas' early-morning round table has seen better days. For thirty years the USGS water expert, Bobbie Trible, would stop by for coffee and provide a current commentary on "interesting" lounges in Puerto Rico or Reno or across from Columbus into old Mexico. But now Bobbie is finishing his last days before retirement as water master up north at Costilla. To top Trible, the expert photographer Joe Gutierrez claims a membership of thirty-five years. The Texas Aggie Lewis Fields, who knew every town in rural Texas and every ethnic joke now forbidden by civil rights legislation, returned to Texas' Hill Country for health reasons and then finished his days in Santa Fe. Late in the morning strolls in John Greer, whose grandfather was an original investor in La Fonda. But C.B. Ogas, from Silver City and with Apache roots, is the mainstay before his twice-a-week trip to Ojo Caliente for a mineral bath. C.B. introduced us to Tesquina, a Mexican Apache sour-mash lightning, but he doesn't know his real nationality. When he entered the army in 1942, they told him he was an American, and at election time the Democrats told him he was a Spanish-American. But when he tried to get a job after leaving the army, he was told he was a dirty Mexican. Now that he is in the twilight of his life he has moved back to Silver City to live in an imposing house that would cost $500,000 here in the City Different.

But the Palace Restaurant also had a luncheon table of Governor Jack Campbell and Judge Donnan Stephenson—The Poets Club, Piss on Everything, Tomorrow's Saturday.

I fear that normal people, including retired investment bankers, national merchandizing executives, and retired Washington, D.C. personages and accomplished captains of industry and hi-tech are now migrating to Santa Fe. Soon tried and true eccentrics may not be around to fill the vacancies of La Fonda's round tables. Soon it will be hard to replace the lovable pool of characters at my Sunday tennis event at Viscoli Park, named by Richard Mares for his private East-West court *(sic)* and including Cadillac Jack with his $1,100 knee brace; General Gordon Sumner, a veritable foot soldier's hero in Korea and Vietnam who didn't learn from his disastrous Nicaraguan policy; Herb Weinstein, still a formidable opponent at 82; jack rabbit Luis Xavier Alba; erratic Pat Trujillo; and ex-Fred Harvey cook Arturo Maes. Imagine, there are now people in Santa Fe who don't know who Sergio Viscoli is!

24/ THE FRENCH ARMENIANS

ONE DAY IN THE EARLY SEVENTIES I was visited by an explosive, exuberant character named Charles Zadeyan. He had moved from Puerto Rico to the Solana Shopping Center in Santa Fe and opened a pastry shop, which was not doing well at all. After we exchanged some pleasantries in experimental French, I asked, "Where are you really from?" He replied, "We are from Beirut, but we are Armenians." I said, "But there is no Armenia." With a flourish of his finger and pointing to heaven, Charles exclaimed, "But there will be!"

With infectious enthusiasm Charles wanted to lease our Cantinita, break out the walls with windows to East San Francisco Street, and introduce croissants to Santa Fe. In those sparse times I could not turn down any revenue-producing proposition, and there was no dedicated Historical Styles Committee to preclude altering the solid exterior wall with inviting windows. We would have to carve out a spot in our basement for the bakery. We finally negotiated a lease that stipulated that all remodeling expenses would be Zadeyan's responsibility. This would leave our food operation with the Cantina immediately to the east plus the formal Gates of Spain room. No one in Santa Fe was pleased that we had converted Mary Coulter's brick lined Cantinita with its lovely fireplace and hand carved iron chandeliers into the French Pastry Shop. Everyone was convinced that croissants would never replace sopaipillas in old Santa Fe. Senator Joseph Montoya complimented me on my shrewdness in getting this misguided baker to construct a door and windows at his expense since surely the venture would go bust. Montoya's attribution of motives was in error since I have always believed that both parties must benefit from a transaction.

For months Santa Feans ignored the French Pastry Shop, and I feared that the senator's prediction might come true. The place just didn't click, but Charles kept paying his rent and never once came asking for relief. He did finally request an amendment to permit the addition of soups and sandwiches to his bill of fare, and then he secured a worthwhile baker. In an instant the French Pastry Shop became the sensation of Santa Fe. During summer and winter townsfolk and tourists lined up on San Francisco Street awaiting the privilege of being seated at one of the tiny square tables. Now tourists line up outside Pasqual's. The *New York Times* listed the French Pastry Shop as the outstanding restaurant in town, which was not exactly the case even though they said the croissants were better than in Paris.

Charles soon hired as head baker an extraordinary Frenchman named Michel Richard, who quite literally was a genius with food. His ability was first recognized by a Yugoslav artist unique in his own right, Vladan Stiha, who was brought to see me about 1971 by Margaret Jamison, the cultured owner of the gallery across the street. Stiha had left Yugoslavia right after the war because he was a supporter of Mihailovic. His brief stay in Italy was doubly traumatic because his wife Elena, a beauty queen at a very young age, had left behind a cloth sack containing all their resources—a cache of precious stones— when she took the train north from Rome to visit Vladan in a recuperation center. This left Vladan no choice but to be declared fit at his physical examination. He then resumed his career painting metal cafe umbrellas that had rusted while stored in a basement during the war. Stiha could do anything well. He developed a large family of friends even though he and Elena had no children. After he opened his gallery at the old railroad ticket office at the corner of Water and College Street, he suffered two serious floods but stoically accepted the standard water damage exclusion clauses in our leases. He contributed the two Indian panels on the north and south firewalls of La Plazuela, supplying even the canvas and wood frames. Several times he made valuable suggestions concerning La Fonda's dedication to heritage. His philosophy included: "Mistress is mistress but wife is wife." It was Stiha who arranged Michel Richard's "coming-out party" at his home, where Stiha hosted a dinner consisting of Richard's culinary creations.

The food was almost too beautiful to eat. Richard's presentations were unsurpassed. Besides his obvious talent as a chef, Richard was also a pleasant, cheerful type with just the right combination of engaging French simplicity and French *joie de vivre*. His attributes were supplemented by those of an attractive blond French wife. For reasons not entirely clear to me, Charles Zadeyan moved to La Jolla to open another French Pastry Shop and leased the La Fonda shop to Richard, whose wife sat on a stool at the cash register. But then Michel Richard moved to Beverly Hills to open Richard's French Pastry Shop. The long-time women's dress shop tenant, Suzette, asked me, "Why

did you let Michel leave? He could have run your whole food operation?" I replied, "That's what I wanted, but I didn't know how to talk
to him." "Oh, gosh, he wanted to stay here, but he didn't know how
to talk to you."

Michel's Beverly Hills shop was an immediate success, and before
too long he was hired to cater the Academy Awards dinner. This
recognition was followed by fancy cars, a divorce, and thirty pounds
too much around his girth. But it didn't take long for Michel to regain
his stride, and he then opened Citrus, one of the most popular high-
priced restaurants on the West Coast and a frequently written up
success story in the trade literature. Everyone in the business acknowl-
edges Michel as the prince of chefs.

Charles Zadeyan's successes as a recruiter also included Guy
Mazire, who ended up as director of all food services at the Santa Fe
Ski Basin, as well as the Belgian Waffelaert twins, whose tours have
included their own restaurant Chez Edward. Now they have a fish
restaurant on St. Michael's Drive and they opened the first
newspaper-coffee curbside bistro in Santa Fe. Gilles was another hard-
working baker imported by Charles and influenced by the success of
the others. Gilles opened a restaurant on San Francisco Street across
from the Lensic and worked like a dog to provide customers with
three meals seven days a week. We really feared he would work himself to death, but he failed financially in time to realize he was not cut
out for business. So now there are four genuine croissant shops in
Santa Fe's core area and three magazine-coffee browsing places, but
it all started with Charles Zadeyan's confident intuition and foresight.
He created a central bakery near Laguna Beach but became a whole-
saler, shipping beautiful pastries and breads all over southern
California and even east of the Rockies. The purists in Santa Fe have
by now forgotten that the French Pastry Shop was originally the site
of La Fonda's main dining room, so I don't have to apologize for our
variance.

The relationship with Charles was mutually satisfactory, but I
was not at ease with their reporting of sales on an overage rent formula.
I decided to just tread water when they failed to take notice of a
deadline to activate a renewal lease. Sure enough, their competent
attorney, Saul Cohen, came to see me one day and prefaced his request
for a late renewal with the statement that I was known for fairness
and not the type to stick to formalities. Once that ego massage and
the breast beatings of the lessee were out of the way, we were able to
negotiate a satisfactory new lease that did not depend on reported

overages. At one point they wanted to expand into the Cantina but then fell back on the time-honored principle that it is better to have customers waiting to be admitted than to have empty chairs.

Charles' brother, George, now owns the French Pastry Shop and his third brother, Jacques, came to Santa Fe and opened the Cafe on the Trail at the Desert Inn, occupying a location where other restaurants have inevitably failed. But Jacques is very talented and hard-working and was quickly a success. So he sold out to his creative baker, who is married to an energetic Tahitian waitress. Jacques went off to play in Puerto Rico and has now come back to open an antique shop with French furnishings.

In 1995 five superb new restaurants opened in Santa Fe. Whether existing marginal places can survive remains to be seen. But their problems are compounded by the cheap buffets offered by the Indian gambling casinos.

25/ HISTORY

Prepared for the Historic Santa Fe Foundation in 1994

TWENTY-FIVE YEARS AGO when we excavated for our shops on Old Santa Fe Trail, copious pottery shards were uncovered, and the same was true when we dug the deep supports for the steel beams of La Plazuela. This confirms our suspicion that there was a pueblo on this site before the Spanish arrived in the Southwest. In historic times many writers have dated La Fonda back to 1610 as the literature does include a reference to a *fonda*, wayside inn, here in Santa Fe. A booklet published by Peter Hertzog thirty years ago describes La Fonda's famous guests and he refers to such a startup. It is likely that there was a place here to tether a horse and wash down an enchilada with some tequila. Hertzog was the pseudonym for Phillip St. George Cook III, member of a famous pioneer family who used to live here in Santa Fe. He moved down to Mexico and died, and his booklet is out of print.*

Our last permanent guest, the artist Horace Akin, is my source for 1610. His spare time was devoted to studying in the state and city libraries. Horace was pretty certain that the *fonda* referred to in the literature describing the area in 1610 was actually at this site. But he based this belief on a correlation of early maps of questionable authenticity.

In February 1740 Maria Francisca Fernandes de la Pedrera bought the site and a three-room house for $200 from Antonio Montoya. When Maria's brother, Salvador Montoya, owned a piece of the property in 1716, he was cited by the authorities for obstructing the alley of Shelby Street, which ran south to the Santa Fe River. Maria de la Pedrera married a Frenchman, Juan Bautista Alariy, later documented as Alarid, who had arrived in Santa Fe in May 1739 with the Mallet expedition. She constructed a house with a parlor, three living rooms, and a zaguan, which is an entry wide enough for a wagon. By 1822,

---

* Recent evidence from a bookshop in London indicates that a Captain Montoya established Santa Fe's plaza three years before the accepted date of 1610.

the Alarid home was called La Fonda. An adobe maquette of their home, created by a descendant now living in Denver, sits in our lobby. So apparently an inn of some sort existed at the site for another 100 years until the Exchange Hotel came into being in 1846.

In late 1857 William S. Messery who had a trading post on the south side of the Plaza, sold the Exchange Hotel to Tom Bowler for $5,000. Two years later it was sold to Leonard Rose for $7,000 who then sold it to two cattlemen from Arkansas. It was way behind in its accounts payables during the Civil War but the Kingsbury and Webb General Store assisted by J.S. Marsh held it together.

The proprietor of the Exchange Hotel was Nancy Thornton, who was the grandmother of Leonard Valdes, the previous executive director of the Public Employee Retirement Association and an initial member of the board of directors of our Corporacion de la Fonda. Nancy Maitilde Thornton arrived in Santa Fe from Kansas in 1907 as a widow with two deaf daughters. She was a graduate from Gallaudet College for the Deaf in Washington, D.C. She opened a restaurant where the DeVargas Hotel was located and created a boarding house on the La Fonda site. Her boarding house became the Exchange Hotel. She was an industrious lady and homesteaded 140 acres near the Puye Cliffs, where she built a house of volcanic tuff. She died in 1920 at the age of 63.

Major and Mrs. John Martin were responsible for the property in 1874 and leased it in 1878 to Mrs. S.B. Davis. Mrs. Davis came to the property from the Hot Springs Hotel in Las Vegas, New Mexico, as a widow from Ohio. She had a young son and daughter to help her at the hotel, as well as ten employees, including two black cooks. She was with the Exchange until 1882, when she returned to Las Vegas to the Plaza Hotel and then to the elegant Montezuma Hotel. By 1888, John and Belle Forsha were running the Exchange. He was a Civil War veteran and came to Santa Fe as a driver for the Ballow and Anderson Stage Lines. At the age of 34, he acquired the Exchange and also married 21-year-old Belle King from St. Louis. He died at the age of 56 in 1902, but his widow continued to manage the hotel with some financial assistance from Henry Dendahl. Belle died in 1932 and is buried at our local national cemetery.

With the coming of the Santa Fe Railroad to New Mexico, other hotels were built in Santa Fe and the Exchange went into serious decline. It was a one-story hotel and corral with gaming tables. The entrance was at the intersection of San Francisco and what was called either College Street or Shelby or Seligman Street, all of which we now call the Old Santa Fe Trail. The hotel's old billiard table is now in the basement of General Kiley's home on Camino Piñones. The Exchange became a definite eyesore, and its walls were propped up with heavy timbers. But in its better days it was well appreciated. In 1873, J.H. Beadle described it as follows:

"We stop at the Exchange, the only hotel in the city for white men or rather Americans. The other distinction, though perfectly accurate, not being well relished here. There was an archway between the kitchen and the dining room, connecting to two courts. On the human side, women and children take their recreations and men of acquired or literary taste can sit and read while the stable side is sacred to dog fights, cock fights, wrestling matches, pitching Mexican dollars and other exclusively manly pursuits. The people of Santa Fe evidently do not take in their philosophy the statement that 'Man was made to mourn'."

In October 1880, President Rutherford B. Hayes and his wife stayed at the hotel, where a gala banquet was held in their honor. In that same year the Dutch explorer of the West, John J. VandeMoer, stated that the one-story Exchange had enormously large rooms measuring 24 feet by 20 feet. They would be large even by today's standards. The rooms opened both to the plaza and to the indoor patio—a delightful setup.

When Captain William Becknell arrived from Missouri in 1821, a La Fonda was operating, but after the conquest of Mexico its name was changed to the U.S. Hotel. In 1857 a man was lynched in what is now our Plazuela; and in 1867, after the U.S. Hotel became the Exchange Hotel, John P. Slough, chief justice of the Territorial Supreme Court, was shot to death where our newsstand is located by the attorney W.L. Ryerson. Ryernson was then acquitted. Even in those days it was rare for a Santa Fe jury to convict a murderer. After five years the chief justice's widow finally collected on his life insurance. But there were other unrecorded violent acts at the site. N. VanHaselin found a loaded Smith & Wesson pistol and a liquor bottle and a skull when in May 1928 he was construction foreman excavating the basement for the hotel's $250,000 addition. By the close of World War I there was widespread interest in Santa Fe in building a community hotel to replace the Exchange Hotel. At a victory bond rally on May 5, 1919, a World War I tank called the "Mud Puppy" destroyed the existing structure. Some years ago a citizen in Santa Fe, whose name I unfortunately lost, told me that he was seven years old at the time of the rally and had been permitted to ride in the tank when it was smashing against the Exchange's walls.

In February 1920 the La Fonda Building Corporation was organized with Arthur Seligman as president and Carl Bishop as secretary. They sought to raise $250,000 to construct the hotel. I believe they were successful in raising $175,250 and borrowed the rest from the First National Bank of Santa Fe, whose president was Arthur Seligman. At that time it was necessary to search the title in a more formal manner, and a complicated chain of ownership was discovered. Downtown Santa Fe was patented on February 16, 1901, by an act of Congress with the deed signed by President William McKinley. The square block on which La Fonda stands had numerous property owners, including St. Francis Parochial School, Duran, Thayer, Baca, Ortiz y Ortiz, Longwill, Catron, and Archbishop Pierce Bourgade. Part of the property was owned by J.B. Lamy and his wife Mercedes Chavez de Lamy. He was the nephew of Archbishop Lamy. When he believed another Frenchman was fooling around with his wife, he fatally shot the man in the back at the entry to the hotel and then walked to a bar across the street and ordered a drink. The remains of J.B. Lamy rest at Rosario Cemetery in a mausoleum commissioned by his wife and still bearing the engraving of the name Lamy. His land went to the church, which built a two-story brick school where our Carriage House sits.

A part of the property along what is now Cathedral Place was carved out and dedicated to the city. Conversely, Albert T. Daeger, the archbishop of the Santa Fe Archdiocese, deeded property owned by the Catholic Church for the La Fonda site to Charles Springer, Arthur Seligman, and Solomon Spitz, who were trustees for the Santa Fe Building Corporation. All of these documents bear a notation on the bottom of the page that it is a "Free Translation from the Spanish." Well, in no time at all the La Fonda Building Corporation was broke.

The fact is that community cooperative efforts to build hotels invariably fail. In the post-World War II years that was true of the Community Hotel in Hobbs and the Ski Resort at Rio Castillo, and the same is the experience all across the country. A reorganization committee consisting of Edgar Street, Levi Hughes, Dan Kelly, Henry Dendahl, and O.W. Lasater called in the Santa Fe Railroad for assistance. Fortunately, the Santa Fe Railroad had employed Charles Whittlesey in 1901 to roughly sketch out what became the Alvarado

Hotel in Albuquerque. After his concepts had been transformed into working drawings by the Santa Fe Railroad's architecture department in Chicago, the Alvarado was completed in 1905, apparently to the railroad's satisfaction. So, with Rapp, Rapp & Henrickson from Trinidad, Colorado, as architects, the La Fonda was completed and leased by the Santa Fe Railroad to Fred Harvey. Its proper name as a corporation is Fred Harvey. The lease to Fred Harvey commenced in 1926, and the Indian Detours started up the same year, providing tourist trips from Las Vegas, New Mexico, to Santa Fe.

From the beginning, talented Mary Coulter decorated the hotel in her unique Hispanic-Indian style. She subcontracted some of the large iron lamps to Lou Reynolds' Blacksmith Shop in El Paso. This was the same Lou Reynolds who organized Reynolds Electric here in Santa Fe and became the prime electrical contractor for the Atomic Energy Commission at the Nevada Test Site even though he was not a graduate electrical engineer. She brought in Earl Altarice from Kansas City to hand paint 798 pieces of furniture. Mary also seized on dipsomaniac Bruce Cooper to make many of the lamps in the dining room and bar. She commissioned the German Arnold Ronnabech from Denver to make the marvelous terra cotta panels in the Santa Fe room opposite the portal. A unique first-class hotel resulted and generated an international following after opening its doors in 1923. PBS plans to show a film on Mary Coulter in 1997.

Peggy Jones, a famous interior and industrial designer from Kansas City, used to spend a month each summer at La Fonda. I found Peggy to be totally reliable. She claimed to have been the very first person to sign the register at La Fonda and was still coming here in the late seventies. The last time I saw Peggy she was almost in tears. She had come here in the winter to decorate a private residence in Santa Fe and was shocked to find the hotel practically empty in the winter—since all her previous experiences at La Fonda had been in the summer when the hotel was sold out and hectic crowds filled the lobby.

Early on, William G. Sargent was the manager, and the daily room rate was $2, or $2.50 with bath included. The telephone number YUcca 2-5511 remains the same today, 982-5511. The property then became a superb operation under the leadership of General Manager David Cole with Russell Wilson as room clerk and Tommy Thompson as assistant manager. Earl Fordum, a former railroad security officer, became the house detective. Then the two African-American Banks brothers became bartenders. One of them was reported to be a captain in the infantry in the Pacific. I am not aware of any black infantry units in the European Theater, where I served. Later on, there was the famous black bartender from Cuba, Alfonso. And, of course, the cuisine under Chef Conrad became famous. The restaurant featured a special menu printed each day, as on a cruise ship. So anyone who was anyone signed the register as a guest at La Fonda with its famous Fred Harvey housekeeping and waitstaff. John Gaw Meem came on board and took care of a 1928 expansion as well as a 1951 expansion; the latter, however was rather seriously flawed because the rooms were too small. I believe the working drawings on that expansion phase were handled by the Santa Fe Railroad's drafting department in Independence, Missouri, and that was also true when they built the Gates of Spain Room at the eastern corner of the property. Elmer Embry was an excellent successor manager, as was his secretary, Amy Meadows, who was actually running the hotel although she was part of the secretarial staff.

Surprisingly, this world-famous, highly admired enterprise entered a period of stagnation and deterioration, as had the Exchange Hotel. We can only speculate as to the reasons for the decision by Fred Harvey to milk the operation and allow it to go into disrepair without proper maintenance. There was a reluctance to bring the property up to contemporary standards, which required a private bathroom for every room as well as the installation of air conditioning and a quiet steam system. In any case, at that time an old hotel was considered a liability, and with the post-war exodus to suburbs adjoining freeways, a property in the core of a city was considered a likely place for riots. The end result was that the Santa Fe Railroad decided to dispose of all of its hotels other than those at Grand Canyon and Death Valley. When La Fonda was put on the market, every experienced hotel operator in the United States turned it down.

In 1968 Marc McAuliffe put me in touch with Walter Keesing, who, with the noble Van Scoggin from Las Cruces had the listing to sell La Fonda. I convinced my associates at Electrical Log Services, Inc., that we would be making a contribution to society by acquiring La Fonda and keeping it from becoming a parking lot. There was maybe a chance the venture might become successful.

Just the year before Judge Donnan Stephenson and Houston Frith had worked out a deal that only required $100,000 for working capital but they could not entice any professional hotelmen to join them, including the San Francisco Swigs of the Fairmont, so they backed off the deal. On December 9, 1968 Electrical Log Services purchased La Fonda from the Santa Fe Railroad for $150,000 cash less a $1,250,000 one-year note kept by the Railroad. We had an obligation to spend $250,000 that first year on improvements. When Elecrical Log was liquidated, the La Fonda stock was distributed to the Electrical Log shareholders. We then made all kinds of managerial errors and stumbled and groped thorough an environment where on some days this entire complex did not gross more than $800. The property was really run down. There were electric panels functioning with copper pennies instead of fuses and sinks in the kitchen not connected to plumbing drains.

To get things rolling, we announced a $300,000 intrastate offering of convertible debentures. We required a financial statement. Next door to my office in Sena Plaza was the Registered Public Accountant, James Gaskin, the former manager of the Trinchera Ranch in southern Colorado lying between Mount Blanca and Culebra Peak. Gaskin kept promising his audited statements, but two days before the Prospectus was to go to the printers, he came in and pleaded that he didn't know how to audit Corporacion. So I told him he had to accept our internally prepared statement and sign it, and that is just what he did.

Arthur Quinn bought the first convertible debenture, then John Gaw Meem and then Pauline Pollack, but it hit a stone wall and the subscriptions came up to only $30,000. I was embarrassed to report this to the board of directors, so I bought the rest of the offering myself. This enabled us to commence the air conditioning of the hotel on a primitive basis even though all the old timers said that you didn't need air conditioning in Santa Fe. About this time the local chapter of the Rotary Club held its fiftieth Anniversary meeting at La Fonda with three charter members, Dan Kelly, Bernard Spitz, and Ferd Koch, keeping their perfect attendance record.

For three successive years I tripped to Chicago to request some leeway on our note with the Santa Fe Railroad, and they were cooperative without making me grovel. Their vice-president Scott told me at the third visit, "Ballen, I don't want to see you next year." But during this time I had an experience not permitted to every man. With convergence of the leaking Magic City gas line and the evaporation of the ELSI collateral, I almost went broke but my wife didn't leave me.

The real march towards the successful rejuvenation of the hotel occurred when Hershel Linsky stopped off here and said that he was a well-known decorator in Chicago now moving to Prescott, Arizona. In order to establish himself in the Southwest he would decorate our

Trails End dining room for no fee. All references reported that whether I paid him or not, if I could get Hershel Linsky on board, we shouldn't waste any time. He ingeniously redecorated the dining room and then, on a fee basis, started redecorating the guest rooms. He accomplished things for $10 that would have cost somebody else $50. Then his health soured and he could not return to Santa Fe's 7,000-foot altitude. But he continued to provide guidance to my wife, who was by then somewhat free of rearing our five girls. Ethel turned out to be a tough supervisor of our maintenance crew and at the same time was able to inspire them to exciting ethnic creativity. After six or seven years she really accomplished miracles in restoring the unique quality of La Fonda's guest rooms. But she had the advantage of a very loyal staff, many of whom really felt a part of La Fonda's family. Her greatest accomplishment was magnificiently executing my ideas for our 6,000 square foot Ballroom. She encouraged Ernesto Martinez to create our 52 mimbres panels and inspired Albuquerque glass and tin craftsman Ted Arellanes to assemble our glorious and wierd chandeliers.

Our employees receive a cash bonus at Christmas and are beneficiaries of an Employee Stock Ownership Plan. We provide paid vacations that run up to four weeks as well as a health and dental plan. We also have a scholarship plan at the College of Santa Fe. We created it in honor of Nina, our first daughter. Many remember our waiter, Freddie Martinez, who finally retired last year and was noted for giving customers their check before he had served their food. Life has its pitfalls and its rewards. His son shot himself, but his daughter graduated from the College of Santa Fe on one of our scholarships with a 4.0 average. She went on to Yale with a scholarship and earned a Ph.D. On her first return trip from Yale, I asked if the better preparation of the students from the East turned out to be a problem. She said, "No, they are just less friendly." Although it is hard to believe, from the time we acquired the hotel from the Santa Fe Railroad in December 1968 to December 31, 1993 we have capitalized expenditures of $15,371,364. When the North American Institute held its meeting here a year ago and the billionaire from Monterrey, Mexico, de la Garza, flew up here with two jets, we found an emergency suite for him. He reported that even though he owned many hotels in Mexico, he could not have been treated better than he was here at La Fonda.

Now we are committed to the final stage of our master plan, which consists of enclosing our summer restaurant, La Terraza, on top of the Carriage House while at the same time preserving its outdoor ambiance, and adding some 14 rooms averaging 550 square feet per unit on the top of our Carriage House, all surrounded by native gardens. We are a supporter of the Historic Styles Review Board and have worked with the board on this final addition. We have addressed their concerns that these room additions not cut off the tops of two towers of St. Francis Cathedral when viewed from the Loretto Chapel.

A full report on the history of La Fonda would have to include some reference to La Fonda's involvement in the Manhattan Project in World War II, when Colonel Boris Pash posted an intelligence man at our front desk and two of his intelligence men worked in our bar. We would have to reveal why Moore's Clothing brought a pair of trousers to the room of one of the leading physicists, and we would have to describe the time when our main transformer blew its 18-inch-long fuses every two hours because of some acid contamination on the bus bars. We have to speculate why a most respected and courageous judge wrote a four-page opinion that the suit of a local gallery owner had no likelihood of success and then one month later recused himself so that the case foundered for two years before it was resolved on the second morning of jury selection. We would have to tell why the *Dallas Morning News* in 1972 said that no visit to Santa Fe would be complete unless you entered La Fonda's men's room, which was located on the spot of Señor Murphy's candy store. And we would have to mention that we pay for exterior lighting of St. Francis Cathedral so that when Fray Angelico Chavez was asked what kind of lights they were, he answered Israelites. We would also have to include the reason the Bullring's cocktail waitress who ran for the state legislature had to sneak out of La Fonda at 5 a.m. attired only in a sheet. We would have to include the many chefs and entertainers who got their start here and went on to great success. We would have to explore the statement by our original chief engineer that there is a passageway from our basement to the Palace of the Governors. We would have to mention that Roy Varrow, a previous general manager, leased an office to a tattoo artist who posted on the office walls pictures of tattoo markings on women's genitals. We would have to describe how a state liquor director settled his two-years-past-due account in six hours when we said we would go to court.

We would have to elaborate how I returned from Italy in 1970 to a cash crisis and walked over to Tim Skinner at the First National Bank and asked for $25,000. Said Tim, "No, and here's why." "I don't have time to learn why" as I walked over to Buddy Ragely at the

Bank of Santa Fe. "I don't know you, Ragely, but you come from Texas, so you must know something and I need $25,000 right now." "That means you need $50,000." "OK you're right." "Here's the fifty, come back in two weeks and we'll both find out what mistakes we've made."

We would have to mention others who helped out at critical moments, like Bill White and Bill Lumpkins and Eugene Zacher and Joe Schepps and Bill Federici and Ned Wood. But as Stanislaw Ulam used to say, even a beautiful leg must end somewhere.

26/ STANISLAW

LET'S FACE IT, just like many other men and women, I was in love with Stan Ulam. Stan was a unique combination of intelligence, kindness, rascality, humor, sportsmanship, common sense, and a youthful love of life combined with a charming detachment from life. Much has been written about Stan by others and by himself in his successful book, *Adventures of a Mathematician*. An entire issue of *Los Alamos Science* was published by Los Alamos National Laboratory as a memorial to him, so nothing would be accomplished by my repeating the other accounts. This chapter will be limited to my own joyful and maddening experiences with him.

Our next-door neighbor to the southeast is the twice Pulitzer Prize winner, Bill Mauldin, known to every GI from World War II. Bill is an intriguing neighbor, with some eccentricities, which include an extensive gun collection. He volunteers to take care of the neighborhood when there is a breakout, as seems to occur periodically, from the state penitentiary eighteen miles to the west of us. Next to Bill Mauldin lived a famous chemistry professor named Mossman, who became a bit sticky in his advancing years. He made the distinct mistake of selling out and moving to a retirement home in Oakland. Because the retirement home was located in a deteriorating minority neighborhood, he and his wife were confined within their own walls. But before he left Santa Fe, Mossman sold his house on Old Santa Fe Trail to the talented mathematician Stanislaw Ulam. Stan's French wife, Francoise, handled the negotiations. Mossman felt he had been outwitted, but I am sure such was not the case.

It was after reading the *Wall Street Journal*'s review of Stan's *Adventures* book that I wrote to the Ulams and mentioned that my mother and father were both from Poland. This proved to be a correct opening, and I was invited over immediately for tea. The Ulams and their household had an Old World charm even though the precocious vitality of a teenager flowed from Stanislaw. Shortly after that meeting, St. Johns College announced an evening lecture by him titled "Scientists I Have Known." The lecture Stan gave would have been more aptly titled "Scientists Who Have Known Me." Even though Stan was fair in everything he undertook, there was not an ounce of modesty in him.

My almost immediate next encounter with Stan was when we both went to our local Sangre de Cristo Tennis Club, four blocks away. He was no match for me, even though I am only a mediocre player. This was a bit of a surprise–all of the stories about Los Alamos during World War II emphasize the tennis episodes. *Sports Illustrated* printed a glorious photograph of a foursome that included like two tall gazelles, Stan Ulam and Jim Tuck. Jim was a British physicist who came to Los Alamos during the war and then accepted American citizenship. His British diction brought forth deep smiles in his listeners even when he was very serious. When Tuck pioneered the concept of controlled thermonuclear energy, the developing project was appropriately titled Sherwood in honor of his British roots. There were excellent tennis players at Los Alamos and excellent climbers and excellent kayakers, but these particular scientists really had no basis for publicizing their prowess at tennis.

In my first time on the courts with Stan we just volleyed–but with more than tennis. We also exchanged stories, bon mots, flippancies. After several repeat scenarios I suggested that he might want to call Ethel and consider playing with her. And with his good common sense, he did not protest at all. So Ethel started playing with Stan although they did not keep score. Stan would always have some excuse for just volleying, and frequently the volleying took the form of his hitting his serves and Ethel running after the ball. She protested to me that she was going to tell him she'd had enough. I tried unsuccessfully to persuade her to the contrary, saying, "Suppose you had an opportunity to volley with Galileo and chase his balls?" Well, Ethel tolerated no nonsense from anyone, as I had found out for myself early in our marriage. Thus, Stan and I were soon back out on the tennis court, and in all the time we played I was never able to get him to keep score. Eventually I protested and told him I would not play with him again unless we could score the games, since that added to the enjoyment. He would agree with me in principle, but when we got to the court, he would always have some excuse: a cold, a stretched back, or a crook in his elbow. Since he was ten years my senior and I did consider it a privilege just to be with him, I would always weakly succumb to his petitions for unscored play. I never did end up scoring a game with him! The only explanation is that, psychologically, Stan could not afford to lose and that would be the outcome if we had kept score.

While driving to and from the court, we would tell outlandish, off-color stories to each other, and we both enjoyed them immensely. But as we approached his home, he would excitedly caution, "Please don't tell that to Francoise." Francoise had a reflex action of moving to another room as soon as I entered the house. Then she would get up her courage and rejoin us with an offer of tea or lemonade or something like that. Because we played in winter as well as summer, Francoise got hold of some peculiar tennis gloves that we could wear as well as some lovely knitted wool caps, so she did solicitously look after our welfare. Once when we returned from the court and Francoise and I were chatting in her dining room, in walked Stan, wearing the briefest bikini and stretching his muscles like Charles Atlas. He said that his real talent in life would have been as a sportsman and that if he had gone into sports, he would have exceeded even his mathematical achievements. I think he actually believed this fantasy. Francoise was always in control, deeply intelligent, but I would have preferred some impetuousness to offset her French civility. As the years go by, I admire her more and more. Ethel's eyebrows arch at my weekly drop-ins to her. I always viewed her as deeply reserved, but she surprised us with her uninhibited memoirs, still in manuscript and in some respects more interesting than Stan's *Adventures* and deeper in concept. They are now deposited in the Bohr Collection in Virginia.

Stan's appreciation of me came when I inquired about a puzzling comment he made about Oppie (J. Robert Oppenheimer, director of the Manhattan Project at Los Alamos) in *Adventures*. Stan: "I never wrote such a thing." Sam: "Oh, yes, you did." So it went until Francoise came in with an open book and showed Stan the pertinent page. I walked out without saying a word. When I entered our house, the phone was ringing. "But you misinterpreted," pursued Stan.

When Stan died, Francoise remained stoical in her sadness, but surprised me by asking, "Do you think I should call a rabbi to participate in the memorial at Los Alamos?" "Why, yes, I think Stan would like that." Rabbi Helman at Santa Fe's Temple was scheduled to leave for a convention in New Orleans but, as was typical of his devotion to all supplicants, cancelled his trip and had a small role in the service. I was surprised at Francoise's thoughtfulness because she was absolutely ignorant of Jewish matters although I believe a relative of hers was chief rabbi of Paris. I couldn't help but join audibly in the Aramaic Kaddish, despite some frowns from others in the audience. Several of the non-Jewish Jewish physicists on The Hill accused me of defaming the memorial by including a rabbi. I had to protect myself by revealing I was only complying with Francoise's wishes. Although Stan was strongly pro-Israel, his attitude was, "There's no one more pleasant than a pleasant Jew and no one more unpleasant than an unpleasant Jew." When Stan met Rabbi Helman at our house, they entered a chess game. On the sixth move, when the rabbi took Stan's queen, Stan said, "Oh, a mistake," and restored the queen to its place on the board—much to Helman's anguished frustration. Eccentric Rabbi Helman proved too spontaneous for his congregation, which is now composed of East Coast and West Coast newcomers. It is amazing how he has touched all segments of Santa Fe and did not swallow that hogwash of not officiating at interfaith weddings. After leaving for Pennsylvania and Alabama, he returned to Santa Fe under peculiar circumstances; he officiated for a spin-off congregation while he was still rabbi emeritus of Temple Beth Shalom.

Stan's strongest quality was his untamed self-confidence, which of course, had a tinge of enticing arrogance. In fact, he would express his definite opinions on everything, whether he knew anything about the subject or not. High on his list of straw men were people in the oil industry, whom he detested. His idea was that they were not motivated by greed or money but by hunger for power and that was a quality in man to be feared. I was probably the first and only oil man whom he knew, but that did not diminish the frequency with which he leveled his barbs at the profession. Following close behind his dislike of oil men was his disdain for politicos Reagan and Meese, and he constantly pleaded to know who was behind these Lilliputian nonentities of Reagan and Meese. It was as if he felt that somewhere there must be a *Protocols of Newport Beach* calling the shots.

The people he really admired were Johnny Von Neumann, and George Gamov, and Fermi. He said that Von Neumann had a better brain than Einstein but that Von Neumann had sold his contributions as a consultant to IBM too cheaply. One day he said that Von Neumann sheepishly regretted that it was Stan who discovered radiation implosion as the solution to the hydrogen bomb trigger rather than himself. Obviously I don't appreciate the nuances, but it seemed logical to look to the energy emanating from X-radiation to compress the lithium-deuterium-tritium and so all the to-do surrounding the Ulam discovery is a mystery. The first Soviet hydrogen bomb designed by

Sakharov and Zeldovich did not use the Ulam-Teller technique. I tried to pursue with Stan and Francoise why there was so little mention of Ulam in "In The Matter Of," the verbatim report on the Oppenheimer hearing. They both said that the only explanation was that there was such great fear of not violating security regulations in the early fifties that fear kept even the high-placed witnesses before the proceeding from even mentioning Stan's name. They both agreed that this unpleasantness, which was exaggerated by Teller's animosity toward Stan, contributed to their leaving Los Alamos to go to Harvard. But then later they left for Boulder when Stan felt it unjust that the sale of residences for private purchase at Los Alamos did not include their home on what was called Bathtub Row. They returned to their friend Professor David Hawkins, whose wife, Frances, took care of the Ulam's two-year-old daughter Claire when Stan underwent his serious brain surgery in California.

It was about 1981 that a week-long symposium took place at Los Alamos to honor Harold Agnew's sixtieth birthday. Somehow or other I was invited to attend. One of the talks was given by Lowell Wood, Teller's protege at Lawrence Livermore Laboratory and the father of many of the speculative devises evolving for Star Wars, including the X-Ray Laser and Brilliant Pebbles. The particular talk given by Wood was about computers and he said that he was fully prepared by 1990 (*sic*) to have a computer bank of memory physically implanted in him and connected to his neurons. This would fantastically elevate his ability to think and solve problems. Stan said to me, "What an idiot; no one knows how the brain functions."

For me the low point of the week-long sessions was a talk by Eugene Wigner, Nobel physicist, in which I understood not one syllable. I think he had even the rest of the audience buffaloed. He would frequently turn to mathematician Nick Metropolis, gaze at him piercingly, and ask, "Do you follow my equations?" to which Nick would lamely nod assent. After having not said a word during the five days of sessions and feeling very sheepish about it, I finally got up just before the session was to come to a close. I offered, "One needs to understand intimately what the data meant. Simply manipulating raw data without appreciating what it meant would be exposed to failure. For instance, oil is found by geologists from Texas A&M and not by Ph.D.s from Harvard." I'll never forget the look of pity I received from Wigner, but at the intermission, Morgan Sparks, the director of Sandia Laboratories came up and said he absolutely agreed with me.

On perhaps the third day of the sessions, which were held on the second floor of the Laboratory's library, I was walking down the hallway with Stan toward the coffee dispenser when Teller rounded the opposite corner. I know that both he and Stan were surprised to see each other, and in a fraction of an instant Teller turned on his heels and disappeared. When Stan went up to Chicago to see Fermi, who was dying of cancer, Fermi told Stan that he expected to see Teller in a few hours and would try to save his soul. Somewhere in the literature there is a reference to this, and it may possibly have something to do with Teller's ultimate joining in the recommendation to President Kennedy to present the Fermi Award to J. Robert Oppenheimer. Incidentally, this was almost the last act by Kennedy as President—he signed the document before leaving his Ft. Worth hotel for the Dallas parade.

Of course, Stan's intelligence was qualitatively superior to my own. That I was no threat to him may have contributed to his letting down his guard in our private times. One day he said that he had the richest imagination of anybody on the planet, and that, combined with some early teen-age luck in proving some mathematical theorems, contributed to his success in his profession the rest of his life.* He contrasted his imagination with what he called "a lack of creativity in Oppenheimer which Oppenheimer recognized and was the source of deep sadness in Oppenheimer." He tended to belittle Oppenheimer's capacity as a scientist but acknowledged his considerable strength as an administrator at the Laboratory. He praised Von Neumann's proper testimony in support of Oppenheimer at the loyalty hearing even though Von Neumann was a strong advocate for the hydrogen bomb.

Von Neumann had Jewish origins in Hungary but had been baptized early and never had any empathy for Judaism. At the time of Von Neumann's death from cancer, he lost control of himself and became incoherent to the point that the navy had a guard stationed outside his hospital room in case he became delirious and revealed atomic secrets. Just before he died he converted to Catholicism, and his final visitors were members of the Catholic clergy. Stan said the only explanation for this was that Von Neumann was in a deep depression and could not contemplate the end of his thinking power. The only faith that promised some tangible afterlife was Catholicism.

---

* I don't know if he was aware of Einstein's "Imagination is greater than knowledge."

One day I mentioned to Stan how incongruous it was that intelligent people would believe some of the outlandish fables of Christianity or Zuni faith and expressed fear that people who believe such things might believe other monstrosities. Stan said, "That is true, but Judaism has an equal number of childish fables." Upon reflection this seemed quite true to me. The converse to this is when I.I. Rabi refused to attend a symposium on Science and Religion by saying he would not trash the faith that had supported his ancestors for a millennium. But I do not ignore Goethe's assessment: "He who possesses art and science also has religion. He who does not possess them better have religion."

The principal essay in the Ulam volume of *Los Alamos Science* was by Stan's close friend and colleague, the MIT mathematician Gian Carlo Rota. His essay was a very courageous psychological exploration in which he tried to explain what made Ulam tick. I admired the effort by Rota but did feel that on a couple of points he was too cutting.

The Laboratory held a cocktail reception to introduce this volume in honor of Ulam. The main talk was given by the much respected Carson Mark, who once said to me that Teller was the mother of the H-bomb since he held it inside of himself for so long and that Ulam was the father since he fertilized the notion, but that Mark was probably the midwife, since he brought it to fruition. Mark's address was a vitriolic attack on Rota for talking about things that were false and for relying on impressions for which he did not have the supporting facts. I had never before witnessed such an uninhibited attack on a colleague (yes, Rota was present). I then appreciated the beauty of science, in which integrity is paramount and human manipulation is secondary. One of Rota's points dwelled on Stan's laziness, which undoubtedly had an element of truth but was not described appropriately. Rota's subsequent revisions of this article were even more critical, almost hateful. What is behind this treachery remains a puzzle. Stan's colleague from Poland, the mathematician Mark Kac (pronounced Katz, and whose wife was named Kitty!) from the Rockefeller Institute, said very lovingly that Stan had never done an honest day's work in his life. Well, Stan just didn't labor like the rest of us; he sat back and contemplated and let his intuition play and somehow came out with wonderful improvisations. He always needed to work in harmony with some other mathematician who would do the Jimmy Higgins calculations.

We had many memorable dinners with Stan. He appreciated

Ethel's cooking and said in a nonbelittling way that when it came to food, he preferred quantity to quality. Maybe this is because Francoise's table never overflowed. One of the dinners at our house included as guests some Texas presidents of oil companies. The discussion either was boring or an anathema to Stan, for he suddenly started to cough. In an instant he jumped up and ran out of our house. A few seconds later Francoise walked after him. The rest of us just looked at each other and continued our evening with the unspoken realization that the aberrations of geniuses need to be tolerated.

At another dinner we had invited our friends, Shirley and Padriac Frucht. Padriac was an economist whose background included professorships at Brown University, Harvard, and the University of Chicago and an appointment as the economist for the State of Maryland. Paddy had an Irish Catholic mother and a Jewish father. I used to affectionately taunt him by saying that he had inherited the worst qualities of two races. We played tennis with some regularity but he had an adept drop-shot that devastated me and I finally told him that I would no longer play with him if he continued to use his drop-shot. He was unwilling to give up part of his armor. Paddy, compulsively, had to be truthful and, unfortunately, he would search for evil motives in others even when they did not exist. Once we listened to a lecture from the Nobel economist Kenneth Arrow, and it was awkward how Paddy attacked him in the question-and-answer period, and not too convincingly either. On this particular evening at our house we did not have occasion to explain to the Fruchts who the Ulams were. Somehow the conversation led by Paddy drifted to the H-bomb, and Paddy proceeded to explain all kinds of things about it to Stan, who would just quietly reply, "No, you're wrong." This did not deter Paddy. He continued to describe complicated nuances about the H-bomb while Ethel and I and the Ulams just looked at him with a growing chuckle. About this time Shirley recognized that something was embarrassing and beseeched Paddy to stop being the professor and to ask Stan what he knew about it. Finally Paddy blurted out, "What do you know about the H-bomb?" But Stan's only reply was, "Sam will tell you later."

Another dinner was also a disaster. The discussion got around to the minimum wage, which Paddy, from the Chicago School of Economics, claimed did not help the vulnerable members of society. I probably did not entirely disagree, but Stan cried out, "What a shame—such ideas from petty capitalists! You probably made your money anyway by cheating people." Never in my life had anyone said such a falsehood to me. My lame response was, "Since you inherited your wealth from your family, you would not know what fair business dealings are. Anyway, I would sooner rely on a businessman than an academic scheming for tenure." We did not speak to each other for a month. I waited for an apology but then realized that it would never be forthcoming from someone who would not score a tennis game. So I said to myself, "I have to take him for what he is." I then initiated the resumption of our friendship. Similar to my appreciation of Stan is that of a Los Alamos computer analyst, who told me about the time Stan was invited to talk to a convention of New Mexico high school math teachers. He assembled his blackboard and announced he would talk about Bayesian equations. When he saw the blank look on the faces of the teachers, he asked for a show of hands from those who knew about Bayesian equations. When no hands were raised, he erased the board, put on his jacket, and walked out.

Stan had no tender feelings for Indian dances or arts. At one exhibit of pottery by the famous San Ildefonso potter, Maria, at the Wheelwright Museum in Santa Fe, Stan said that his granddaughter could make such things. I cautioned him to quiet down while we still had our scalps. Stan criticized Oppenheimer for interjecting Latin or Greek into a conversation and said that he would do that only with Americans and would not try such a cheap shot with cultured Europeans. Stan did exactly the same thing in his *Adventures*. And when his publisher wanted a sequel volume, Stan said it would have to be posthumous, to which the publisher replied, "I hope it won't take too long." This publisher may have been Robert Maxwell.

At one of the Los Alamos reunions a blond reporter showed up and the physicists started talking without realizing that it was Sally Quinn from the Washington Post. She was noting every piece of trivia, including Agnew's remark that Oppie was a snob who rode around in an expensive car, showing off. Stan then followed by saying that he felt Oppenheimer lacked sex appeal. This was patently absurd. Jean Anderson followed Oppie by about two weeks on a tour through Scandinavia. When people learned she was from New Mexico, all the women asked if she knew a tall, slender physicist named Oppie. Stan considered himself an expert on the subject of pulchritude. He said if he were a woman, he would be a lesbian. After his death I mentioned to Francoise that it was good that he had preceded her since he never could take care of himself. Francoise's retort was that there were any number of Polish women who would welcome the opportunity.

I was always surprised when women suggested generous hospitality to me, but with Stan it flowed as his natural prerogative. The way he flirted with the young lady attendants at El Gancho Tennis Club was one of the highlights of these visitations. It caused a bit of a fracas one day when I mentioned my surprise to Ethel and Priscilla McMillan that the movie beauty Ina Balin said she did not find Stan physically attractive and was actually frightened a bit by him. To my surprise Ethel and Priscilla agreed, but they in turn were not prepared for my assertion that Stan had legions of female admirers, starting with the Grand Dame of New Mexico high society, Concha de Ortiz y Pino de Kleven. This conversation took a dangerous turn when Ethel and Priscilla criticized the roving of husbands beyond their household. Ethel and Priscilla didn't show much sympathy for my alternative argument that just as it was proper that men should be prepared with understanding and support when women traveled through their menopause, so in the same way women should understand man's natural impulse toward being an innocent libertine. I did not mention that there's a bit of the dog in most men. Anyway, while causation may not apply to sub-atomic particles, it surely does in human relations. One of Stan's last speeches was at a computing symposium in Brussels. During his talk Stan pointed to his head and said, "When you get older, the software turns to hardware." Then, pointing to his crotch, he cried, "And your hardware turns to software."

Unfortunately, I never did complete a last promise to Stan. It all involved Ten Thousand Waves, an oriental-type bathhouse on the Ski Basin Road out of Santa Fe. One Sunday when I had a deep crook in my back, Ethel suggested I go for a massage. The only place we could locate on Sunday was Ten Thousand Waves, and I called for an appointment. But when I showed up, the attendant told me the masseuse would be an hour late and asked if I would like to go to one of their hot tubs in the interim. When I assented, they asked whether I would prefer outdoor or indoor. I replied, "Outdoor." Would I prefer co-ed or just men? "Co-ed." Would I prefer the nude or the swimsuit tub? This was a bit of a surprise, but my answer was "Nude." And so, after showering and receiving some directions, I walked out into an area where there were about a dozen unclothed young men and women in this hot tub. Then I had a good lesson in biology. It reinforced the adage that the sexiest part of a human is in the brain. No anticipated physical evolutions whatsoever occurred as I walked to the edge and lowered myself into this pool. Slowly, one by one, the others left, until the only occupant besides me was an appealing twenty-six-year-old girl, quite proud of her body, who then raised herself to the wooden deck and proceeded to spread her legs as if she were going to get a sunbath on her private parts. I didn't know whether this had some hidden meaning or merely represented her disdain for my gray-haired seniority.

When I subsequently reported this to Stan, he became excited and insisted that I take him up there. I told him, "All you need is a pocketbook with some money, and that is the only examination necessary to get into Ten Thousand Waves." But he still insisted that he couldn't go up there alone and I would have to take him. It so happened that he was scheduled to go to a meeting of the National Academy of Science in Washington, preparatory to going to England to receive a medal from some scientific assemblage. By coincidence, Ethel and I also had an invitation to go up to that National Academy of Science meeting. Not long before we were to leave, Francoise asked me if I would take Stan up to that innocent orgy at Ten Thousand Waves. I consented but said that we would have to wait until after the trip back east.

The key meeting in Washington was an informed forum of five top men discussing Star Wars. I shocked a few people when I announced my name and asked a question about the reliability of accepted statistics on the number and throw-weight of missiles in the U.S.S.R. It was at this meeting that I met the mathematician son of Earl Browder and said something to the effect that Browder Senior had an aspect of grace in him that was missing in the run of-the-mill American Communists.

Stan agreed to meet us for dinner in New York City, where Ethel and I splurged on a luxury room at the Pierre. I invited to this dinner Newberry Award Winner Maia Wojciechowska and her adopted daughter, Leonora, who came in from New Jersey. Maia is a fierce Polish patriot, consumed by an overweening Catholic faith and an uninhibited counterpoint to the broad-brush sentiment in the United States of Polish complicity in the Holocaust. Maia was livid in support of the Poles and felt it a crime that the Jewish defense agencies in the United States had lost sight of the fact that the first nation to rise up in opposition to Nazi Germany was Poland and ignored how Poles had suffered at the hands of Jewish Communist officials. Stan said that the experience in Poland in World War II was a mixed bag: there were examples of bestiality and examples of nobility. I guess he should know since he lost so many colleagues and family members in Poland. He had gone back there about 1982 to receive a gold medal from the Polish Mathematics Society.

Stan was in an exceptionally youthful and vigorous condition, and all of us walked down to a restaurant on 44th Street that was owned by the Argentinian father of the artist Castagna, who was living in the wilderness near Picuris Pueblo in northern New Mexico. We tried to keep pace with Stan's lead. He told Maia in Polish a ditty from the city of LWOW of off-color rhymes of the alphabet and then let us hear how he had progressed to the letter "J" in English. When we left him after a glorious dinner, I told Stan that I would take him up to Ten Thousand Waves after he returned from England. However, Stan suffered a fatal heart attack immediately after his return to his home on the Old Santa Fe Trail. The memorial service was scheduled for Los Alamos. It included some beautiful remarks from George Bell, Norris Bradbury, Gian Carlo Rota, and David Hawkins. Rota said, "Stan knew everything about the biggest and the tiniest in this universe but nothing in between." I guess I somewhat occupied the in-between for him. Hawkins said, "Those who don't live much don't die much, but Stan died a great deal." I never did live up to my promise on Ten Thousand Waves, but prominent in my library is Stan's photo with his salutation, "And so to the man who is almost as often right as I am."

In the summer of 1994, when the Kosciuszko Foundation of Denver came down to La Fonda to commemorate the tenth anniversary of Stan's death, Francoise presented a tender speech. It was no surprise when she revealed that Stan spoke but that she wrote *Adventures*. We mortals knew all along that Stan would not have the patience to sit with pen and paper.

27/ KISSING COUSINS

ONE EVENING IN 1972 I was working behind the front desk at La
Fonda when the loveliest brunette I had ever seen walked past and
into La Fiesta Lounge. Her friendly beauty was attraction enough,
but I really thought I knew her. She was seated with the architect
John Midyette when I interrupted with, "But don't I know you?" "No,
you've made a mistake." "But I surely have seen you." "Do you ever
read *Life Magazine*?" And then it hit me: this was Ina Balin who had
adorned *Life*'s cover a few years previously.

Ina had come to Santa Fe for the annual water meeting of property owners at Vista Redondo, which was up the road from Rancho
Encantado in Tesuque. Lade and Peggy Ladenburg from Dallas had
acquired this canyon-cut land, inhabited only by sparse piñon and
juniper scrub, at the foothills of the Sangre de Cristo Mountains from
the Indians for next to nothing. They were the very first developers
to sensibly subdivide their land into five acres minimum per lot and
to establish underground utilities and a property owners' architectural committee. Ina purchased her lot for $15,000; they are now
selling for nearly $300,000. When monies got tight, Ina subsequently
sold her lot to Robin and John Rubel, who built an award-winning
two-million-dollar home on the site. There are so many retired physicists and engineers and artists and investment managers up at Vista
Redondo today that I say it's not just dollars to get you in there, you
also need a superior IQ. Texas Instrument's Mark Shepard has an
enormous house in which all the electrical appliances can be controlled
from his desk console in Dallas. But when the architectural control
committee protested that his tile roof was higher than permitted, he
told them he had more attorneys than they could ever corral and to
get lost.

There are many beautiful Hollywood actresses, but what distinguished Ina was her ability to put men and women at ease despite
her spectacular looks. She hailed from Philadelphia and made her
mark after World War II as the female lead in *Compulsion* on Broadway. She had a successful career in the movies, playing opposite John

243

Wayne in the *Comancheros* and taking the lead in the *Greatest Story Ever Told.* For a while she was a warm friend of one of Hollywood's top moguls. When she showed up in Santa Fe, there was not an ounce of snobbery in her. Her chums were from every walk of life; she felt bound to reciprocate any favor extended to her. Her closest friends, an intelligent and humanistic but plain-appearing wife and her writer husband, had previously moved to Santa Fe.

When Ina made several trips to Vietnam to entertain our troops, her experiences there changed her life. During the collapse of our South Vietnam allies, Ina became involved with an orphanage at Ohn Loc. Then, despite her mother's violent objections, Ina adopted a sixteen-year-old girl and two five-week-old girls and manipulated her connections to get them on one of the evacuee planes. The oldest, Nuyette (Nu Nu), was beautiful and endearing and rather obviously had a black soldier for a father. Today she is divorced from a GI in Hawaii and has two daughters and one son who thrive despite their affliction with sickle-cell anemia. The younger adoptees, Kim and Ba-Nhi, are intelligent charmers in different ways, but they were captivators before their first birthday and still are. For several years Ina raised these kids in Los Angeles while she tried to develop a travel agency—she was at that difficult in-between age for an actress. But Santa Fe was pulling her and finally she rented a house on Mansion Ridge Road and volunteered for the drama department at the College of Santa Fe. Inexplicably, she could not adjust to the easy Hispanic ways. The worst side of her emerged. She could not go through Furr's Cafeteria line without getting into a verbal fight with the Hispanic servers: "Why did you put the potatoes next to the beef?" "What took you so long?" "This tea is not hot enough." To Ina's credit, she knew what was happening and saw the irony that, having lived her entire life devoid of prejudice of any form, she was becoming a bigot. Having great hopes for her daughters, she was also concerned about their education since she couldn't afford to send them to Santa Fe Preparatory School. Their schooling at Pojoaque was a disaster. So they all moved to Westport, Connecticut, where her friend Paul Newman lived.

In the interim she went into partnership with Pietro of the Palace Restaurant in marketing some exotic sauces under the name Palace Seasoning. She made a number of successful marketing trips to Dallas and both coasts. But troubles and petty complaints became a black cloak covering Ina's effervescent good cheer. Ina's many warm friends knew that Ina's entry to a conversation was a litany of the slights she

suffered and the problems she faced. Money pressures were significant despite a generous check each Easter from a long-time admirer
in Paris. Her children were spontaneously friendly and sensible individuals so her periodic family vacation trips to Santa Fe in her Jeep
Wagoneer were widely welcomed. Her family and ours became the
closest friends: her daughter Nu Nu was married in our house by
Supreme Court Justice Bill Federici. Nu Nu's first child was named
Ina Ethel. When anyone wanted to know if we were related, our joint
response was "We're kissing cousins."

Every August 4 we go down to the Corn Dance at Santo Domingo
Pueblo and have lunch either with Angie Reano or Ernie Coriz. This
particular August Ethel went early with the originator of the first Santa
Fe tourist periodical, Ruth Leakey of *La Tourista.* I escorted Ina down
there later in the day, and we joined Ladybird Johnson's brother,
Tony Taylor, for lunch. Everyone gave me a dirty look when I introduced Ina Balin. The artist Ford Ruthling couldn't contain himself
and remarked, "We all like Ethel." By the time we got back to La
Fonda, Ina was in a cloud of rapture from experiencing the dance
and asked if I wanted to show her one of the newly decorated guest
rooms. I wisely mentioned some commitment in the office. This was
a lucky break, and we were able to remain the closest of friends.

Financial problems were pressing on Ina. Her half-brother retired at a young age from the Solomon Brothers trading desk with
more than $30,000,000, but he had a fatal crash in Westchester in a
new plane he had just purchased. Ina was not included in his will. So
when she began complaining of not feeling well at Santa Fe's altitude, we all thought it was just sour grapes. Her friend, Dr. Roger
Smithpeter, worried that it was hypertrophic pulmonic sterosis, a
diagnosis which was confirmed by the result of an echo cardiogram.
The prognosis was early death unless she could have a lung and heart
transplant. Her friends in Santa Fe could not accept this possibility,
but she went up to Yale where it was rather cruelly confirmed. Not
really believing the worst, I called her in the New Haven hospital
and said her girls could come down and spend the summer with us.
Her reply was "You're sweet," and she hung up. Four days later she
was dead—at the prime of her life.

Guardianship of her children went to a wealthy and respected
theatrical agent with a penthouse on Fifth Avenue. Kim and Ba-Nhi
have spent the summers abroad, and by a fortuitous twist of fate,
their education is guaranteed. There was a beautiful memorial service

at our house and one in Connecticut. I was asked to lead one in Hollywood, but I thought it would have been awkwardly theatrical of me to accept. Ina's wide range of loyal friends, who loved her most dearly, know that her best memorial is the fine children she saved from Vietnam, who are honoring her with their own lives. Ina's exceptional beauty, courage, decency, strength, and sacrificial love remain a legacy in Santa Fe for all of us.

Paradoxically, Dr. Smithpeter, her friend and attending physician in Santa Fe, grew up on a ranch near Cheyenne, Oklahoma. He had no knowledge of the massacre of Indian old men and women and children there by General Custer and his Seventh Cavalry. Smithpeter had no inkling of this historical event although he attended school in Cheyenne. Fortunately, an encyclopedia was handy when he challenged my story.

Our last visit in New York with Ina's daughter Kim was ironic. She had come down from an exclusive prep school for an AIDS march on Broadway. It was raining cats and dogs, and we would need a cab to get from her home on Park Avenue to a friend's apartment on Eighth Avenue. Kim said she was returning to school and would drop us off. We were bewildered by her offer until we accompanied her downstairs to her limousine and chauffeur.

28/ A $40,000,000 PRESSURE COOKER

EDDIE J. SMITHSON WAS A RESPECTED MOTEL MAN from Las Cruces who turned his large girth into an asset by naming his bar and grill Fat Eddie's. He had a delightful blond wife, and they were close to each other despite the fact that she once found him spellbound by a shapely guest. He came to his senses when she poured a pitcher of water on his thinning scalp. Together with two local investors, he had just sold their Las Cruces Best Western for a profit when he approached me early in 1980 about getting involved in La Fonda. We had made real progress in renovating the hotel so it was ready for a professionally experienced general manager. I was impressed by Eddie. My initial evaluation proved accurate...he had lots going for him and was upright in character. But he was vulnerable: a tender ego and a deep caution, the latter surviving from financial setbacks with his father at a young age in a carpet store in Farmington. After he left La Fonda, he was properly honored as State Director of Tourism.

Our then general manager A. S. was not working out. When I hired her she was an executive secretary at the Classic in Albuquerque. The trade gossip was that she was really running the place, and I felt a quantum jump in her title would propel her to her full potential. But she didn't have the confidence to initiate innovations. She was so distressed when Eddie came in above her that she left without saying goodbye. Despite a phone call and two letters from me, she never showed up for her bonus check and I was not prepared to mail it under such ungracious circumstances.

We worked out a game plan for five years. Eddie made a significant installment investment in Corporacion's common stock, his title would be managing director, and in five years we would sell the property to a buyer who would respect La Fonda's ethnic staff and preserve its unique regional style. I told Eddie he would make a million dollars, and that is exactly how it turned out. He and his wife redecorated a fine suite for themselves. It was an expansion of Mary Naylor's

247

fourth-floor apartment. But when they painted the brown-stained vigas to a modern white it indicated that truly they did not cotton to La Fonda's decor. My partner, Jim Fouts, facilitated the transaction by selling some initial stock very cheaply to Smithson. This helped Smithson lower his average cost and enabled Fouts to cash in some of his holdings.

Around 1984 Tom Catron and Coe Newman introduced me to their client Nitan Madhvani, who wanted to buy La Fonda. Catron was someone to take seriously and respectfully. Grandson of the famous-infamous Thomas Benton Catron, Tom was senior partner of the senior law firm in town, chairman of the Santa Fe Opera, chairman of the Museum of New Mexico Foundation, and chairman of Sunwest Bank of Santa Fe. I viewed him as a likable and humorous buddy and a pleasant fellow member of the men's social club, Quien Sabe. Coe Newman was an admired long-time Santa Fean with whom I really was comfortable. I had confidence in her integrity and judgment. In his turn Madhvani proved to be charming and intelligent. He was born in Uganda of Indian parents who fled to Kenya after Idi Amin's genocide. The Madhvanis were one of the largest East African conglomerates, with executive offices in London. Nitan was a graduate of Oxford with a French wife. Through a local, nonpracticing attorney he was introduced to Santa Fe. He bought some lots on Tano Road and wanted to pour monies into La Fonda. But I feared he would turn it into a Ritz Carlton and destroy everything native we had tried to preserve. So in a very polite way the Madhvani overture was discouraged.

Such was the setting when I was invited to lunch by Gerald Peters at his Casa Sena restaurant in Sena Plaza. I had not previously met him, but he was the central topic of conversation in Santa Fe. Although he was the subject of much criticism, he also had many young admirers, who recognized him as a daring entrepreneur who leaped on the bandwagon of downtown Santa Fe's growth early on. More than any other entrepreneur, Peters seized on the transformation of quiet, cultural Santa Fe into a place where fortunes could be made. This brought him critics and jealous adversaries. A story of his destitute financial condition circulated when he entered St. Johns, but I suspected the facts were otherwise. His grandfather was the senior partner of the Denver securities firm Peters, Writer and Christianson. I had authored an appraisal report for that firm on Mountain Fuel Supply Company after it made an important gas find at Church Buttes. Peters had made a superb purchase of Sena Plaza from the School of

American Research but there was envious street talk questioning aspects of the transaction. The same jealously surfaced when he sold the former Los Llanos estate to the aging Georgia O'Keeffe. The secretarial pool of downtown Santa Fe was convinced a young lady had been captivated by his self-confidence and she then was physically decimated when the relationship did not deepen. Quiet Santa Fe could not keep up with his astute aggressiveness, but his enemies calmed some when he married the decent daughter of a long-time leading Santa Fe physician. Undoubtedly some realtors raged when Peters turned eight-dollar-a-foot rental space into forty-dollar-a-foot rental space, and some gallery owners were left at the starting gate when Peters sensed the surging market for the Taos Masters. At this lunch I was impressed by a very ingenious and exciting young man. I was surprised at the depths of his financial sophistication. Yes, he wanted to buy La Fonda, but I turned him down since I knew I would risk losing most of my friends. The wags were already calling our town St. Petersburg.

Some nine months later, Peters called me again for lunch. By then he was the leading real estate investor in downtown Santa Fe. He had completed some admired commercial remodeling in honest Santa Fe style. He proposed that he buy some stock in La Fonda, if the hotel wasn't for sale right then. My thoughts about him had changed somewhat. He obviously was a growing power in the city. I thought that exposure to our civic-minded board members would be a good influence for a maturing presence that could not be ignored. I told him that any purchase would have to recognize that he could not interfere in our selection of a prospective buyer when we got around to selling. If he wanted to enter the bidding, he would first have to resign from our board of directors. Further, he had to accept our determination to protect our native staff and decor. All of these covenants were agreeable to him in writing, but I was still bothered by some stories of a Millicent Rogers Art Auction he had supposedly manipulated for his own profit.

So I went to see Ed Lockhart, vice president of Santa Fe National Bank, who reported that Peters lived up to all his business dealings with the bank. Yes, they had heard unconfirmed rumors concerning involvements at St. Johns but they were only rumors. They were pleased with the lender-borrower relationship between Peters and the bank. Essentially, the identical report came from Tom McGreevey of Smith Barney and the young Allan Ball at the Bank of Santa Fe. When the prospect of selling a stock position to Peters, together with his written negative pledges, was presented to La Fonda's board, Jim Russell objected strongly, saying, "You can't trust him to cross the street." But, I emphasized the positive reports from the bankers and the Board consented unanimously. Dave Sierra knew the next day what had occurred and said at breakfast, "You will rue the day you let him in."

In fact, Peter's presence on the board was helpful. When we got ready to construct our $4,000,000 Carriage House, he introduced me to Jerry Ford (no, no relation to Gerald), the head of the United New Mexico bank system. We worked out some attractive Industrial Revenue Bond financing at an interest rate that was only 75 percent of Chase Manhattan prime. At the time, Ford was dating stately Susan Dupepe in Santa Fe. When he called for a weekend reservation prior to a trip to Washington, the girls in our executive office were all agog that Jerry Ford was calling me. When I asked, on the phone, "Is your girlfriend going with you?" their gasps could almost be heard over the telephone lines.

Peters tried several times to become leasing agent for our commercial tenants but we discouraged that subject. He wanted me to become a limited partner in his Plaza Mercado on San Francisco Street, but I showed no interest. When he proposed I join an art syndicate, my attorney asked for secured liens on the art and he dropped the matter. Then he flew me on his jet for a day of skiing at Aspen and asked that I purchase a one-third interest in the jet. I told him, "Jerry, your father was a stockbroker and mine a grocer in Harlem. Owning a jet does not fit my image." Meanwhile, Madhvani was making repeated social visits to Santa Fe. Catron had been his house guest in Nairobi and had returned with impressive reports of Madhvani's family's standing. Both Smithson and Fouts were reminding me that our five-year game plan was coming toward a close, and their wishes could not be ignored.

Therefore we executed an agreement with Madhvani giving him an exclusive right to investigate the hotel and provide us with a copy of an Appraisal report at his expense. We would be obliged to negotiate in good faith until February 1, 1987, to see if we could agree on a trade. This agreement was subject to our board's approval. A meeting was set for Saturday afternoon at my home after a dedication luncheon of the Carriage House. At the luncheon I told an unsuccessful joke that Smithson may have incorrectly interpreted as a barb in his direction. I reviewed the Madhvani agreement with the directors and was amazed to see Smithson protest in an unseemly way the buyer's commitment to respect our native staff and decor. "That's stupid," he said, "A buyer should be free to do whatever he wants with the property." I was stunned at Smithson's insulting language and suspected he must be under some tension from the bank loans he had arranged to buy his La Fonda stock. Peters had not arrived for the board meeting, but the directors present approved the Madhvani agreement. Ten minutes later Peters walked in. I informed him of the resolution just passed and told the Secretary to read him the agreement and resolution at the close of the meeting.

Slowly, the unpleasant implications of the 1986 Tax Reform Act dawned on us. A buyer could get a stepped-up cost basis only through December 31, 1986, but the Madhvani agreement extended to February 1, 1987. I offered Catron a reimbursement of Madhvani's costs if he moved the expiration date backwards or surrendered the agreement, but he said his client had a deal and insisted we abide by it. Peters then came over to La Fonda for lunch and asked for the right to buy the property, but I reminded him Madhvani had an exclusive. Anyway Peters had not resigned as a director. Fortunately, Dr. Ralph Lopez joined us for coffee, and when Peters again sought the right to be a buyer, Ralph said, "We operate honorably and Madhvani has an exclusive until February 1, 1987."

Peters then attempted to buy Smithson's stock on an installment basis with an immediate proxy on all his stock, and I knew we were in for a potential squeeze play. We might not have the requisite vote for a liquidating sale of assets. I informed Catron that things were passing out of my control and said, "Perhaps I will make an enemy of everyone." But Catron again refused to release us from the Madhvani agreement or to follow up on my suggestion that Madhvani buy Smithson's stock and we would extend Madhvani's period of exclusivity.

By mid-December 1986 Peters delivered an Arthur Andersen tax opinion letter on the necessity of a 1986 transaction which implied I would be irresponsible to the shareholders if I let the crucial December 31, 1986 date pass with no sale. Peters then proved his ingenuity by proposing that we sell our stock to him, in which case he would inherit the good faith obligation to negotiate with Madhvani on sale of assets. Our attorney advised that the distinction between stock and assets would not hold up and we so informed Peters. A firm turn down then would have avoided subsequent grief for all the parties. But two days later our attorney said he had reviewed the question with his senior associates and they felt such an arrangement was legal and permissible. So, recognizing the dangerous parallels to the Texaco-Getty-Penzoil quagmire, we agreed to negotiate a sale of stock to Peters for all the shareholders if he would honor a good-faith commitment to negotiate a sale of assets to Madhvani. For sure, in hindsight, it is obvious that we were not wise or noble to succumb to such convoluted reasoning.

On the evening of December 21, 1986, Peters asked me to come over to his house, where he was huddled with his wife, attorney Gene Gallegos, and financial consultant Milo McGonagle. They proposed a one-third cash, two-thirds note secured by a third mortgage on La Fonda's assets for the stock of La Fonda. Gallegos was a powerful and adroit attorney, so I asked, "Gene, how can you provide a corporate lien when not all the stockholders may be involved in the sale?" He replied, "Oh, we can work that out." I said, "Gene, you will have to demonstrate that to the content of the selling shareholders." We agreed that Peters would present a written proposal, and we would meet on the twenty-sixth. Since the terms appeared interesting, Peters and I decided to call in attorneys. Our hotel attorney continued to represent us. Peters said he would use the Jones firm.

Peters was represented by Manuel Rodriguez, a former monsignor, since his law partner, Gallegos, had gone off skiing to Purgatory. Our attorney said, "Remember, Manuel, I will want your firm's legal opinion on this third mortgage at closing." The next several days were frustrating and really troublesome to me since I had a bad case of the flu. There were appointment conflicts and scheduled meetings did not occur. Rodriguez wanted to alter aspects of the trade in order to meet certain tax influences. We objected to warranting that the plant was in compliance with code. We could not give such an assurance on a sixty-five-year-old building. Then Gallegos returned and proposed that our law firm, not his, deliver a legal opinion on the third mortgage. It dawned on me that this trade could not prudently close in 1986, and our tax advice was that it had to be a 1986 finite sale and not contain any resemblance to an option. Thus, the Memorandum of Understanding between the selling La Fonda shareholders and Peters said it would be null and void if the transaction did not close by December 31, 1986.

To compound difficulties, Tom Catron went to England and his son, Fletcher, had learned of the Peters' interest. Fletcher submitted a rush draft contract on behalf of Madhvani that we felt was filled with uncertainties. From Nairobi, Madhvani sent a lengthy telex that had all the earmarks of setting us up for a lawsuit and contained self-serving recitals that were not completely accurate. Even though Peters said he would monetarily indemnify us from any Madhvani claims, I knew this transaction was not set to close. Such was the opinion of Smithson's own attorney, Mel Eaves, a man who represented his client 120 percent of the time.

Undoubtedly, Peters imagined that we had a better offer from Madhvani and Madhvani figured we had a better offer from Peters, but they were both wrong. Neither contract was suitable for closing although the dollar considerations were about the same.

Gallegos sent us a demand letter that smelled of another threatened lawsuit. I feared a schoolboy scam based on a promissory note that had fictitious collateral and that could be contested for years. On the evening of the thirtieth, "C" returned the contract intended for closing with all the necessary changes marked therein. Arthur Andersen said they would fax us a comfort letter, but by December 31, 1986, it had not arrived. Around 10 a.m. of the thirty-first the response Gallegos contract was received with the unacceptable clauses unchanged. Our attorney hand-delivered a sober letter outlining the reasons the transaction could not close in time and expressing a willingness, when things quieted down, to resume negotiations in 1987. Instead, early in January, Peters went off to Hawaii and Gallegos prepared a lawsuit. Several attorneys refused to represent Peters, but then a highly respected Albuquerque attorney, Frank Allen, Jr., filed a $40,000,000 breach of contract suit against the La Fonda directors. Now we were at the mercy of some uninformed local journalists happy to attack the establishment, and they published a most unflattering photo of me with descriptions questioning our integrity. But I was not the only target. The downtown crowd shifted the jest of why a former governor could not be circumcised, "There's no end to that Peter."

Ballen, Fouts, and Smithson shook hands in agreement that we would all act together. We correctly assumed that Peters would try to fragment us. But then my son-in-law, whose marriage was breaking apart, committed a serious error of judgment that we are all capable of. He sent Smithson a stupid letter accusing Eddie of padding his expense charges and not attending to business. Smithson undoubtedly imagined this letter was my handiwork, which was not the case, and neurotically feared for his vulnerability. Because our hotel attorney was going to be our chief witness, we sought other defense counsel and were able to secure the very capable Dave Olmsted, who delegated the case to Larry Maldegen. That was a fortuitous turn of events for us. After Frank Allen deposed me, Fouts, and our hotel attorney, he knew there was no valid legal complaint. He withdrew from the case and was replaced by a tough streetfighter, Tom Simons. During Allen's questioning of me, he asked what words in the contract required a legal opinion on the soundness of the third mortgage. I blurted out, "That's an obscene question," and Maldegen gave my shins a kick that still hurts.

Peters requested an injunction against us before Judge Bruce Kaufman. Simons handled himself impressively even though he had only four days to become familiar with the case. To our amazement Simons called Peter's tax adviser and our hotel attorney's partner as his witness. The tax adviser testified that he had met with Peters twice at the tail end of the year and advised him not to provide a guarantee of the Peters Corporation. I thought Judge Kaufman would erupt out of his seat, but there was nary a ripple. Our capable attorney, Maldegen, asked the tax adviser if he had the permission of La Fonda or Ballen to counsel with Peters and he replied, "No." Our hotel attorney had suggested that, regardless of what we felt about the tax adviser, he would be 100% truthful; he was an honest witness but, as it turned out, somewhat less than 100%. Just before I testified, Peters stopped me in the hall and pleaded, for his children's sake, not to mention his net worth. I said, "Well I'm a father and I'll have to think on that." In my testimony I referred to "an enormous net worth."

Judge Kaufman denied Peter's request for an injunction in a four-page opinion stating that the parties had not reached agreement on a trade and it therefore appeared unlikely Peters would prevail in a trial on the merits. We were elated because the trial was scheduled to open before Judge Kaufman. It looked like this coercion would soon be over. Madhvani's friend, David Carlson Smith, seemed to know precisely what was going on in Simons' office. Coe Newman relayed from Smith that Peters would not lie down as a result of Kaufman's ruling but would keep the legal pot stewing forever. But then a month later Kaufman told the attorneys he was recusing himself because our law firm was representing one of the parties in his daughter's dispute on an unrelated real estate brokerage fee. Maldegen attempted to dissuade the judge. The canons state that recusal should occur only where there is clear-cut conflict of interest and that was not the situation here. Kaufman said that anyway he had a heavy docket and it would be a long time before he could get around to hearing the case. I always admired Kaufman as a most courageous and honest man who had devoted many years of worthy service to Santa Fe, but there were others who found it a trifle confusing.

Relations with Smithson had deteriorated. He wanted out of this lawsuit, and his attorney, Eaves, told me that Eddie had an obligation to his wife and had to seize this opportunity to play me against Peters. I hung up on Eaves. We arranged a meeting at my office to reach a settlement with Smithson, but our attorney noticed Eaves' distinctive car outside of Rodriguez' office. We correctly assumed that Peters was buying out Smithson and also his testimony. I kept telling our attorneys that Smithson was inherently honest, but we were all shaken. Many a witness, by a shrug of a shoulder or an inflection of the voice, can drive a nail into a coffin. My courage was fading. I knew that Eaves would exploit any weakness to enhance his client and, as an opportunist, he was far more adroit than any of the other players.

Judge Vernon Frost from Tucumcari was then mutually selected to hear the case. He was perhaps the most distinguished district judge in the New Mexico court system. But, before that, Peters won an appeal to the New Mexico Supreme Court entitling him to a trial by jury. Our position was very inadequately argued by Dave Olmsted, one of the finest attorneys in the state. As much as I liked and respected Olmsted, I could not ignore his amateurish performance before the court. We decided to add Paul Bardacke, a former attorney general, to assist Maldegen and to handle the jury trial itself. This really angered Olmsted, but within three months Dave was in the hospital for a cardiovascular operation and a few years later he was dead. There is no doubt he was not functioning at his best before the Supreme Court.

In later tenacious questioning by Maldegen, Peters' tax adviser revealed he held a powerful structural role in the buyer's Corporation. This incredible revelation cleared up an ongoing mystery. Three days after Peters filed suit, a young attorney whom I knew socially came over and said, "You were not exclusively represented in your negotiations." I replied, "Oh, but you surely are wrong." "No, I am not." I could not believe that there were not strong procedures to enforce a Chinese Wall among the participants, but now we had our own "Deep Throat."

Maldegen continued his discovery efforts against determined opposition. I was beside myself with rage, but all the attorneys somehow or other took it in stride. I felt we had to listen to their advice on how to conduct our defense. Their strategy was accepted by Richard Freling of the powerful Dallas firm of Johnson & Gibbs, whom we called in for an overview. While I felt there was no legal justification for this lawsuit, I was afraid of how Smithson or Eaves would come across as pro-Peters witnesses. A jury could lose all sense of proportion for a landmark like La Fonda, and everything we possessed could be wiped out. Ethel knew the risks but said we would not crater and would fight this pressure-cooker. Then I was concerned that one of the defendants was over eighty and the other closing in on seventy. I felt it wasn't fair to load a $40,000,000 joint-and-several lawsuit on their estates. Not one of them ever complained. Maldegen said he wasn't afraid of Smithson because Smithson's sale contract required him to be a cooperative witness for Peters. Maldegen said he could tar it as bought testimony. But then Bardacke pulled a miracle in visiting with Eaves, who became a totally supportive witness for us and was backed by extensive and accurate notes. Just before the trial Simons spent ten hours trying to shake Eaves in a deposition, but all he accomplished was to reinforce our position. Now three years later, Bardacke and Eaves are law partners.

The first day of jury selection did not bode well for Peters. He had at his side a Philadelphia psychologist jury appraiser at a rumored cost of $120,000. When a Hispanic native potential juror said, "This Peters has destroyed my town," Judge Frost reprimanded, "You shouldn't say that." But the next native juror also said, "No, I cannot be impartial when it concerns this Peters." And then an intelligent nonpracticing lady attorney was maneuvered onto the panel although it was clear she was an enemy of Peters.

At 6 a.m., on the second day of jury selection, Peters called my partner Jim Fouts, with a conciliatory attitude. He would drop a separate case challenging the legality of Corporacion de La Fonda paying our legal costs, which by now exceeded $800,000. Our attorneys said it was doubtful whether we would prevail on this aspect. Judge Frost kept pressuring the parties for a completed settlement before the noon hour because he did not want to buy the jury panel lunch! So in a completely uncontrolled, intensely emotional atmosphere, we retreated a centimeter and the complaint was dismissed. Immediately thereafter Ballen and Fouts agreed not to sell La Fonda during the century but to continue to improve the property. My daughter Lois, one of the defendants, pointed out serious typographical errors in the midst of six of the most astute attorneys in the city. Many folks were inaccurately informed that withdrawal of the case involved cash payments.

I was incensed about what had been discovered concerning this tax adviser. But I also knew that Maldegen's firm and the tax adviser's shop shared a juicy pot on overturning an artist's Will. It was no surprise when Maldegen advised that he sympathized with our feelings but his partners would not permit him to represent us in such a complaint. Even in law, things are not black or white. Maldegen's former senior partner insisted his name be withdrawn from the masthead when he learned a contribution had been given to a charity of a sitting judge. I was exhausted by these three years of legal entanglements and knew that everyone was entitled to learn from an indiscretion. I asked a former Supreme Court Chief Justice what to do. "Well, Sam, you have reason to be angry but bear in mind that our Supreme Court is not set up to discipline top-line players. Maybe that isn't how it should be but that's how it is and you need to bear that in mind." So, Saul Cohen succeeded in resolving any irritations.

Some have asked if from the beginning this was our slick scheme to neutralize Peters. That is like asking if FDR sucked in the Japanese at Pearl Harbor or if George Bush's ambassador importuned Saddam Hussein to invade Kuwait. Although he persists in derogatory references to us, he has behaved properly since the trial and has not harassed management. He has mainly acted in a responsible way in the community but continues to be involved in litigation. He has a superb food manager and has developed an excellent restaurant. In time he will likely build the finest art gallery in the country on the Paseo. He has achieved his ambition of being the major private employer in the city. All of us who are entrepreneurs in business learn as we grow older. We eventually replace daring with the wisdom to distinguish when to be a bull in a china shop and when to elevate to wiser standards of conduct. Or, as Anatole France said, many of the great benefactors of Notre Dame Cathedral sitting in Place Vendome are ex-madams.

29/ *ENTER OPPENHEIMER*

AROUND 1955, THE SUCCESSFUL INDEPENDENT OIL MAN, Bruce Calder, George de Morenschildt, and I organized the Bohemian Club in Dallas. It consisted of twenty men who met each month. Each member in turn served as host of a gourmet meal and delivered a controversial paper. Jake Hamon, who was a member of the Bohemian Grove outside of San Francisco, assisted by giving us some ideas as to do's and don'ts. It was an eagerly sought after monthly event, and occasionally we were permitted to invite a visitor. One of the meetings was devoted to a hypnosis demonstration by Dr. Andres Goth. A visitor, A. L. Barnett, Jr., performed like a robot–to our anxious curiosity. Later he died of a malignant brain tumor, which perhaps explained his peculiar behavior that evening.

Back in those days, when Texas friends got together, sooner or later they would be talking about Negroes after they finished reciting sex exploits. (When the race question was the subject of a position paper at one of our meetings, it did not result in the same confusion that occurred at a similar gathering in Houston when a recent arrival from New York–junior partner of the investment firm, Fridley & Hess–splashed cold water on the party when he said he wasn't fearful of competing with Blacks.) It was the custom for ensuing discussion to take place by going around the room. That night it got to the tall and handsome native Dallasite, Dr. Jabez Gault, who in essence said, "I am not against Blacks, but I detest niggers. I am sick and tired of having to provide free medical attention to niggers." Sitting next to him was the beloved cellist, Lev Aronson, from Lithuania. Aronson had been interned at Buchenwald during the war and had appeared on a "This is Your Life" TV segment. Lev was the first cellist at the Dallas Symphony and a professor at Baylor. His intimate friend was Piatigorsky. Lev was sitting next to Jabez Gault. When Lev said, "I was the nigger of Berlin," that ended the discussion. The Bohemian Club died after the FBI became more than suspicious of us. The fact that George de Mohrenschildt was one of our founders didn't help matters.

259

For my dinner, I was given the assignment of summarizing the Oppenheimer loyalty hearing at a time when I really knew nothing other than what had appeared in the newspapers. After concentrated reading, I devoured the 800-page verbatim testimony published by the U.S. Government Printing Office, which had pledged to the witnesses it would be kept secret. I concluded that an erroneous decision had been reached in revoking Oppenheimer's security clearance. So I once again read the 800 pages and was reinforced in my first impressions. I delivered to the meeting of the club a rather complex and partisan summary and ended with my conclusion that the case was lost by Oppenheimer's naive and gentlemanly attorney, Lloyd K. Garrison. Bill Hudson, a very conservative individual and one of the initial backers of the *National Review*, was skeptical and borrowed the volume. He then reassured me by stating that he had arrived at the same conclusion. Garrison never billed Oppenheimer for his lengthy legal services, and Oppie never thanked Garrison. As Vickie Weisskopf said, Oppie was the most complex person he ever met.

About December 10, 1963, the First International Congress on Gravitational Collapse was scheduled for the Statler Hilton in Dallas. It was organized by Ivor Robinson, a Lithuanian refugee who had been brought up in England and parlayed a strong English accent. He was a mathematical relativist with the Graduate Research Center and organized this Congress with Oppenheimer as chairman. There was an impressive group of invited lecturers, like Fred Hoyle from England, Margaret Burbidge from California, and John Wheeler from Princeton. At first there was debate as to whether the Congress should be cancelled—the November 22 assassination of President Kennedy was fresh in everyone's mind. But they decided to go ahead. I wrangled an invitation from Chaim Richman, who had done his doctoral work under Oppenheimer but was not going to attend the conference. I later learned from Nobel physicist I. I. Rabi that Richman was one of those victims of Oppenheimer's sharp tongue. I guess he never really got over it.

In 1939 Oppenheimer and a post-doc student, Snyder, had written a famous, controversial paper predicting what we now know as black holes. Oppenheimer then produced a follow-up paper with another talented graduate student, Volkoff. Thus, Oppie was the logical chairman. The second-floor ballroom at the Statler Hilton was packed to capacity. Oppenheimer went up to the podium and started talking. When someone shouted out from the back, "The microphone is not working," Oppie's response was, "That's not my problem," and he continued talking. This just added to his magnetism because what I saw was the smartest and saddest face I had ever run across. During Fred Hoyle's lecture Oppie gradually drifted from the podium over to the blackboard and without any fuss reached over and took the chalk from Hoyle's fingers and completed Hoyle's subsequent equations himself. What a look of angry puzzlement shone in Hoyle's eyes.

I was mesmerized by this Oppenheimer and trailed after him on the mezzanine during the first coffee break. An attendee with a heavy German accent came up and said something like the following: "For the past six years I have been measuring X, comparing it to Y, and hoping to prove Z. What do you think about it?" Oppie pondered awhile, said, "You have wasted the last six years," and then walked off. So this Oppenheimer never really left my thinking thereafter. We ultimately met his carpenter son Peter and his brother Frank and also the latter's daughter and even visited their beautiful ranch in Blanco Basin near Pagosa Springs, Colorado. This is where Frank lived in "deprived" isolation after being fired from the University of Minnesota immediately after admitting before a Congressional Committee that he had been a member of the Communist Party before World War II. I was certainly not the only one captivated by Oppenheimer. Dorothy McKibbin, the well-known manager of 109 East Palace Avenue and the person who greeted all the greats assigned to "The Hill" (Los Alamos) during World War II, was invited to lunch at La Fonda early in 1943 by George Stevenson. "Dorothy, there is an important war project starting and we need you to work there." "What is it?," Dorothy asked. "I can't tell you." "What will I do?" "I can't tell you, but it is vital for the country." "When do you need my decision?" "Tomorrow." So, lunch over, they walked into the lobby where they saw a tall, thin man with a porkpie hat. "You will be working for that chap," said Stevenson. So hesitating but a few seconds, Dorothy said, "I'll take the job." That was Oppenheimer.

Two years after we moved to Santa Fe, our good friends, Chaim and Betty Richman, returned to Los Alamos where Richman was going to be group leader of one of the units connected to the meson physics facility. Subsequently, he realized he wasn't a strong enough science manager and relinquished that post. When Betty asked me how things were going, I said I had problems. She asked if they were connected with health, and when I answered in the negative she said, "You have no problems." Of course, she was correct. Betty and Chaim and their children were very close friends of ours in Dallas, and we had provided many niceties for them, including a grand farewell party when he went off on a temporary assignment back to the cyclotron in Berkeley. When Betty's brother's oil company went belly-up unexpectedly, I feared she did not know this and awkwardly advised some caution in her spending. She responded, "Oh, heck, many's the time in Tulsa when I was growing up with three Cadillacs in the garage and no gasoline for a one of them." Unfortunately, I had seen where they had closed off friendships either because of change of scenery or because they misjudged the motives of other people. I saw this happen with the physicist who had gotten Chaim his job in Dallas with the Graduate Research Center, Dr. Lauriston Marshall, and the Indian physicist, Raju. When they left Los Alamos to retire near Santa Cruz, California, Ethel and I gradually evolved onto their nonentity list, an occurrence which is very saddening. Old-timers said Betty was the prettiest girl on The Hill during the war. It was a pleasure how well she liked me until I suggested some psychosomatic basis of her frequent illnesses at Los Alamos.

Chaim told me that the J. Robert Oppenheimer Memorial Committee, which was in the process of formation in Los Alamos, needed a business type on the board. I was interrogated in a friendly but direct way by Norris Bradbury, the savior of the Laboratory and its second director. I joined their board and have been a member ever since. I served one term as committee chairman. The committee annually presents a world-class public lecturer at Los Alamos. When I introduced John Wheeler as lecturer one year, I mentioned hearing a previous colloquium of his and remarked that I didn't understand his quantum explanations of light waves canceling each other. Said Wheeler, "If that's all you didn't understand, then you are indeed the most brilliant attendee in the audience." I met many of the greats in science, including perhaps a dozen Nobel Laureates, and pointed out a nonscientific error in one of Hans Bethe's papers. Harold Agnew, the third outspoken director of the Laboratory, intended to be pejorative but I took it as a compliment when he called me a physics groupie.

Anyway, I arranged to have published a rather elaborate fundraising brochure after my English construction was corrected and improved by Priscilla Duffield and Carson Mark, long-time leader of the Theoretical Division. There were not too many who could match Priscilla's unique career. She was personal secretary to Ernest Lawrence, when he was in charge of the cyclotron. She then became personal secretary to Oppenheimer at Los Alamos and finally ended up as personal secretary to a West Coast biologist named Revelle. Her appraisal is that Revelle was the greatest of the three. In order to distribute this fund-raising brochure I asked for a list of industrial suppliers to Los Alamos National Laboratory. Lo and behold, out came a computer readout listing each supplier and the dollar amount each had collected during the previous year. I, not so jokingly, said we could perhaps raise more money if we sold that list to Soviet Intelligence. But the solicitation proved productive, and we received some checks from Xerox, IBM, and other major corporations. Willard Kruger, who had made his money as architect for Los Alamos during World War II, was very enthused about the project, thinking that there were some architectural commissions involved. But, when he learned otherwise, he didn't send a penny.

With some trace of rascality I sent the fund-raising brochure off to the widow of Admiral Strauss, who, many said, was Oppenheimer's essential nemesis. Back came a letter from Strauss' son saying that they appreciated the invitation but their philanthropy had already been spoken for. He added, "By the way, we object to this sentence that the FBI had violated the client-attorney privilege during the loyalty hearing. We are sending the brochure on to Judge Roger Robb, and you probably will hear from him." Roger Robb was the brilliant and combative government prosecutor who proved more than a match for Oppenheimer and his attorney, Lloyd Garrison. As a reward for his lynching of Oppenheimer, he received an appointment to the federal bench. In due course came a letter to me from Judge Robb, who stated that the sentence in the brochure about client-attorney privacy was false and that there would be a libel action unless I retracted it. I told him to give me a bit of time to confirm the facts.

Attorney Harold Green turned out to be the source of that allegation, which was included in a book by Stern on the Oppenheimer affair. I went up to Washington to see Green, who was a member of the Fried Frank Kampleman law firm. Green was the young attorney in the Atomic Energy Commission who had been preparing charges on low-profile disloyalty cases within the agency. He was just sitting there when General Nichols, Deputy Director of the AEC, told him he had to draft loyalty charges against Oppenheimer. A file of supporting material was furnished to him from the vaults. While he was reviewing the file and drafting the charges, which was a most unpleasant assignment for him, he noticed that there were some files of reports from FBI agents who had trailed and bugged Oppenheimer continuously. Some of the reports covered meetings Oppie had with his own attorneys and summaries of these reports had been presented to J. Edgar Hoover and Lewis Strauss. But a security clerk came in very distressed, seized those specific files and removed them from Green's purview. Green told me I should not succumb to Judge Robb's request and that if it came down to a legal issue, he had corroborating evidence. He then opened his private safe, pulled out some papers, and said, "Here is an affidavit from a former FBI agent confirming what I have just told you, just in case it is ever needed." I asked, "Who is that FBI agent?" "I cannot tell you, but he is now retired in the Southwest." So I told Robb we would not withdraw the brochure. No further word from him. He did not file suit against me. Gordon Grey, chairman of the Loyalty Review Board, told me Robb was too honorable to be so involved, but Grey was proved wrong.

When I received permission from the FBI to inspect their records under the Freedom of Information Act, Ethel accompanied me to Washington. The FBI could not have been more helpful and did not charge me for copies of several hundred pages. The file clerk assigned to me said the Oppie file was in the same room with the Kennedy and Martin Luther King files. When I told him the focus of our inquiries, he directed me to a particular file cabinet and said, "Where the agent reports an unimpeachable source, that means electronic eavesdropping." Even though a quarter of the agent reports were blacked out for national security, it was immediately obvious that the allegations of FBI wire-tapping were correct. Strauss wanted J. Edgar Hoover to intervene with the board during its final private deliberations, but Hoover declined and said it wouldn't be cricket. It was also obvious that during the 1954 Loyalty Hearing copies of these FBI reports were going to Admiral Strauss, and, by implication, to Judge Robb.

After I reported all this to the Oppenheimer Committee, Green asked if we could help get him a forum, so we invited Harold and Beverly Agnew to dinner. I said, "Harold, you've invited everyone from Billy Graham up or down to the Lab's morning colloquium and you should invite this fellow Green." Beverly agreed. It was no surprise when Agnew replied, "In life you must be responsible for your actions and I will not encourage anything to defend Oppenheimer." When our daughter Joanne (now Lee), a ballet dancer, tore into Harold for his cowardice, that alone was worth all our involvement in this drama.

When we intervened with Jane Wilson in Chicago, the *Bulletin of Atomic Science* changed its editorial decision and published a piece by Green, which generated minimal attention. My friendship with Betty

Lilienthal (no connection to the AEC commissioner), wife of an early engineer at LASL, now paid off in a surprising way. Betty was highly regarded on The Hill. The respect shown to her by Bradbury, Agnew, Bethe, and others was noticeable. She was head of the Wednesday Irregulars, our hiking club. Among its incidents: Ethel broke her ankle, Mary Argo had a fatal stroke, and Helene Suydam suffered an ugly dog bite. Betty and a few others were hospitalized after an unfortunate Wednesday auto encounter with a school bus. Participation in these hikes became a high priority with me. The hikes included a four-day backpack around Navajo Mountain, which I led, and a two-day 70th birthday hike for Bob Walker up to Lake Lily in Colorado. Our group had a near-fatal descent from Wheeler Peak on a scree slope, led by a Taos pediatrician. Memorable were several glorious trips to the McNally's cabin on Wilson Mesa, west of Telluride. But, if anything, Betty engendered confidence. At a cocktail party in Corrales, a momentary acquaintance at her elbow revealed that he was the former FBI agent involved in that Oppie bugging and that it bothered him. When the three of us had lunch at La Fonda, Lee Hancock repeated to me what he had told Betty at the party. Betty joined with me afterwards in writing an affidavit with notary acknowledgment in case something happened to either of us.

Ethel and I were invited to dinner at the home of Dave Davenport who also had Priscilla McMillan, his cousin, as a guest. I had not seen Priscilla since she had interviewed me in Dallas on the Oswald matter and since she had married and divorced George McMillan, who had produced the NBC Anniversary TV show on the Kennedy assassination. Like many others, I had the highest possible opinion of Priscilla's intelligence and reliability. David Davenport was a former CIA man who had become disenchanted and was now semi-retired to his youthful locus of Santa Fe. He had remarried the charming Scottish ophthalmologist, Ann Thompson. When Priscilla asked what was of interest, I implied that I had some explosive documents on the Oppenheimer affair and was searching for an honest journalist to complete the investigation and let the chips fall where they may. "Well, Sam, I've always been intrigued by Oppenheimer and the Manhattan Project even if I know absolutely nothing about them."

So Priscilla is now nearing the end of thirteen years of research. We look forward to her book, for which she received a MacArthur grant. When she started, she didn't know a proton from a neutron. Now she is an expert on the Oppenheimer Affair and the decision to produce the H-bomb and the decision to create Lawrence Livermore

Laboratory. She can open more doors than any researcher I know. I introduce her to people, and she ends up as house guest in the homes of such people as John Manley, Rabi, Francoise Ulam, and Weisskopf. *Scientific American* assigned her to review Blumberg's second authorized Teller biography. She also did the *Sunday New York Times*' review of David Holloway's book on the Soviet nuclear program. Her book will be a documented bombshell. It is curious how connections emanate from her. The wife of associate Joe Downer was at college with Priscilla; the researcher of the BBC Peter Goodchild TV docudrama was her goddaughter, and so on.

When the Schector-Sudoplatov book came out accusing Oppie, Fermi, Bohr, and Szilard of being conduits to the Soviets, I felt immediately that the Schectors were ignorant of science, and some poor Freudian slips on their part reinforced my opinion. When protests poured into McNeil-Lehrer for their dramatic presentation of the Schector/Sudaplatov drama, they never apologized even though the editor of *Time Magazine* did so after learning of all the demonstrated errors in the Schectors' book. Priscilla McMillan became one of the leaders of the coterie of atomic historians in trying to correct the public misunderstandings from Sudaplatov's disinformation.

I expected fireworks at our monthly committee meeting after the Schector slander, but it was not mentioned until the very end and then rather dispassionately. I suspect this may have caused one resignation from the committee but even our three very conservative members remained loyal. These scientists are committed to intellectual maturity and do not surrender to media smears. Probably the committee's key anchor is my warm friend, Harold Argo, who is also the deepest admirer and friend of Oppie's executioner, Edward Teller. In our area, members of the "in" crowd just refer to first names. They may say, "I had coffee with Murray" (Gell-Mann), or "I had lunch with Edward" (Teller), or "I skied with Stirling" (Colgate), or "I climbed toward Lake Peak with Hans" (Bethe), or "I was at the symphony with Francoise" (Ulam), or "I had a call from Sig" (Hecker). How humiliating to have to query for further identification.

Naturally, the brilliant staff at Los Alamos includes some unorthodox ducks, but they are calmly tolerated. When Norm Rosen opened the first liquor store in Los Alamos with Senator Montoya's quiet assistance, he told his very first customer that a fifth of scotch was a shrewder buy than a quart. But the scientist ran some calculations on his pocket slide rule and said, "You're wrong." Once the leader of the Weapons Testing Group, Bill Ogle, was on a Reeves Airways flight to the Aleutians when Reeves' daughter was chief stewardess. When she announced everyone should buckle up for takeoff, an occupant of the restroom refused to return to his seat. So the stewardess used her security key to open the door. She then put a hammerlock on this fellow, and dragged him to his seat with his trousers around his ankles. The Los Alamos physicist was so impressed that he left his wife and six children and married the stewardess. Bill's later memorial service was attended by everyone, but not by his first wife! Reeves was a legend for flying the foggy Aleutians. On one bush-pilot trip he asked the control tower how he could find the terminal. The controller replied, "Man, this place is locked in—you can't land." "Heck, I'm already on the ground. How do I find the terminal?"

My friend Jim Walzel was president of Houston Natural Gas Company but was given a proverbial Golden Parachute by Enron after they purchased the company. However, Enron failed to protect the name Houston Natural Gas with the Secretary of State in Austin. So I shared a chuckle with Walzel, sitting once again as president of Houston Natural Gas Company and still in the Houston Natural Gas Company Building. I pondered on this while flying home. Did the Department Of Energy protect the name Los Alamos Scientific Laboratory when they changed the name in the late seventies to Los Alamos National Laboratory? Back in Santa Fe, in the Secretary of State's office I was advised the LASL name was unassigned and, after providing a twenty-dollar cashier's check, I received a certificate duly embossed as proprietor of the venerable Los Alamos Scientific Laboratories: Samuel B. Ballen, Director, and Ethel Ballen, Deputy Director. I never did receive a congratulatory letter from Harold Agnew, not even after writing to him on our new letterhead.

The cold war still had its frostiness in 1987 when the J. Robert Oppenheimer Memorial Committee was meeting at Cathy Strong's house to decide on the next year's speaker. I blurted, "Let's invite the head of the Soviet Academy of Science." After some incredulous expressions of "Will he be permitted into the country?" and "Will he be able to come to Los Alamos?" and more central, "Will the Soviets let him depart?" the members courageously decided to give it a try. "Who is the President of the Soviet Academy of Science?" Nick Metropolis came to the rescue: "His name is Marshuk, a world-class mathematician and I met him once—a decent and cultured chap." Then Nerses Krikorian, head of Intelligence at Los Alamos National Laboratory, supplied the address. I speculated that the Soviets respected private enterprise more than another committee, so I sent the invitation letter on La Fonda stationary. This brought down the wrath of Nicolas Metropolis. In the letter we enumerated the previous eighteen well-known annual lecturers, about half of whom were Nobel Laureates. After five weeks without response, a follow-up was sent through DHL at a cost of seventy-five dollars but delivery to Moscow was guaranteed in four days. The concept of going right to the top rather than through secondary intermediaries paid off. A qualified acceptance letter came from Marshuk explaining that it would be possible to come in December rather than August 1988. His topic would be Worldwide Ecological Concerns. Fortunately, he did not argue with our offer of transportation expenses within the United States.

Although each formal Oppenheimer Memorial Lecture was set for the first Monday in August, the Committee recognized a unique opportunity and decided to schedule a special December meeting. Several times we tried to call, but the lines to Moscow were always busy. Long delays in the mail became an ulcer-threatening routine. By now several members on the director's staff were concerned about protocol and how the Lab itself could participate. As the time came closer, we heard that Marshuk would have a party of eight scientists with him. Our treasurer got the chills. Then, manna from heaven, his visit was to include a stop-off in Washington with the head of the U.S. Academy of Science for a discussion about improving relations. Marshuk's group would be accompanied by a U.S. Academy interpreter, and we would split the expenses. Sig Hecker, the director of Los Alamos National Laboratory, is a soft- spoken, well-liked, quiet leader. He does not confront the bureaucracy of the Department of Energy in Washington, which has a strangle hold on the Lab's affairs. Many of the 1800 Lab Ph.D.s travel the world, including trips through the Iron Curtain, but normally the consent from DOE does not come until two days before scheduled departure. I think that Harold Agnew would tell the Washington gang to shove it and Norris Bradbury would delicately do the same, but now we live in more structured times. So this was the background for the charade which followed.

Marshuk's plane landed in Los Angeles one day after the devastating earthquakes in the Crimea. Since he was a member of the Central Committee, he was immediately called back to Moscow, but his entourage was permitted to come on to New Mexico. The protocol section of the Lab had not yet received permission from DOE for the Soviets to visit the Lab *nor* had protocol received a monetary allowance for a banquet. They were frantic. We were talking about obtaining $2,000 from the Lab's $900,000,000 annual budget. Fortunately, the Committee had scheduled the lecture at the high school auditorium rather than in the Lab's symposium hall. We decided to house the visitors at La Fonda rather than in the Los Alamos Inn—a decision that proved fortuitous.

Marshuk's speech was delivered by Kirill Ya Kondratyev, head of the Limnology Institute of Leningrad, a distinguished figure with near-perfect command of English. The *Los Alamos Monitor* had head-lined that morning that Marshuk was called back to Moscow, so the audience was sparse. Kondratyev gave a good talk. Shortly after he commenced reading Marshuk's paper, he realized it was dull and boring. He put it aside and gave an excellent spontaneous commentary with some interesting slides, pointing out that they reached opposite conclusions from the Americans vis-a-vis the influence of supersonic aircraft on the ozone. He had arrived at Los Alamos at dusk and drove back to Santa Fe in the dark. He uttered, "I've been to Los Alamos but haven't seen Los Alamos." Protocol had still not received DOE permission for the director to host a banquet or for a tour of nonclassified facilities to take place. Santa Fe, on a spur of the moment, came to the rescue. The School of American Research opened its fabulous vault of ancient Indian pottery, and Dr. Riccards of St. Johns College hosted a tea at which he made some splendid remarks about human rights. Kondratyev countered, "In many respects our people have more rights than yours. Our people will not work and there's nothing we can do about it." I didn't realize they really would have preferred a trip to Wal-Mart.

The head of the delegation, Dr. Makarov, arrived separately with a friendly chap identified by Los Alamos Intelligence as KGB. Makarov was a different type—elegantly clothed in the equivalent of an Oxxford suit—and never had to lift his bags since his associates would leap to oblige on such occasions. He was filming everything on the way up from the Albuquerque Airport on his video camera. Yes, he would like to see an Indian pueblo. So we drove into Santa Domingo Pueblo. All my Indian friends were away, so as a last resort we stopped at the store opposite the church. The Soviets had seen a horno and wanted some Pueblo bread. The thirteen-year-old girl tending the store said that they were all sold out. I said, "Well, these are visitors from Russia." "I'll speak to my mother." She came back five minutes later and gave each of them a loaf of bread but refused to accept payment. Makarov then spotted some simple jewelry behind a counter. I asked, "Can you give these Russians a break? They don't have too many dollars." The young girl just cut all the prices in half and the Russians went on a buying orgy. I had to insist they leave so we could get to Santa Fe in time for dinner.

La Fonda's banquet crew had done wonders with a delicious cocktail-dinner party in the Santa Fe room, which was packed with sixty guests. The chemistry was just right. Makarov, through the KGB interpreter, sure knew how to talk and gave a moving after-dinner speech concluding that the only ones who would object to these improving times were those "who required we be enemies." Walter Kerr, the part-time Santa Fe author of the definitive work on the Battle of Stalingrad, responded with some good words in Russian. Then Makarov presented to Hecker and me medallions of the 18th century creator of the Russian Academy of Science. Hecker rose and courageously said, "I'm sorry I was not able to entertain you as I wished or to escort you through suitable portions of our Lab. I will accept your invitation to visit your country but hope you will not be forced to treat me as I did you."

Someone in Washington who obviously was ignorant of geography of the west had plotted their next leg to Denver. The Russians had a 7 a.m. flight from Albuquerque west to Phoenix and then northeast to Denver. Ethel and I had to pick them up at La Fonda in two cars at 5 a.m. As we drove south, I turned on my radar detector. "What is that?" "It's to detect the police." "WHAT? YOU DEFEAT THE POLICE?" "Yes." "How much does that cost?" "Oh, now only $120." "Do you have one to offset the radar?" "Yes, but not in automobiles."

By 1991 relations with the U.S.S.R. had improved dramatically. Marshuk was in Oregon to receive an honorary doctorate. He wanted to come to New Mexico and give the talk he had committed to in 1988. This time he was introduced by Hecker in the Lab's symposium auditorium. Marshuk's talk was a paean to Oppenheimer's quest for cooperation and was delivered in hesitant English. When Marshuk and his aide were offered a trip to Bandelier or to Pecos National Monument, they asked, "How about that place with inexpensive Indian jewelry?" So again we went down to Santo Domingo. This time my friend Ernest Coriz was home with his beautiful wife and lovely children. Marshuk purchased some fine silver jewelry at normal prices, but Ernie was moved to give Marshuk his beaded belt buckle and was elated to receive Marshuk's calling card in Cyrillic and English.

As we left the Pueblo, we stopped once again at the store across from the church. The same girl—now two and a half years older—

opened up the jewelry shop and offered some steep discounts; seven dollars for rings and thirty dollars for silver bracelets inlaid with heavy turquoise. "Why are you treating these Russians so decently?" "Well, they've come a long way and are guests here." A few months later came a fax message from Marshuk in which he invited Ethel and me to the U.S.S.R. as guests of the Academy at their expense. Because we were then absorbed with the completion of the La Fonda ballroom, we replied that we would take a raincheck and instead proposed that the Academy assist us in a lengthy 1992 trip at our expense to Tanna Tuva, across from Mongolia. Bureaucratic hurdles had kept Richard Feynman from making a similar trip, so we were keeping our fingers crossed. Ethel and I intended to fly from Anchorage to Khabaraosk, then to Lake Baikal, and finally to Kyzyl in Tanna Tuva, where we would send postcards to all our science friends to let them know that we pulled off something that Feynman never could accomplish. But along came the breakup of the Soviet Union, and the Soviet Academy of Science evolved into the Russian Academy of Science. Today we do not know what transpired with Academician Marshuk.

Louis Rosen is an insufficiently appreciated hero at the Lab. Early on he invited top Russian and Chinese physicists to the Lab. His doing so undoubtedly contributed to the piercing of the Iron Curtain. La Fonda had a Chinese waiter when Louis planned to bring down a dozen senior Chinese nuclear physicists for dinner. I asked our Chinese waiter if he would serve them. He asked, "Are they from the Mainland?" Affirmative. "Oh, no, that is not my scheduled day." But then he reconsidered and said he would be happy to do it. He set up the banquet tables and stretched a banner with Chinese script. We couldn't decipher its meaning but the waiter said it was a welcome greeting. Louis' last trip to Russia involved missile disarmament. Although they really had no modern computers, the Russians were doing powerful science. One of them said, vis-a-vis our Western handheld computers, "You guys have forgotten how to think."

30/ *MR. STANLEY*

Stanley and Linda Marcus joined Judge Oliver Seth's 10 a.m. coffee table. Fortunately, Dick Morris, the former president of El Paso Natural Gas Company, was present. Morris' friend called Marcus the most brilliant man in the country. I had countered that, since he really had little appreciation or understanding of science, the accolade should be limited to the wisest and most civilized man in the country.

Mr. Stanley's real forte was in public relations, but I don't think he would argue with Einstein's assessment: "It would be a sad situation if a bag was better than the meat wrapped in it." Previously, Morris had told us that when he had his executive offices in Houston, his personal secretary, a lady who hailed from Louisiana, had never been west of Houston. When Morris moved his executive office to El Paso he pleaded with his secretary to move with him, but she had no enthusiasm whatsoever. So he arranged for the corporate jet to fly her on an inspection to El Paso. It was a clear day, and looking out at the landscape, she simply refused to get off the airplane at El Paso.

Present at the table this particular day was Tom Moore, originally from Wyoming and the co-proprietor of Moore's Clothing Store on the Plaza. He had served as the executive director of the National Men's Clothiers' Association in Washington, DC, but was now retired. I told Moore and Marcus that I had a story just for them. "There was this storekeeper from Oklahoma City who made his annual buying trip to Chicago but unfortunately had imbibed too many drinks at lunch. When he got back to the market, the manufacturers had palmed off on him some outlandish garments. He knew that he had been taken once he got back home and tried desperately for two years to get rid of the lemons. There was one orange plaid jacket that just wouldn't move. So one day he called over his chief salesman and said, "Look, I will be going to lunch and will be back in two hours. I don't care what it takes, but I want you to get rid of that hangover jacket." When he returned from lunch, he looked at the rack and saw that the jacket was gone. Then he looked at the salesman who had some scratches on his face and some tears on his shirt, and asked if it had been that difficult to have gotten rid of the jacket. "No," said the salesman, "that wasn't the trouble, but his seeing eye-dog almost ate me alive."

Stanley said it was a good tale but not the best. That concerned a most difficult buyer for Macy's. The buyer, named Ginsburg, would always report some soiled merchandise in a shipment to her or a numbered garment missing or a parcel coming in too late to meet a sale and, therefore, Macy's required a rebate from the supplier. So one day a manufacturer walked into Macy's and asked for Mrs. Ginsburg. "She's dead," the counter girl replied, and the manufacturer left. At noon he returned to the store and asked for Mrs. Ginsburg. The counter girl said, "Look, I told you she was dead. She died yesterday." And the manufacturer went away. That afternoon the manufacturer returned and went up to the counter girl and asked to see Mrs. Ginsburg. The counter girl again with some anger said, "Look, I told you she is dead. Her funeral is going to be tomorrow. What is wrong with you? Don't you know what I told you?" "Ah, yes," said the manufacturer, "but it just sounds so good to hear it."

I casually met Stanley Marcus a number of times in Dallas. Although my partner, Jerome Crossman, was a favored friend of his, I really did not achieve any intimate recognition until an incident occurred at La Fonda about 1970. The designer Alexander Girard and I were chatting one day at a cocktail party when he asked, "Don't you agree that Santa Fe deserves a fine hotel?" He said that since we had the location, La Fonda should be knocked down and he should be employed to design the successor hotel. I feebly told him that the historic ordinance would never permit the destruction of La Fonda. But then in order to repair the discussion, I mentioned Stanley Marcus' description of Girard as a genius because of the puppet display he had installed at Hemisfair in San Antonio. Said Girard, "Why, I don't know what you are talking about." I then said, "Surely you saw that open letter to you which Marcus ran in the *Dallas Morning News?*" "No, I never received such a letter and I don't know what you are talking about." Shortly afterwards Stanley and his wife Billie were walking through the lobby and entered our newsstand. I came over and said that I had confidence in my memory and, "I'm fairly sure that I saw your advertised letter to Alexander Girard but Girard said he had never received it." Stanley said, "Why, absolutely. I sent him that letter, or I intended for my secretary to send him that letter. I have it in my files and will send him a duplicate." And that is exactly what he did.

Actually my respect for and wonderment at Stanley occurred soon after we had moved to segregationist Dallas when he permitted the store to admit black customers on certain hours on Saturday. Then I recalled the commotion about a Bertoia sculpture that was installed in the new Dallas Public Library. When it was revealed that Bertoia had an extensive leftist affiliation during his residency in Mexico, the city council passed a resolution not to pay Bertoia his $8,500 fee. Mayor R.L. Thornton went over to look at the modernistic sculpture and described it as a poor welding job. Stanley and brother Edward resolved the embarrassment by saying they would pay for it, and the city council decided they wouldn't be outmaneuvered and so the steel, brass, copper and nickel construction was installed. Amongst the other incidents that I recalled when we were still living in Dallas was the time when a high school student with long hair was expelled from classes until he met the dress code. Stanley announced that he would pay the young man's attorney to contest the ruling, but I don't think the youngster prevailed.

Many years later I asked Mr. Stanley where his fundamental view of life had changed. "But it hasn't. While at Harvard I learned to respect the Bill of Rights and that has been my yardstick ever since."

When we came to Dallas, the most impressive local Jews were members of the anti-Zionist American Council for Judaism. Although I never joined the organization, we attended many of their functions and became close to many of their stalwarts. It was readily apparent that its officials had become ideological extremists and had moved away from the mainstream Jewish community to the point where they were ineffective. Among the leading members of the American Council for Judaism were Jerome Crossman, who maintained his loyalty to the very end, and Stanley Marcus, who however, had a change of heart. This was publicized about 1966 when I was invited to a private luncheon near the Zodiac Room and felt that I was under false colors since all the other Jewish businessmen there were exceedingly wealthy and powerful. I was certainly not of their stature. After a delicious lunch the prominent Zionist Bernard Schaenen, who had coincidentally gone to City College, got up and said that Stanley Marcus had something to say. It went like this: "I don't know whether it's because I'm getting older and am thinking of meeting my maker, but I want you all to know that I have rethought my position on the state of Israel. Conditions have changed from the time it was evolving as an independent country, and my theoretical opposition is now past history. I am going to support Israel, and I urge you all to do the same." So I filled out a United Jewish Appeal pledge card for $1,000.

I became a good and close friend of Linda Marcus long before I really got to know Stanley. I knew her as Linda Lovely when she was working in the research section of the Dallas Public Library, driving a Volkswagen, and going to SMU graduate school. I knew her under this name for about two years. Ultimately, I learned that her surname was really Robinson. She was such a delight that everyone called her Linda Lovely. Some short time after Mr. Stanley became a widower, they were wed and she still continued to drive a Volkswagen. None of her many admirers had any doubts that she would successfully evolve as the comfortable wife of this world-famous renaissance man. We also knew that he could not look to her for any kitchen duties.

As their honeymoon present I offered one of our best suites at La Fonda plus some private touring of northern New Mexico. On that occasion we drove up in our four-wheel drive vehicle to a Sunday mass at Christ in the Desert Monastery on the east bank of the Chama River, north of Abiquiu. When we got there, Linda warned me that any form of structured religion was repellent to Stanley. I told her to look on it the same as visiting a Pueblo dance. When we entered and went into the chapel it happened that some new-lifestyle Hispanic priests were then conducting the service. We stood in a semicircle while they lit incense and concluded by asking each of the attendees to embrace his neighbor. When I reached over to hug Mr. Stanley, a look of helpless horror came over him. When we exited the chapel, I said to Stanley, "It's just a folk ceremony and they won't kill you." He answered, "Don't give them a chance." We then drove past Cañones to the base of Tsiping Pueblo, which then was rarely visited. It had not been vandalized by inconsiderate tourists. Stanley was still smoking his pipe as we ascended a somewhat difficult climb, but Linda kindly stopped several times saying, "I'm tired. Let's rest." Stanley's physical strength was dissipated. To his dismay, I had to assist him on the descent. I learned much later that he said at a Dallas cocktail party, "That was the worst day of my life." When I repeated this anecdote at Stanley's 90th birthday party banquet at the Crescent in Dallas, Stanley told his table it was indeed the worst day of his life!

Stanley is the wisest person I know, and also the most civilized. The day after the Tsiping Pueblo excursion we had dinner at our house and he was attracted to Mary Argo, the Los Alamos physicist, especially because of her knowledge of Walla Walla onions. Like anyone else, there are many complexities to him. His philanthropy is readily available for all the artistic events, but when I asked him to make a contribution to the Temple Beth Shalom Building Fund, he said, "Please ask me for anything else." I said, "I know how you feel since religion is not my strong loyalty, but these people need a place of satisfactory congregation." He then said, "Fine, let them pay for it." His mind is crystal clear at his present age, yet he carries too much weight and, for as long as I have known him, has not led an outdoor existence.

But that was not always the case, as I learned one day. When the four of us were out driving together Linda asked, "Is it possible that George De Mohrenschildt had some involvement in the Kennedy assassination?" My unsuccessful answer was, "Well, when you talk about possibilities it is possible that the mass murderer at Altoona is present in this vehicle." From the back came Stanley's groan, "I don't like that." But then when we were discussing horses, I had to watch my tongue. In the fifties Stanley had an assistant, Warren Leslie, who wrote a weekly essay for the *Dallas Morning News*. He signed these essays Wales. I instinctively had reservations about Warren Leslie, although I knew he was very bright and he knew it too. He finally left Neiman's and went to work for a notorious perfume manufacturer in New York. He then published a novel *The Starrs of Texas*. It was a poorly disguised story about Neiman's and the Marcus family. Leslie's novel contained vivid descriptions of incest, and rape, and contract murder. It was a piece of pornography without the four-letter words. In the car Linda asked, "Did you know that Stanley used to ride horses regularly?" Without thinking, I said, "Oh yes, I know that because I've read Warren Leslie's book." I then clamped my mouth shut. But Stanley said, "Oh yes, but Warren is doing just fine." "How do you know that?" "Well, I spoke to him a week ago." "My gosh. How could you talk to that fellow after the trash he wrote?" And Stanley answered, "When you love someone you take them with all their blemishes." So it was not a shock that Leslie was included on the guest list for the 90th birthday grand event, which was a wholesome version of Malcolm Forbes' last extravaganza.

Linda has a doctorate in archaeology and really wants, I suspect, to live out here in New Mexico. Stanley had been a visitor to Santa Fe from the 1920s and was not ignorant of the culture or the talented artisans here. So it was no surprise when they decided to buy a second home up in the hills above Hyde Park Road. I have facetiously stated that the decline of Santa Fe can be dated from that moment because so many competent and normal people were attracted to Santa Fe after learning that the Marcuses were living here. People have accused me of knowing everybody, but I am a very distant second to Stanley. Besides corporate executives of top echelon, he also is attracted to artists, many of whom are of the gay community. I said to him one day that there used to be a sign on the Central Expressway entering Dallas that read "Welcome to the City of Excellence," but that in Santa Fe everyone was welcome no matter how humble or lacking in stature. Stanley's reply was, "Well, I tried to make it possible for people to strive for their very best potential and to let them know that they can achieve some degree of excellence."

He is honorable and tough and courageous and unabashedly realistic. As well read and well authored as he is, he is really no idle intellectual. When L.B.J. was being measured for some custom Oxxford clothing, he murmured to Stanley that maybe now that he was President he would be getting some kind of discount. But Stanley said, "Mr. President, we price our merchandise properly and the prices are fair." He made no secret of the fact that even when John Connelly was governor of Texas, Marcus had no use for him. When it became known that his long-time personal secretary had embezzled a very substantial sum of money, Stanley filed his criminal complaint with the district attorney instead of keeping it quiet.

I treasure his friendship and also Linda's, who I know will always speak forthrightly to me even if it's what I don't particularly want to hear. When his doctors were concerned by a pimple on his tongue and urged that he give up smoking, he gave me his private collection of Partagas cigars from his New York City vault.

31/ *LA FONDA'S LAST ERECTION*

WHEN HARRISON & ABRAMOWITZ together with Alcoa from Pittsburgh designed the Republic National Bank Building in Dallas, it was then the tallest structure between the Mississippi and the West Coast. Powerful Fred Florence, president of the bank, wanted to top it off with a replica of the Statue of Liberty. But Harrison & Abramowitz put their foot down and said they would withdraw from the project if Florence insisted on this. A compromise was finally reached. An aluminum-sheathed trylon stood on top of the Republic National Bank Building and from it beamed a rotating searchlight that could be seen almost to the Oklahoma state line. The mischief-makers in Dallas called this "Florence's Last Erection." But bank gossip was not limited to the Republic. It included octogenarian Nathan Adams, head of the First National Bank of Dallas. He would not leave the boardroom when the directors removed him from the helm and he had to be carried out in his presidential chair. The legends included R.L. Thornton, head of the Mercantile National Bank, who went office to office with Christmas greetings. After taking a sip of spiked eggnog at each stop, he amazed the secretaries by standing over a spittoon and unzipping his trousers to relieve himself.

In 1994 we received Historic Styles approval for the final stage of our master plan, which we did not pursue because of financial caution. However, once the bonds of our $4 million Carriage House had been amortized to less than $2 million, we became serious about completing this project. Youngest daughter Marta was made project manager, and our architect had to contend with her strong environmental concerns. The draftsmen proudly packed in forty-two rooms, which were in compliance with the building code, but they hadn't counted on Marta. She took me and Ethel up to our Carriage House and pointed to the view of Atalaya Peak. She convinced us that we had to preserve those views, so the forty-two rooms were reduced to twenty rooms. Then one day she took us over to the corner of Water Street and Old Santa Fe Trail and pointed out the view's impact against the towers of St. Francis Cathedral. The twenty rooms were then reduced to fourteen rooms. Then she said that because of outgassing of toxic materials, there would be no drapes and there would be no carpets and there would be no phony gas-fired fireplaces. We would be allowed a wood-burning fireplace in the library. By way of caution, we had decided to make our enclosed La Terraza a function-banquet room, but Marta insisted that it be a restaurant so that this beautiful site would be available to the citizenry. But here she did not succeed, as we pointed out that just as the citizenry can enjoy our Lumpkins Ballroom, so they would be able to gain access and appreciate our enclosed La Terraza. Then she proposed that the open area between the guest rooms and La Terraza be professionally landscaped. By the time we were finished with all this nobility, the estimated cost bumped against $5 million.

The Cornell Hotel Management School would question our sanity in pursuing this addition. After checking around, Marta learned that Jeanne Crandall was considered the new Mary Coulter as an interior designer. She was employed by Fred Harvey to redo the weary El Tovar at the Grand Canyon. Once Jeanne came on board our project, we appreciated her unique combination of courage and knowledge. We are confident that she will produce something splendid that will harmonize with the Pueblo Deco decor of the existing La Fonda. These guest rooms, averaging 550 square feet, will be the finest in the state. Our present facilities benefit from the native paintings of our maintenance man, Ernesto Martinez; we hope he will be able to assist in the decoration of these rooms. His genius has been recognized with a prominent cover story in *USA Today* and *New Mexico Magazine*. So we hope this taste will prevail and not succumb to a ritzy touch.

Surprisingly, we did not have too much difficulty in getting our board of directors to authorize the pursuit of this venture, even though they know how risky and tenuous the economics appeared to be.

Brian Arthur, the young wonder of the Santa Fe Institute, said, "First-class men hire first-class men while second-class men hire third-class men." Well, over my fifty-year business career there has been an extra thrill in giving second-line executives an opportunity at top management. I succeeded for sure with Electrical Log Services. Marta is showing that she could be a winner as she evolves into La Fonda's top tier. That is our dividend as Ethel and I wind down our direct leadership at the hotel. Cementing our confidence in the family's future at La Fonda is the knowledge that daughter Lenore is completing a hospitality program at Northern Arizona University. The daughters will respect that La Fonda belongs to Santa Fe and not just to its stockholders and that its net profits need to be continuously reinvested in the property.

Assuming fate provides another decade of physical strength and mental alertness for me and Ethel, we intend to build a Trading Post suitable for the 21st century at Navajo Mountain. The Chapter has granted us a lease on five acres, but this resolution needs to overcome the hurdles of sundry agencies at the Navajo Nation's capital of Window Rock. It is always a spiritual experience for me to ascend toward Navajo National Monument and first see the dome of Naatsisaan to the north. In October 1995 a group of us followed Bert Tallsalt to the top of No Mans Mesa. We really thought we were the first Anglos to make that climb but then learned that Arthur Baker had done so in 1928 for the USGS. Verily, there are few places one is first on this exciting planet.

When we annually tripped from Dallas to Navajo Mountain, we would stop off at Inscription House Trading Post to visit with Stokes Carson, who packed 57 years as a trader in Navajo Country. Shortly before he died, he looked at me and said, "Guess you are destined to end up here." He just might be right.

But, of course, we will have to come to terms with genius Leo Szilards' tenth commandment authored October 1940:

"Fuhre das Leben mit leichter Hand und sei bereit fortzugehen, wann immer Du gerufen wirst." *

---

* Lead your life with a gentle hand and be prepared to depart whenever you are called.

*My mother and father (Biegelaisen) and sister Marion
at her graduation from PS 25 at 149th Street in the Bronx
in January 1931, and me at age 9.*

32/ THE REST OF THE STORY

H ERE IT IS January 8, 2001 and Ethel and I are at the Burr Trail Trading Post and Grill, about 70 miles north of Navajo Mountain, preparing the first public edition of *Without Reservations*. The initial private printing sold out in four months with no advertising or marketing whatsoever.[1] Patty Dietrich created this Post with some minimal assistance from La Fonda and Gibbs Smith, the Salt Lake City publisher of the dramatic story of Everett Ruess, "A Vagabond for Beauty." Ruess was the adventuresome young man out of California who explored the Navajo reservation and the area west of the Water Pocket Fold, accompanied by his mule. Ruess ultimately disappeared in a canyon south of Escalante in 1934, and the mystery surrounding his death continues to this day. If you are not a crow, it's 214 miles driving from Navajo Mountain to Page and then up Cottonwood Canyon to Escalante and then to Boulder. The latter paved 30 miles between Escalante and Boulder must be one of the most spectacular stretches of highway in the United States and despite its isolation has now been included in the itinerary of German tourists wandering about the Southwest.

Patty Dietrich is the daughter of Sue and Don, the late friends who introduced us to Santa Fe in 1949. About eight years ago, she wrote from Chicago sounding us out for an invitation to our home, where she then spent several months. Our previous contact was at Cornwall, New York, where she was walking around with a bare bottom since her parents did not believe in toilet training. She was moved by her mother's notes as an anthropologist (Sue having been adopted into the Sioux Nation) to get reacquainted with the Southwest. At our urging, she went out to Shonto on the Navajo Reservation to manage its Trading Post. Her desire to become a pioneer woman of the west was reinforced and it didn't take much of a suggestion about Boulder, Utah for her to drift up there, and the rest is all her unique accomplishment. Boulder is on the northern edge of The Grand Staircase-Escalante National Monument created by President Clinton

---

[1] The known corrections are quite few. This was surprising since I authored the story entirely out of memory.

and a lasting achievement of his, even if the Mormon natives are distressed that there was no environmental impact due process. It will be surprising if in the next decade Patty does not become an accepted official of Boulder's government or the subject of a Hollywood special.

~ ~ ~ ~ ~ ~ ~ ~

I was never able to implement our desires to recreate a Trading Post at Navajo Mountain. The local Navajo Nation Chapter passed the requisite resolutions granting us an adequate lease at two different sites, but the charming, friendly officials at Tuba City and Window Rock imposed requirements that no prudent person could accept. For instance, their lease stipulated that we would have to take out fire insurance with the Navajo Nation as beneficiary, even though the closest fire fighting facilities were 2½ hours away. We spent several years trying to pursue every hopeful tactic, but we were unable to successfully contend with the Navajo bureaucracy. I suppose on the other hand they felt that we were being disrespectful of their sovereignty and not flexible in accepting their requirements. The final straw was a meeting in Gallup where the Bureau of Indian Affairs recognized our motivation to be of assistance and agreed to give their consent to anything which the Navajo Nation approved, but the representatives of the Navajo Nation would not budge a centimeter. I threw up my hands and backed off the project. But inasmuch as the road from Inscription House to Navajo Mountain is in process of being paved, it will then be possible for the residents of Navajo Mountain to do their shopping either at Inscription House or Page, and the lack of any convenience store at Navajo Mountain will not be distressful. Moreover, there is now a very impressive Navajo executive from Many Farms who has been appointed director of the school, which is now under local jurisdiction, rather than subservient to Window Rock or the BIA. He has a package of plans to make the school the center of social activity and included in his vision is the reactivation of a mini-store near the community water faucet.

~ ~ ~ ~ ~ ~ ~ ~

In the midst of this frustration I was able to develop an intimate friendship with Dr. Fred Begay, the only Navajo Ph.D. physicist in the world and a staff member of Los Alamos National Laboratory.

Fred Begay organized, with the assistance of the late Glenn Seaborg, the Seaborg Hall of Science, an effort to bring mathematics and science to secondary education on the Navajo reservation. I am privileged to serve as a trustee of the Seaborg Hall of Science. Fred Begay, of Navajo and Ute background, did not graduate from high school, but nevertheless he received a legitimate Ph.D. in physics from UNM. There is not a trace of arrogance in the way Fred approaches his Navajo brethren and he more than respects their traditions and their religious practices. The key difference between us, which is not a source of any conflict, is that I believe all organized religions are vulnerable to becoming cults and should be avoided. But Fred counters by saying that each of them has something beneficial for mankind and they should all be accepted. I early on learned that if Fred read something or heard something it would stick with him indelibly.

With Fred's assistance, I tried to expand my competence in the Navajo language, but age has taken its toll of me and that proves very difficult. I have the greatest respect and affection for Fred, his wife Helen, and several of their children. It was my pleasure to take Fred Begay out to Paiute Mesa, where we camped for the night, which was a moving experience for him since he felt that his ancestors had come from there. Then one year, Fred and Jenny Wise joined us at Navajo Mountain's Pioneer Day and I four-wheeled them up to the top of Navajo Mountain where Fred had his corn pollen and eagle feathers and prayer blanket and performed a ceremony over each of us, but particularly Jenny Wise, who was having some internal physical and emotional adjustments at the time. One day we stopped off at Julia Fatt's place at the eastern rim of Paiute Mesa, just overlooking Naikai Canyon. Over many years Julia had permitted me to leave our cars near her property while we went trekking and I always left something at her residence. Julia spoke no English but told Fred that she called me "the watermelon man," since that is generally what I left at her doorstep. She asked, "I wonder how he lives?" The end result was that Julia came and stayed with us in Santa Fe and we escorted her to the museums and to the Native American Preparatory School at Rowe and to the movies, but after four days she said she wanted to go home.

~ ~ ~ ~ ~ ~ ~ ~

Although Ethel and I were flattered when we were voted *"Living Treasures of Santa Fe"* and although I felt distinguished when presenting the commencement address at UNM Los Alamos, and although it was pleasing when the young Hispanic women gussied over me when I wore an outrageous bikini dress at The Buckaroo Ball, and although I felt awe when designated a lifetime honorary director of the Southwest Association of Indian Arts, and the same when the Anti-Defamation League chose me as their banquet selectee – actually, the real deep spiritual satisfaction came when I was asked to conduct or participate in the memorial services of a number of outstanding Deceased Treasures, shown below in no particular order:

John Rinehart was an accomplished physicist who had nothing to do with the Manhattan Project or nuclear energy. His specialties were conventional explosives and geysers. During the big war he worked on shaped charges and proximity fuses back east. Ruth Leakey said it best: "John is awfully smart but he doesn't think he's smarter than he is." John was living life to the hilt and entirely active when he developed cardiac warnings and recognized that his mortal clock was starting to run out. Therefore, he planned a series of journeys to include the truly exotic: trips to Timbuktu, Ethiopia, Kamchatka and Tibet. His understanding wife Marion tolerated these mostly solitary trips but accompanied him annually to the Yellowstone thermals. When he built an indoor pool as therapy for his wife's arthritis, his Albuquerque physicist son said, "This house is going to be hard to sell." But John retorted, "That will be your problem." John's autobiography was published posthumously by Marion and it revealed a number of surprises from a scientist who was more outspoken and more intolerant than the laid back and easy going person we had known. China invited John to lecture on stress waves and his trip would include Yunan Province's Stone Forest near Vietnam. Ethel and I were distressed by the junk scattered at this unique park when we were there so John cooperated in a request of mine. I asked Erica Jen, the wife of George Zweig, the co-discoverer of quarks, to write out in Chinese script, "Please do not litter." After handing John ten copies of this sign, he agreed to post them in the Stone Forest and did just that.

But this was not an isolated case of posthumous discard of inhibition: The great, great theoretical and practical geologist at UNM, Sherman Wengard, surprised everyone with his memoirs. His long time professional associate, Donald Baars, said about those writings, "You thought you knew Sherman Wengard, I thought I knew Sherman Wengard. Well you are in for a surprise." But then the renowned winner of the Pulitzer Prize, Richard Rhodes, did not wait till he could escape the gasps of his contemporaries in publishing the now out-of-print clinical *Making Love*.

Jack Rogers always wore a bigger Stetson than my own and we would compare the number of X's on the hatband, but I always came out second place. Jack and Nan moved to Raton, to be nearer their cattle ranch, but each summer welcomed scores of friends from Santa Fe to a delectable outdoor barbecue. Jack's health was obviously weakening and we all had a bit of fright when he fell into his charcoal fire at one such outing, but we were able to pull him out with only minimal damage. In Santa Fe, Jack's hangout was the Palace Bar, and that is where we conducted his memorial. He and Nan were childhood sweethearts from Jacksboro, Texas, and somehow my extemporaneous remarks drifted into critical description of the rancher Worthington and his rodeo star daughter, Jackie, when Nan sputtered that they were the best of friends in high school. So I quickly retreated and changed the direction of my remarks.

Dick Slansky's abrupt death at fifty-seven was unfair. An accomplished skier, head of Los Alamos Theoretical Division, a calm but courageous student of philosophy, arts and science, and a beautiful physical specimen with an adoring wife, he was entitled to live out a fuller life. Dick collapsed in California while lecturing at a conference. He started his adult education majoring in divinity at Harvard but then could not avoid seeing his own light and switched to physics.

Stan Livingston was a doctoral candidate at Berkeley under E.O. Lawrence and for his thesis, following some suggestions from his mentor, produced the world's first Cyclotron, which perhaps had a diameter of 5 or 6 inches. Lawrence never mentioned Stan in his Nobel Award speech and never acknowledged the accomplishment of his student. This evident pain persisted in Stan's withdrawn demeanor ever after. He was married twice to Lois, one historian describing her as the most beautiful co-ed in California. Stan's final times were not pleasant and his arm was surgically amputated shortly before his end. Anger gripped him as his time came to a close, and I feel he knew Ethel and I were there for a final visit, but he would not acknowledge our presence. Yet, at his service, I said that he died happy knowing that Congress had issued a Memorial shortly before praising his cyclotron discoveries and, after all, Stan's science was the most important thing in his life.

James Russell was the second person I met in Santa Fe and we were easy going friends from the word go. He invested in all of my activities and he was the best partner one could have, even when several of my start-ups turned out to be lemons. He kept his birth date a secret from his office manager and even his son and wife each had a different date. I think he was well into his nineties when he left us. He held on cheerfully and then told his wife Dee that the end was near and stopped eating. When Ethel and I visited, Dee somehow let him know we were there and he opened one eye and said, "Howdy doody." At his services I told the story involving Jimmie and Greer Garson's husband Buddy Folgelson, but Maurice Trimmer gave me a more accurate version from former Governor Jack Campbell's unpublished autobiography:

> *"It was customary in 1941 for some of the more affluent lobbyists to rent all the rooms on La Fonda's third floor. The connecting doors between the rooms were constantly open; card games were frequent and parties were noisy. It was in that session that Harry Leonard and Buddy Fogelson were in process of purchasing the Forked Lightning Ranch. A violinist was providing musical entertainment for the celebrants but at 1 a.m. he put his instrument in its case and went home. This greatly displeased Buddy and Harry who promptly invited Campbell to go with them to a small bar down the street which had a piano. They proceeded to negotiate the purchase of the piano on the spot, put the cash on the counter and hired a group of local natives to roll and carry it to La Fonda, into the elevator and into Buddy's suite on the second floor and sang and danced till daylight."*

Governor Bruce King and I, joined by her beautiful children and grandchild, spoke at *Mickey Stewart*'s funeral. She had been Deputy Director of Health and Environment for the State and Resident Manager at La Fonda. But the most moving eulogist was a black preacher from Albuquerque. I guess Mickey's father was president of Washington University in St. Louis and she was raised in dignified elegance which prevailed when she married a physician and moved to Albuquerque. But events took a painful turn when she was exchanged for a young nurse. However, Mickey was determined to raise her kids by herself and she established a laudable record of reliable service in New Mexico state government and at La Fonda. Her appealing sweetness remained during the trying times of contending with cerebral malignancy, but Lovelace Healthcare rose to their best and provided air transportation for her several times to a specialist in Tucson. Shortly before her ending, Ethel and I brought her down for lunch at La Plazuela and the word quickly spread throughout La Fonda that Mickey was in the dining room. And one by one her former employees came by with heartfelt greetings. All the good vibes of her Memorial Service were shattered when the hell and damnation Baptist preacher exploded with his conviction that Mickey had reached her nirvana with her God and that the rest of us were doomed to the devil without Jesus. This preacher probably had an IQ of –20, but he thought he was a founder of MENSA. It never occurred to him that Nobelist Eugene Wigner wrote:*"That I will die hardly bothers me. We are all guests in this life, and our culture commits a crime when it persuades us to think otherwise. As a scientist, I must say that we have no heavenly data, so I am afraid that after death we merely cease to exist."*

St. Francis Auditorium was packed solid with every seat and aisle space occupied for Lumpkin's Memorial. They had to close the doors and reject latecomers. If John Gaw Meem was the earlier conscience of Santa Fe, then the later mantle passed to **Bill Lumpkins**. He could get along with the most noble and the most humble and each acquaintance felt he was a special friend of Bill's. As an architect, he probably left his influence on more homes in Santa Fe than any of his colleagues and was a pioneer in solar construction and also double adobe walled residences. As an artist, his colorful watercolors became better and better as time marched on. But what really distinguished Bill from the crowd was his undiluted humanity and respect for the underdog and pride in having grown up on a ranch in eastern New Mexico. Bill created the first chapter in Santa Fe of the American Civil Liberties Union and urged me to accompany him on a visit to the boy's disciplinary school at Springer. "Why are we heading up there?," I asked. "Well, there's a young man with very long hair and they want to force him into the standard Marine Corps barbering." "Well Bill, I really have no empathy and no sympathy with this errant adolescent but I'll ride with you anyway," said I, influenced by my spreading baldness. Over many years Bill was a constant contributor to our various redos at La Fonda, including the roofing of La Plazuela and the windowed wall between the bar and the lobby and it is because of his untold sound critical comments over the years that we named our large ballroom *The Lumpkins Room*, even though he was neither the architect nor the decorator. There is not a mortal who is perfect and that was no exception with Bill, since he did not act in his best nobility when the glass paneled roof of La Plazuela developed a serious leaking problem, but we managed to survive that bit of tension without it affecting our friendship. Unfortunately, no one has replaced Bill as the conscience of the community or the dean of preserving the pueblo deco architectural themes as Santa Fe expands.

It was on a Wednesday Irregular hike that physicist **Mary Argo** collapsed to her death. The autopsy revealed a fatal stroke, so she was gone before she hit the ground. That evening, Harold Argo's son called me out of a dinner party and said his father would like to see me, and I rushed up to The Hill to be with one of my closest friends. It was apparent right off that Harold was in shock at the loss of his distinguished lifetime partner. "We are not church oriented and I wonder if you would conduct Mary's Memorial Service?" I guess my own emotions were on edge because I tactlessly replied "Oh yes, that would be a thrill," but Harold was too wrapped up in his distress to take offense. Mary had raised her three sons and daughter and continued to work while Harold went on for his doctorate. So Mary never had that advanced degree even though she produced some highly classified work at Los Alamos on opacities and she was much admired for her professional competence. I only recall superlatives of Mary as a mother, a wife, a scientist, a hiker and an enjoyable intellectual opponent, since she was most admiring of Edward Teller. Daughter Leslie was also an intimate friend of Teller's, but her personality changed when she went off to college in California and returned grossly obese and with serious psychological trauma. The ill-informed psychiatrist at Las Vegas, New Mexico only made matters worse. Anyway, Leslie revealed to a local woman psychiatrist just before she took her own life, that as a youngster in Los Alamos she had been physically abused by a neighboring boy with threats that he would kill her brothers if she were to utter any revelations and this emotional load remained her private secret. I really liked Leslie and appreciated her keen mind and could not help saying at her Memorial Service at Fuller Lodge that if the mental torment was now over, perhaps her action could now be better understood.

For years **Judge Jose Francisco Torres** sat in La Fonda's lobby and kibitzed with the transient guests. He grew up alongside the Purgatoire River in Southern Colorado and never graduated from high school. Nevertheless, he tried to matriculate at the University of Denver but was told that such swarthy trash was not welcome. Fortunately, he was admitted to Westminster Law School and ultimately graduated and, after its merger with Denver University, received an Honorary Doctorate many years later. He was very proud of having argued with Whizzer White in moot court. Our friendship was cemented when we both knew about the ill-fated Whiskey Creek Pass east of San Luis in Southern Colorado. Judge Torres was in charge of a W.P.A. crew working on that road, which was never opened because a tunnel was not completed at the start of World War II, even though it was listed on many of the Colorado and New Mexico maps as late as 1990. I included that story from the altar of St. Francis Cathedral. His lovely daughter, Eva, continues his tradition of greeting visitors to Santa Fe as a downtown walking tour guide.

~ ~ ~ ~ ~ ~ ~ ~

Although there are only a handful of blacks in Santa Fe, the State Police SWAT team includes an enormous chap who would make the famous Texas Ranger model at Dallas' Southland Center appear puny. Santa Fe does have a chapter of the NAACP and I was invited to talk to them about growing up in Harlem. I focused my story on the really harsh survival difficulties of the depression and said the blacks' salvation was their Baptist church, the hard working mothers, and the Jewish communists. They accorded me an enjoyable reception.

~ ~ ~ ~ ~ ~ ~ ~

The puzzling estrangement between mathematician Gian Carlo Rota and Stanislaw Ulam's widow endured. I attempted, with no success whatsoever, to suggest that Father Time was at work and he should bury the hatchet. Instead, Rota wrote to me with some utterly critical accusations against Francoise, which I am fairly certain were not accurate. He also told me that on his next trip to Los Alamos he would explain the real happenings between Teller and Ulam on the hydrogen bomb, but unexpectedly he died one night at MIT. At his memorial service at Fuller Lodge, Francoise sent a generous eulogy even though she did not attend in person. Included in her remarks was mention of Rota's attempt at suicide, which was fortunately diverted by Mark Kac. But, at the Memorial, physicist J. L. excluded that sentence when he read the eulogy.

~ ~ ~ ~ ~ ~ ~ ~

In those few years since the private edition of *Without Reservations,* Santa Fe has continued its mainlined trend. The gated golf-coursed community of Las Campanas has been a success although Santa Fe natives are distressed that it accounts for nearly 10% of the water consumption of the area. Very prestigious people worldwide in practically every discipline continue to retire to Santa Fe, which greatly enriches the cultural understructure. But the price we pay is the erosion of that frustrating charm of former simplicity, perhaps exemplified by the story of when General Patrick Hurley ran for the Governorship in 1954 and at a political rally in Chimayo kept talking about Chiang Kai-shek and the islands of Kemoy and Matsu. In the back of the crowd, one local asked his neighbor, "You know English, what is that he's saying about Chiang Kai-shek?" Came the reply, "Chinga los checkes," (if you don't vote for him, he's going to screw your welfare check). Of course, Hurley lost. The local Council of International Relations has become a powerhouse of esteemed, accomplished members, even though as in most such entities it is the rare Hispanic other than Ambassador Frank Ortiz and Elizabeth Romero who participate. In recent years, nearly $100,000,000 has been spent on the remodeling of the Opera House, the Chavez Sports Complex, the construction of the Georgia O'Keeffe Museum, the Sanchez Golf Links, the two Museum of New Mexico expansions, the addition of several art and cinema buildings at the College of Santa Fe – all demonstrations of Santa Fe's strong $2.5 billion economy. In the face of this affluence it is a disgrace that the physical plants of our public schools are deteriorated instead of being an inspiration for the student body. But this cannot be accomplished unless residential real estate tax appraisals are brought up to normal scales which is not desired by the populace. The pundits say that Santa Fe will grow fivefold to 300,000, but limited water may save us from a repeat of when Austin exploded into a hectic megalopolis.

~ ~ ~ ~ ~ ~ ~ ~

Now past 96, Stanley Marcus remains intellectually alert and his involvement in civic matters is undiminished. However, he did finally cease his weekly essay in the *Dallas Morning News.* Mr. Stanley still goes to his office every day, works out with a trainer three times a week and goes out for dinner more times than not. Since he embellished the credibility of the Marions when they came to Santa Fe, his role in the creation of the Georgia O'Keeffe Museum has not been adequately appreciated. Although he cannot return to our 7,000 ft., he and Linda continue their vacations to Mexico and Guatemala. He exemplifies Ron Klein's mother's admonition "While you live, live."

Samuel B. Ballen, Private First Class in Louisiana in January 1943, prior to embarking for North Africa.

ONOMASTICON